IMAGES
of America

LA SALLE COUNTY

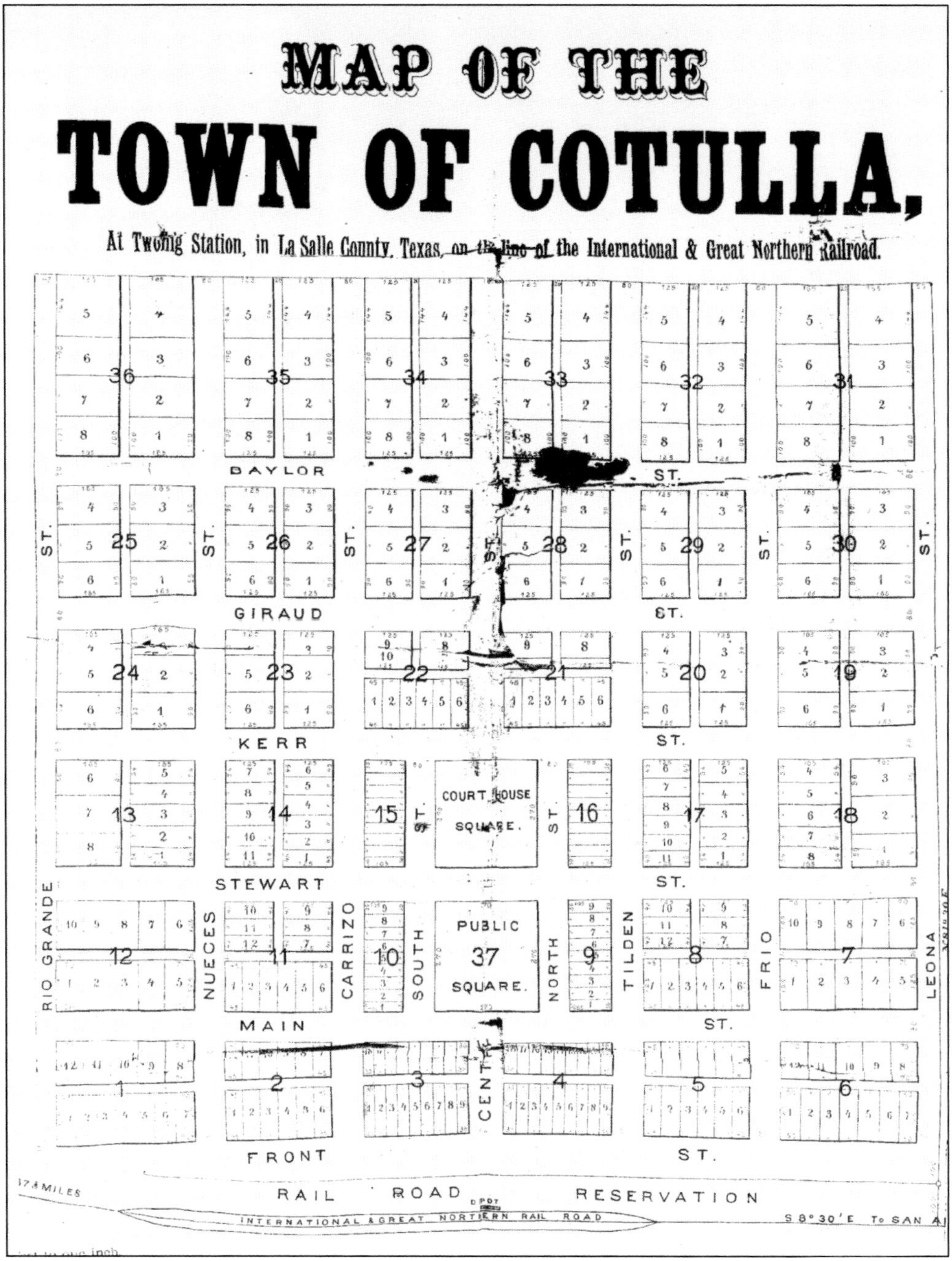

The original town of Cotulla as founded by Joseph Cotulla on the International and Great Northern Railroad in 1882 is featured on this map. (Courtesy of the Brush Country Museum.)

On the Cover: Agapito Alaniz (left) and Jose Lozano were vaqueros on La Mota Ranch. They are pictured breaking a young horse. (Courtesy of the Brush Country Museum.)

IMAGES
of America

LA SALLE COUNTY

La Salle County Historical Commission

ARCADIA
PUBLISHING

ISBN 978-0-7385-7938-2

Published by Arcadia Publishing
Charleston, South Carolina

Printed in the United States of America

Library of Congress Control Number: 2010928861

For all general information, please contact Arcadia Publishing:
Telephone 843-853-2070
Fax 843-853-0044
E-mail sales@arcadiapublishing.com
For customer service and orders:
Toll-Free 1-888-313-2665

Visit us on the Internet at www.arcadiapublishing.com

This book is dedicated to the fearless men and women who braved a wilderness filled with Indians, outlaws, and rattlesnakes to create our county.

Contents

ACKNOWLEDGMENTS

The La Salle County Historical Commission thanks all the people of Cotulla and La Salle County for sharing their photographs through the years with the Brush Country Museum. Without their help and support this book would have not been possible.

All photographs used in this book are from the Brush Country Museum collection unless otherwise indicated.

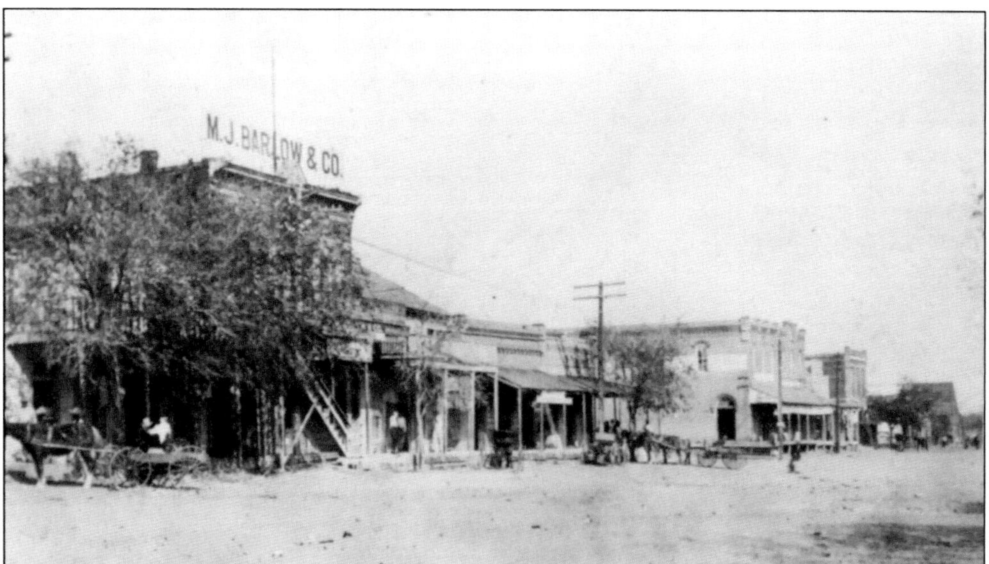

Front Street in downtown Cotulla was where everyone came to shop. This photograph was taken about 1913.

Introduction

La Salle County is located in the heart of the Brush Country. Its county seat, Cotulla, is approximately 67 miles north of Laredo on Interstate Highway 35. La Salle County was named for explorer Rene Robert Cavalier Sieur de La Salle. The terrain is mostly mesquite trees, cactus, brush, and grass. During the 1920s and 1930s, farming played an important part of the county's economy. Today ranching is more predominant.

La Salle County was officially formed in 1858 from Bexar County. The Nueces River runs through La Salle County and was at one time the boundary between Texas and Mexico, throwing much of the county into a no-man's-land. After the Treaty of Guadalupe Hidalgo gave the Nueces Strip to Texas, it remained a haven for Comanche Indians and some smaller tribes and also to outlaws. In 1852, the U.S. Army established an outpost, Fort Ewell, on the San Antonio-Laredo Road where it crossed the Nueces River. The fort consisted of a commissary storehouse, a blacksmith shop, and two sets of company quarters constructed of adobe. The purpose of the fort was to protect the travelers along the road. The army abandoned the site in 1854 because it proved to be unhealthy for the soldiers. Meanwhile a small settlement had grown up around the fort. William A. Waugh settled along the San Antonio-Laredo Road where it crossed Cibolo Creek in 1856. Joseph Cotulla settled along the Nueces River in 1868. William and Amanda Burks established La Mota Ranch in the 1870s.

When the county was formally organized in 1880, Stewart's Rancho near Fort Ewell became the first county seat. Pierce Johnston was the first county judge, James M. Buck became the first sheriff, and J. W. Baylor the first county clerk.

In the early 1880s, Joseph Cotulla learned that the International and Great Northern Railroad was going to run tracks into La Salle County. To induce the railroad to come to his ranch, Cotulla donated 120 acres for a town site. He named his town Cotulla. On the opposite side of the tracks, Jesse Laxson established the town of La Salle. After the railroad came through the county, the town of La Salle became the temporary county seat, and all the records were moved from Fort Ewell. Cotulla and the town of La Salle began competing to become the county seat. In 1883, a special election was held to decide on a permanent county seat. The voters chose Cotulla. Joseph Cotulla had dedicated a block in his town for a courthouse square. Soon after the election, construction of a permanent courthouse began. J. C. Breeding and Sons of San Antonio were the architects, and the building was constructed of redbrick from the Cotulla brick kiln. A jail was built just north of the courthouse.

In the early days, Cotulla was a wild frontier town and La Salle County a haven for outlaws. Shootings and hangings were common. A sheriff was assassinated, and a justice of the peace was accidentally shot during a gunfight. Texas Rangers were stationed in Cotulla to try and keep the peace. Over time things began to settle down. Churches and schools were built, and other settlements began to spring up over the county.

In 1883, the settlement of Encinal on the southern county line was granted a post office. The settlement of Millett received postal designation in 1888. The early 1900s were a period of growth. The towns of Gardendale, Artesia Wells, Fowlerton, and Woodward were established. Out-of-county developers formed most of these towns. Nationwide advertising brought trainloads of new settlers to the county. The population doubled during this period of time. The newcomers bought 10- and 20-acre tracts expecting to irrigate the acreage and turn their land into prosperous farms.

In 1923, Los Angeles, in the eastern part of the county, was established by the F. Z. Bishop Land Company. Many of the settlers of the Los Angles area were of German descent and came from the Central Texas area. By 1928, Los Angeles had 300 residents. A hotel, general store, cotton gin, lumberyard, and school had been built. The population of the county again doubled.

During the Great Depression, the boom of earlier years died. The onion and other vegetable farms were forced to cut back. Cotton production dropped. Many farms were abandoned, and the people left the area.

In the early 1940s, Hugh Roy Cullen and Quintana Petroleum Company came to La Salle County. A large portion of the county was leased for oil and gas, including the town of Cotulla. Numerous wells were drilled in the eastern part of the county. In 1941, the B-1 Washburn in the Quintana field was producing 400 barrels of crude daily. Crude from the well was loaded onto tank cars at Dull, located on the San Antonio and Uvalde Railroad, and shipped out. Many new families moved into the county with Quintana.

Drought gripped La Salle County and much of Texas in the 1950s. Years went by with no rain falling. The remaining farmers moved away, and the ranchers were forced to sell their cattle while trying to hold on to their land. In 1953, the county agent reported that the number of entries in the junior livestock show would be reduced because of the drought. The drought was so severe that citizens of the county would meet, and a community prayer service was held with various individuals praying for rain. In the early spring of 1957, the drought ended. Rain began to fall, from slow, soaking rains to gully washers.

The citizens of La Salle County have always been a hardy bunch, able to meet any disaster head on. Whether Indian raids, outlaws, gunfights, hangings, droughts, floods, train wrecks, or brush fires, the citizens of La Salle County will and have overcome.

One

The Trailblazers

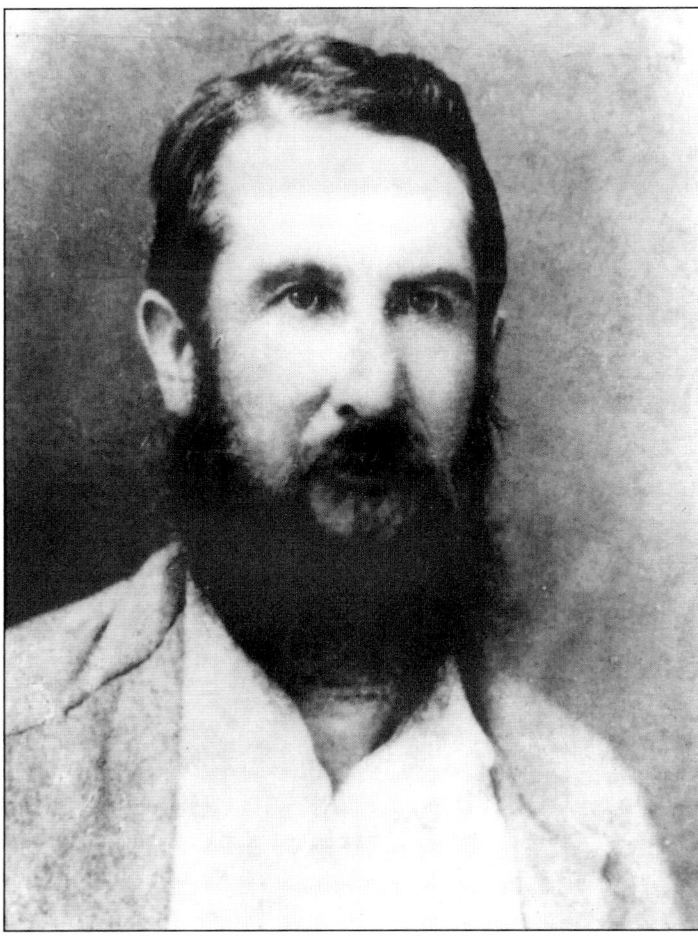

In 1856, William A. Waugh established a cow camp on the Cibolo Creek crossing on the San Antonio-Laredo Road. He built a ranch house and ran his cattle on the open range. When La Salle County was created in 1858 he found himself one of the first residents of the newly formed county. For many years Waugh continued to run his cattle on the open range. In 1877, he purchased the first land in La Salle County. His ranch consisted of 5,340 acres on which he ran 1,000 head of cattle, 60 horses, and mules. William Waugh married Maria Angelita Serna in the early 1860s. William and Angelita were the parents of one son and three daughters.

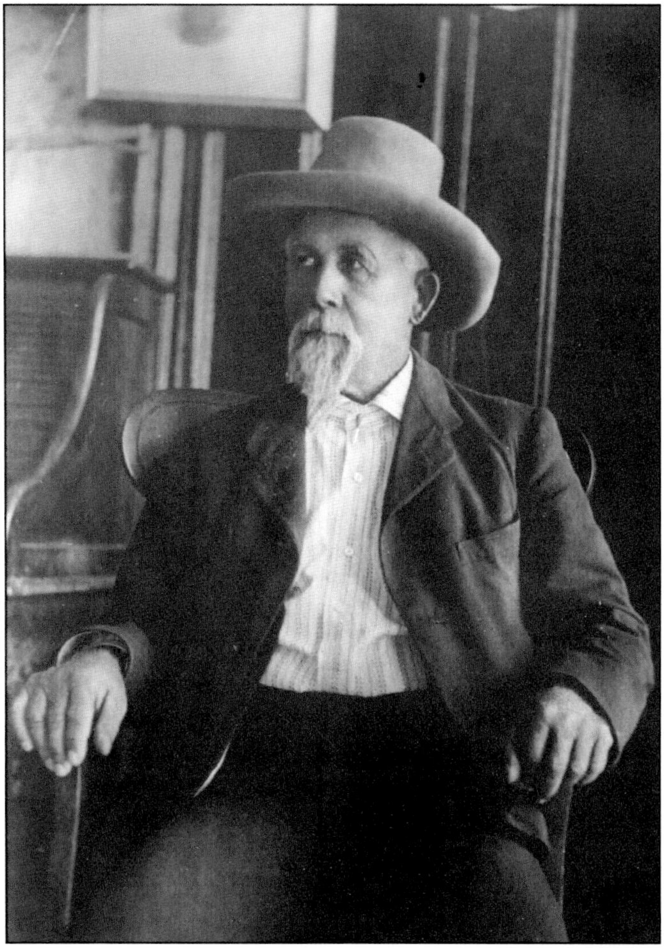

Joseph Cotulla was born in Poland and came to Texas in 1856 when he was 12; he settled along the Nueces River in 1868, where he started farming and ranching. In 1871, he married Mary Rieder in Atascosa County and returned to La Salle County to build his bride a home. At one time he owned 30,000 acres in La Salle, Dimmit, and Webb Counties. When he realized the International and Great Railroad was coming to the county, he donated 120 acres for a town to induce the railroad to come to his ranch. He named his town Cotulla. To help the town grow, Joseph Cotulla donated a block for a courthouse and a public park. He donated lots for the first school, and the Baptist, Methodist, and Presbyterian churches. Joseph and Mary Rieder Cotulla were the parents of four daughters and five sons.

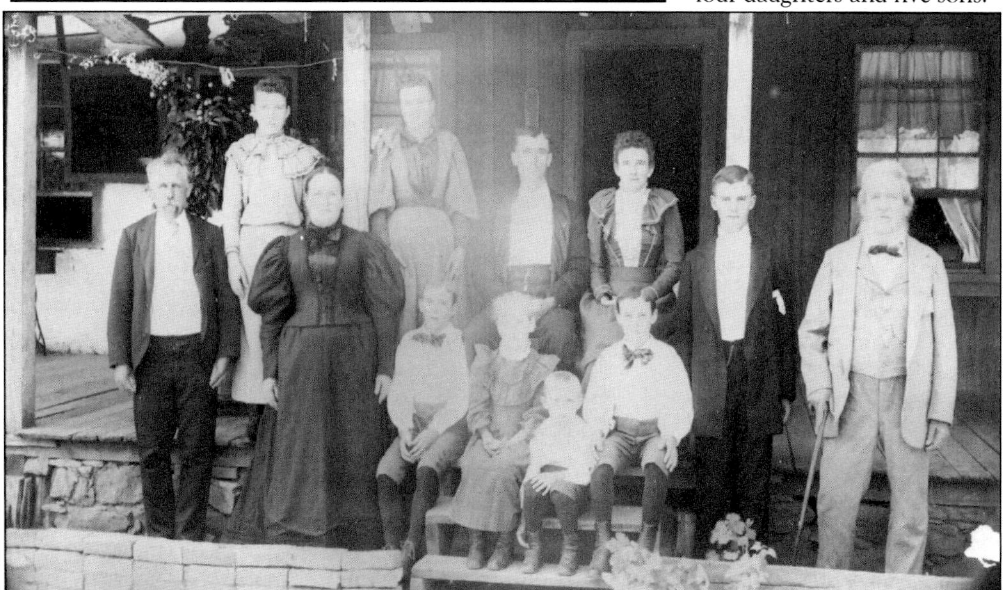

In 1878, Jean Stuart Taylor Steele encountered one of the worst experiences of her life. She was home alone with her young children when a band of Mexicans, Indians, and one white man attacked the Palo Alto Ranch. John Steele, brother of her husband, William Hutton Steele, was killed. Richard and George Taylor, sons by a previous marriage, were captured and later killed and scalped. Jean Steele witnessed the massacre from her home and gathered her other small children and hid them in the tall grass along the Nueces River until the raiding party passed.

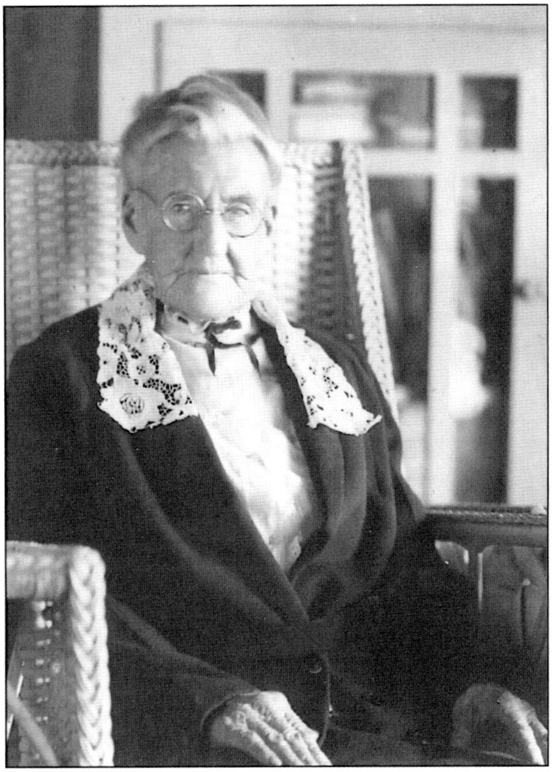

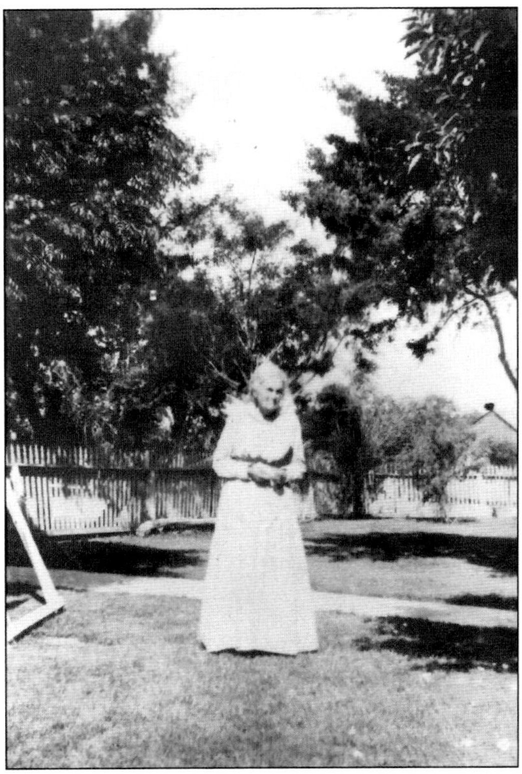

Wanting to settle where the country was more open, Amanda Nite Burks and her husband, William Franklin Burks, settled in La Salle County. He spotted a section of land where the wood and water was plentiful and immediately filed claim on it. In the summer of 1876, Amanda and William Burks came to La Salle County to build their home. Soon after establishing La Mota Ranch, William died, leaving Amanda a widow. She continued to live on and operate the ranch until her death in 1931.

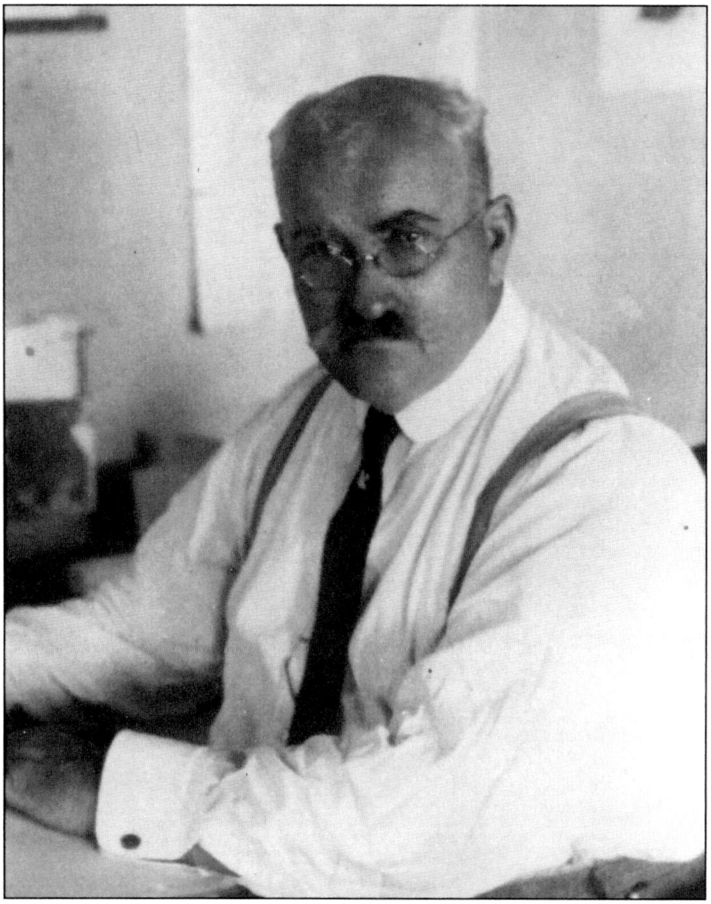

When La Salle County was officially organized at Fort Ewell in 1880, George H. Knaggs was there. He was appointed temporary clerk and took the minutes of the first commissioners' court meeting. In 1884, he married Carrie Jordan (below, in black), and they became the parents of four sons and three daughters. Hospitality was always the word at the Knaggs home. A warm welcome was always extended to all.

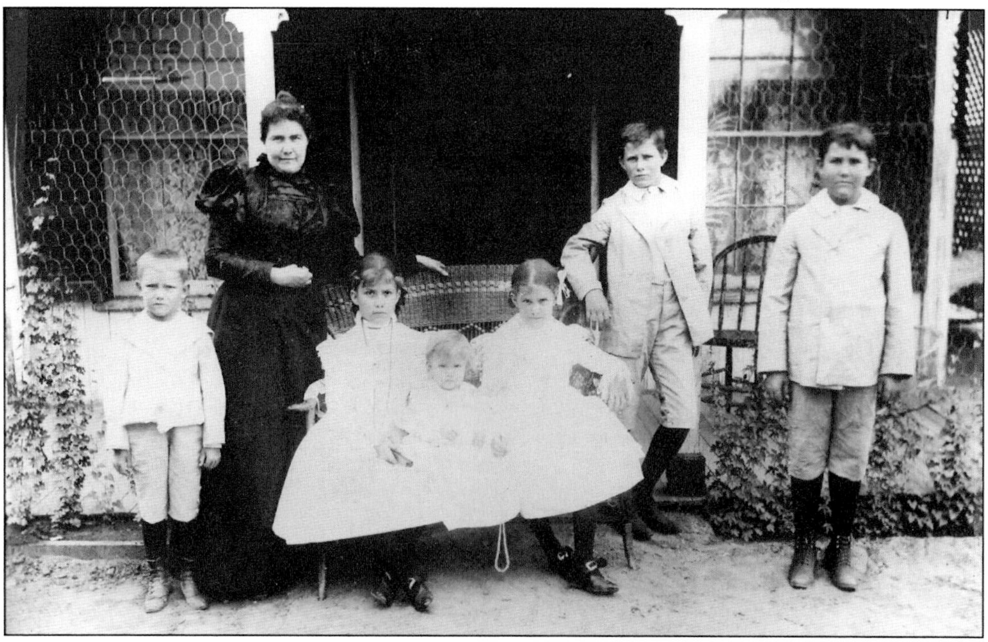

William Henry and Eliza Ann (Scholfield) Keck came to La Salle County in 1880 establishing their home in the western part of the county about 8 miles from Cotulla. Keck was a devout Methodist. When the Methodist church was erected, he preached the first sermon in the new building. He was fatally injured when he was thrown from a hay rake in June 1890. The Kecks were the parents of four children, Henry A., Edgar A., Sallie, and Thomas Randall.

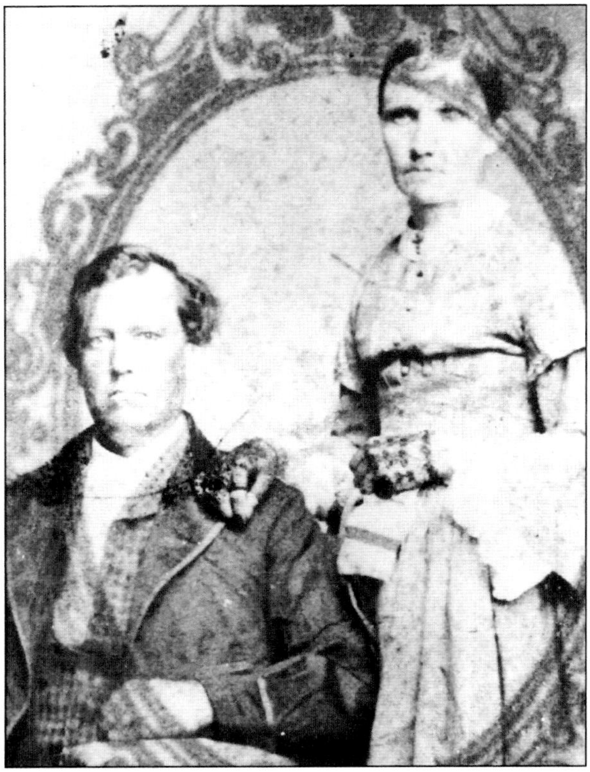

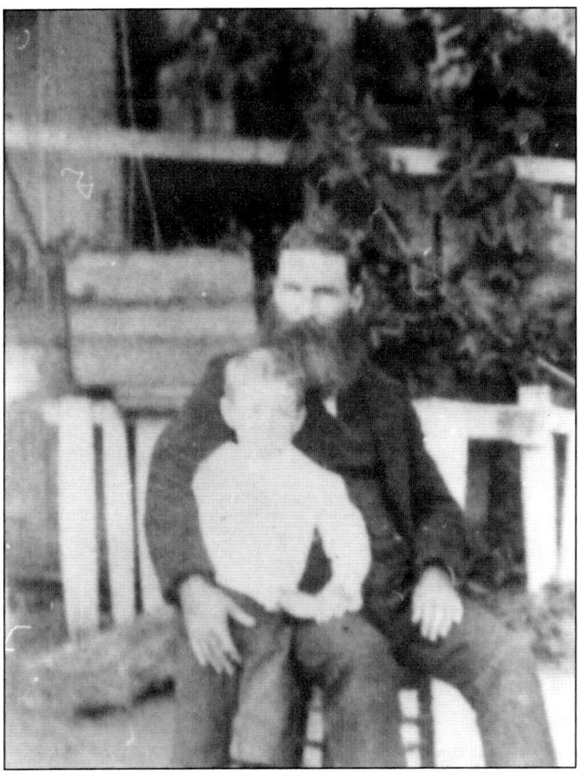

Jack W. Baylor was a captain for the Confederacy during the Civil War. After the war, he made his way to La Salle County. Jack Baylor married Rhoda Burks, and they settled on La Mota Ranch. When La Salle County was officially organized, he became the first county clerk.

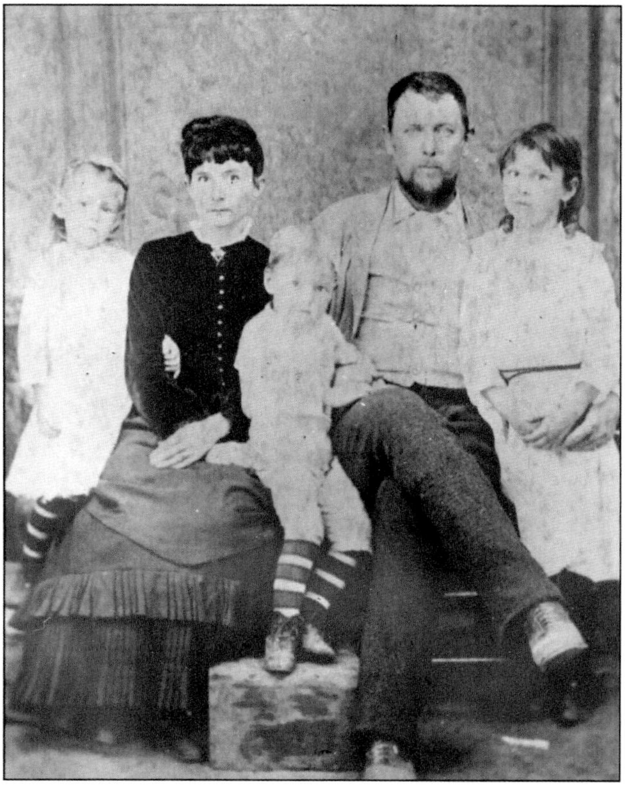

Often led blindfolded into a thicket to treat a wounded outlaw, Dr. Joseph W. Hargus started his medical practice in the brush south of Fort Ewell. The story goes that in the early days of his practice he treated 259 gunshot wounds and examined another 108 gunshot wounds that did not require treatment. He married Saphronia Frazier in 1880. When they moved their family to Cotulla in 1884, they built the first house in the new town. He practiced in La Salle County until 1887, when he and his family moved to Dimmit County.

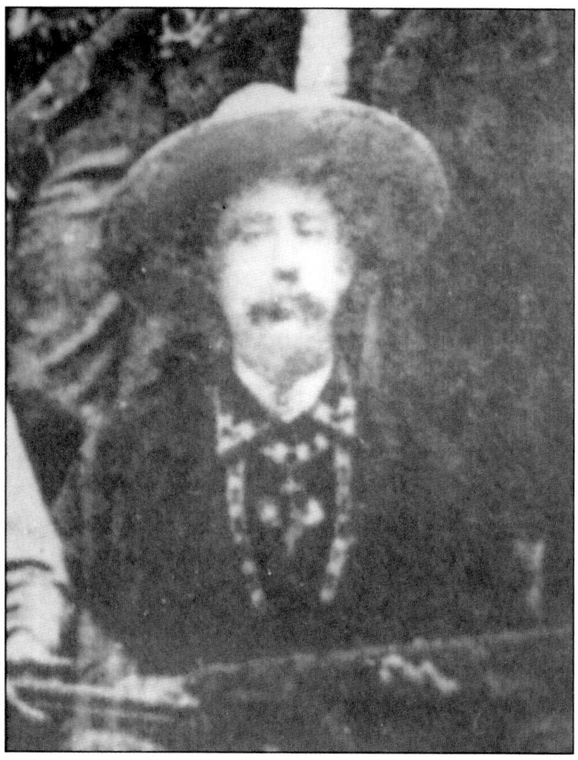

On September 1, 1881, Cecilio Charo was granted 160 acres of land in La Salle County by the State of Texas. Charo served with Company F of the Frontier Battalion of the Texas Rangers. On May 30, 1881, the commissioners' court appointed Charo constable.

J. Guy Reed was the owner of an early newspaper in Cotulla called *Reed's Isonomy*. The newspaper had a wide circulation. Reed printed exactly what he thought in his newspaper and thereby became the subject of many libel suits. He was wounded in a shooting at the Burke Hotel where another man was killed.

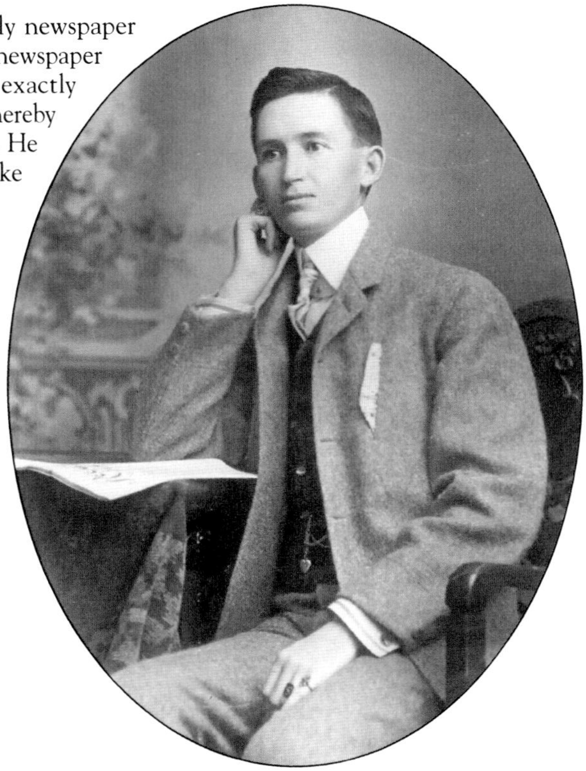

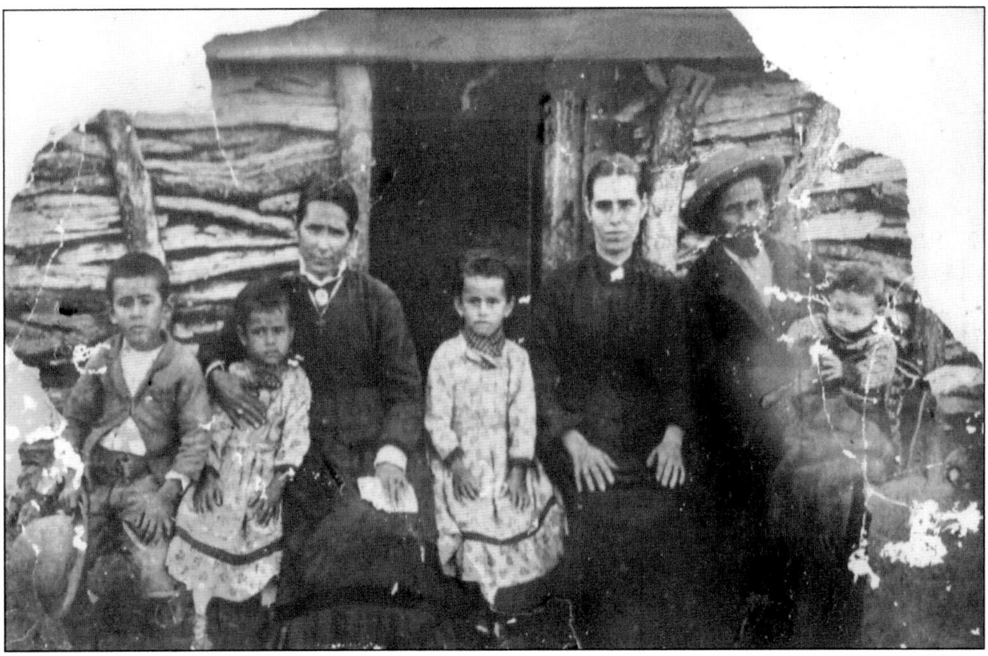

Candelario Campos and his wife, Eulogio Escamilla Campos, were both born in Mexico. Candelario immigrated to Texas when he was 16 years old; Eulogia was in her 20s when she did the same.. In 1880, they were living in the Encinal area, where they proceeded to raise their family and live out their lives.

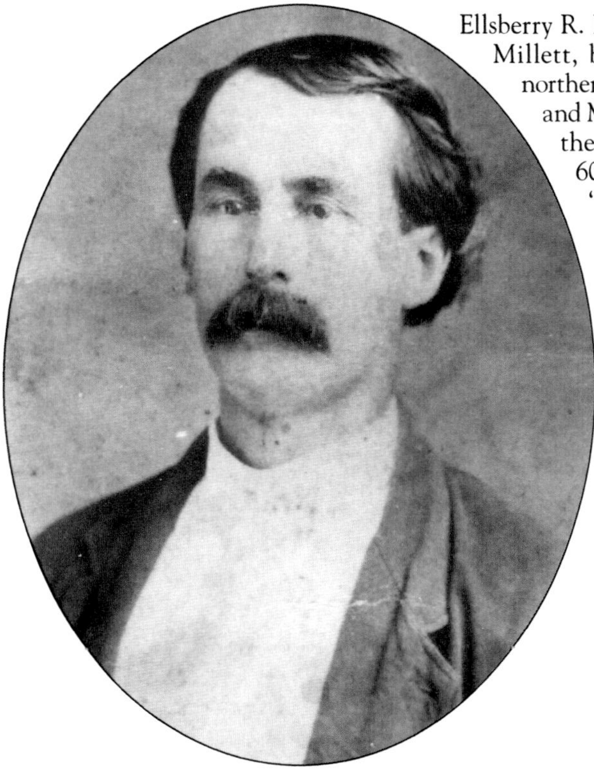

Ellsberry R. Lane, with his brother-in-law Alonzo Millett, bought a large tract of land in the northern part of La Salle County in 1881. Lane and Millett expanded their operations until they owned 125,000 acres and employed 60 cowboys. They became known as the "Texas Millionaires."

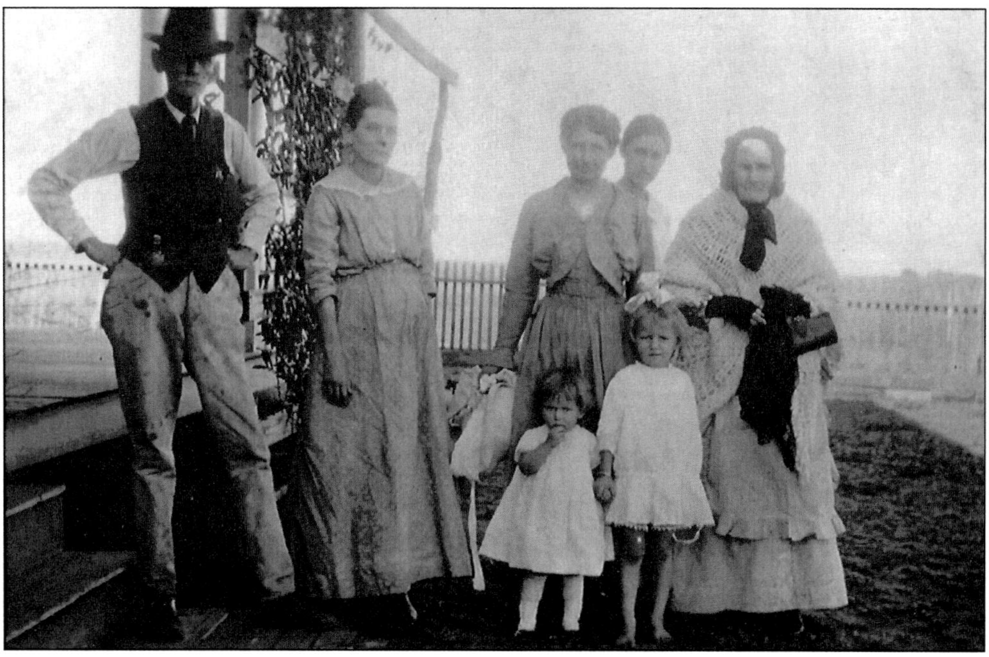

James H. Breeding came to La Salle County in 1882. He first worked for Lee Hall building tanks east of Cotulla. In 1886, he married Laura Alice Hocker and moved to Encinal to take over a mercantile business. James and Laura were the parents of three children, Bessie, Herbert, and Hellen.

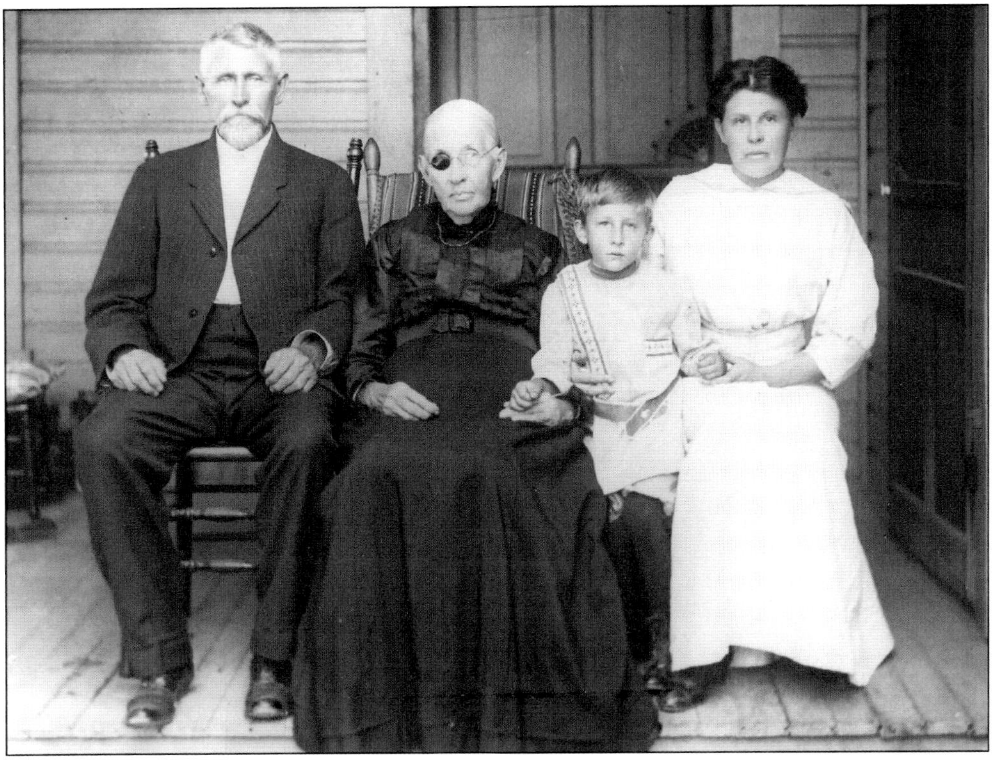

Charles Blair and Harriett Amelia Merrill Burwell were among the early settlers of La Salle County, having settled there in 1884. Pictured are four generations. From left to right are John Armistead Burwell, born 1856; Harriet Merrill Burwell, born 1831; Travis Poole, born 1908; and Winnie Burwell Poole, born 1887.

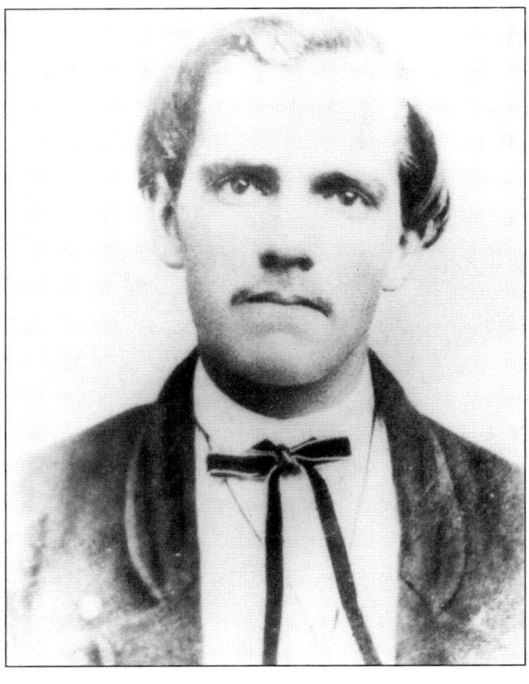

While working as a contractor on the International and Great Northern Railroad, William Barnes Guinn first came to La Salle County. After the railroad was completed, he liked the place and decided to stay. He built the second house in Cotulla. "Uncle Billy," as everyone called him, was a farmer and rancher. He was among the first to irrigate and raise onions. At age 80, he was still driving his Buick around town.

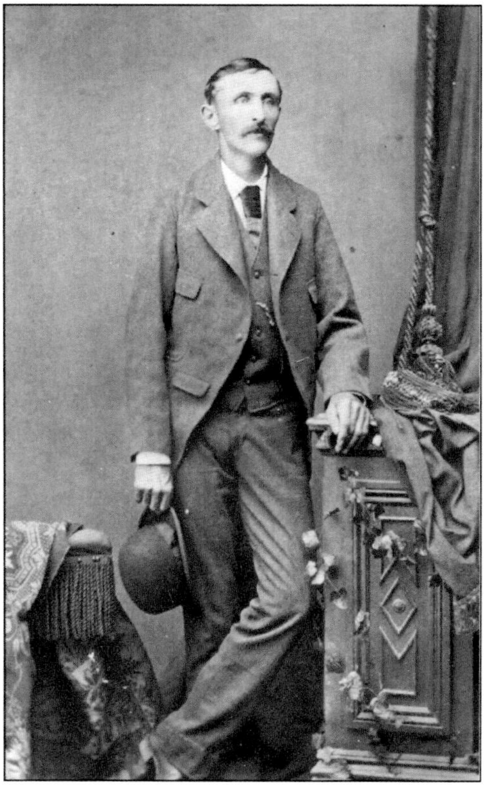

George and Jessie Ann Spence Copp bought property east of Cotulla on the Nueces River in 1885. At one time, he owned land from the railroad bridge to Vincent Crossing. The Copps built a large 12-room house with beautiful grounds on the property. George was an onion farmer and shipped the first load of onions out of the state of Texas. Being a man of many talents, he also owned and operated Copp's Saloon located on Front Street.

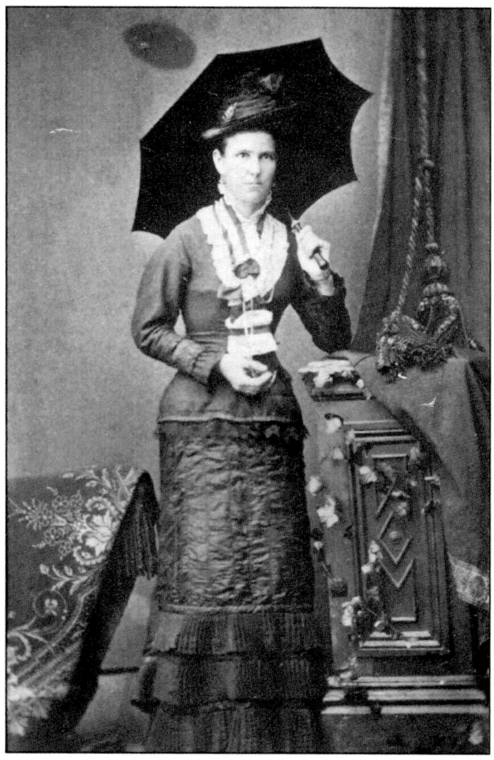

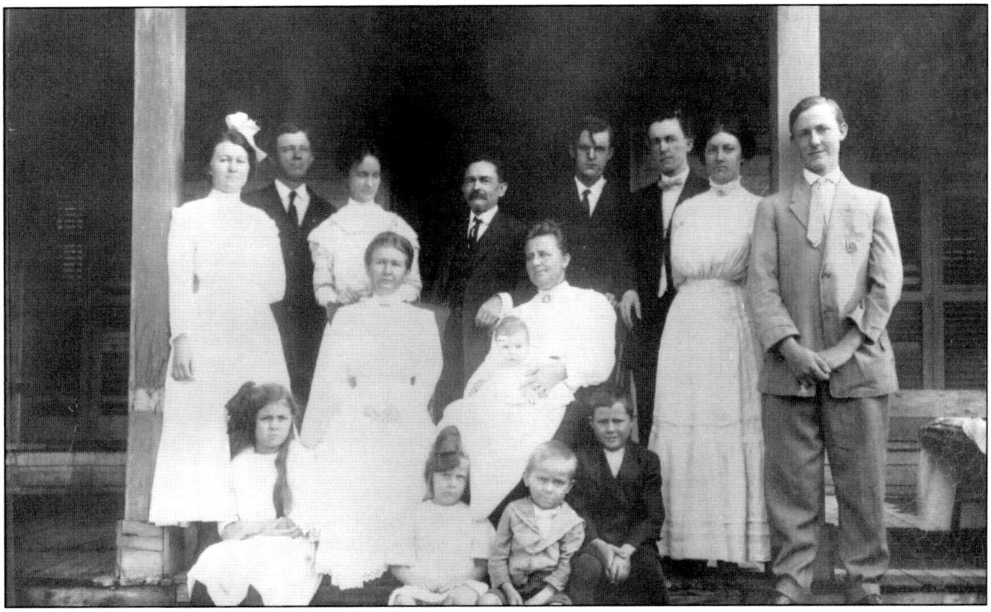

In 1886, Bernard and Aissa Wadgymar Wildenthal moved to Cotulla. Nine children were born to this couple: Arthur, Bernard, Carl, John, Hobson, Bryan, Mary, Adele, and Helen. Bernard Wildenthal became involved with the Stockmens National Bank in 1900 and remained with it until he retired in 1925.

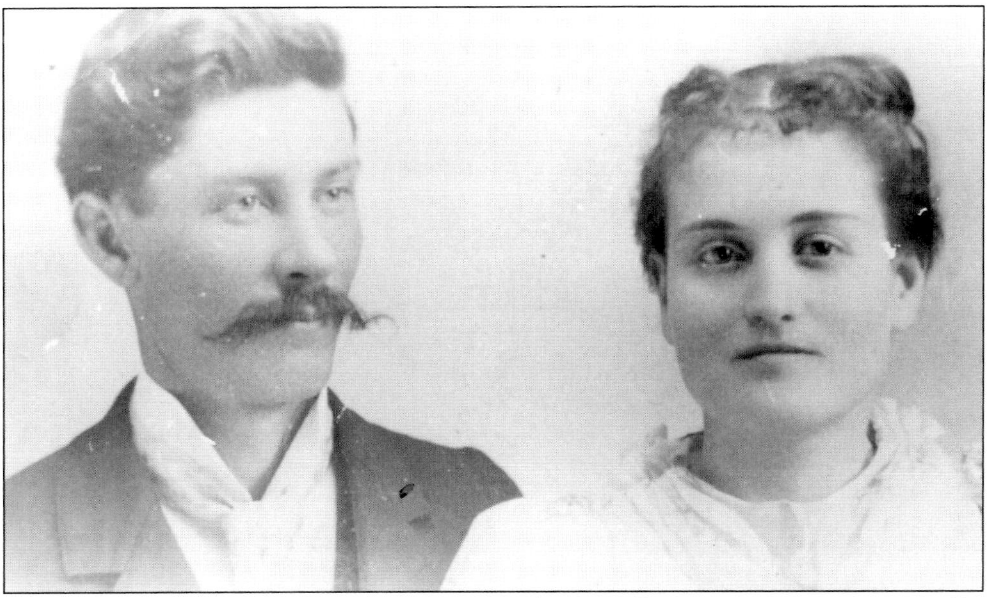

Lewis W. and Mary Louise Passmore Gaddis moved to La Salle County in 1899. Lewis Gaddis worked in the drugstore owned by his uncle, Dr. J. M. Williams. In 1904, he purchased the business and began operating as Gaddis Pharmacy. Lewis and Mary Louise Gaddis were members of the Methodist Church and outstanding civic leaders.

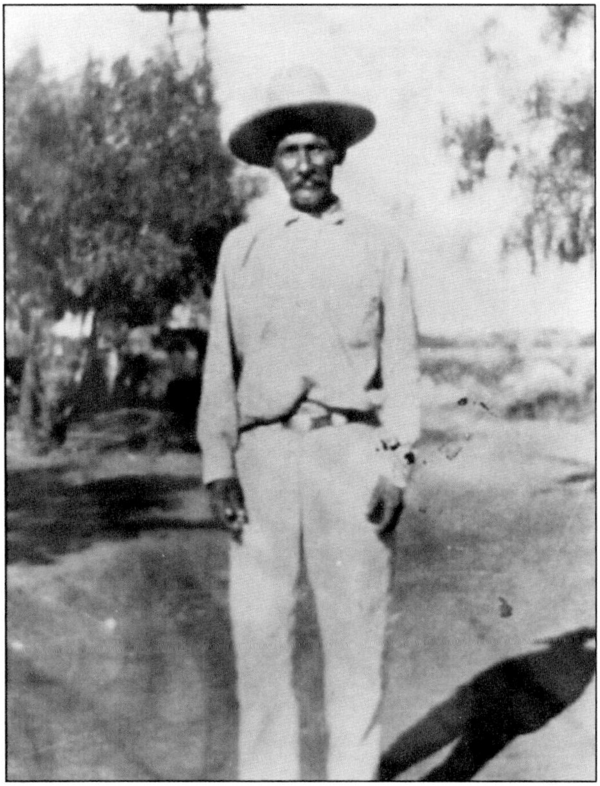

Fortunato Cabello was born in Mexico in August 1874. He came to Texas with his mother and stepfather in 1890. The family first settled and worked on a ranch in the Encinal area. Fortunato Cabello married Librada Barrera about 1898. In the early 1900s, they moved to a ranch near Millett where they raised their family. Both are buried in the Millett Cemetery.

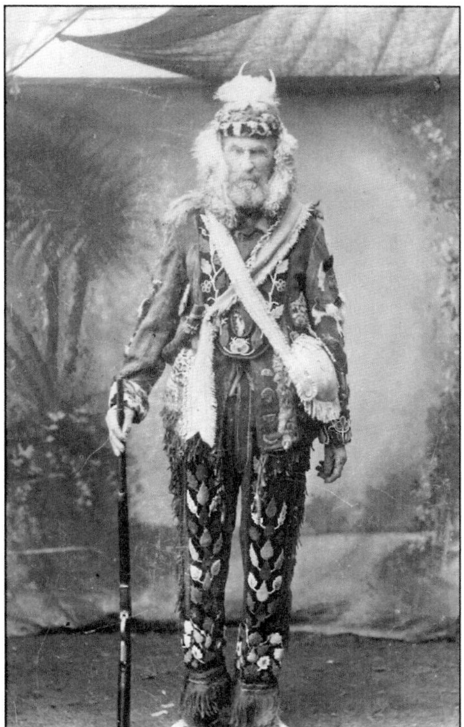

Col. Robert Hall was born April 4, 1814, in South Carolina. He came to Texas in the spring of 1836 and soon became a true Texan. He was a veteran of the War for Texas Independence, the Mexican War, and was a spy for the South during the Civil War. He was an Indian fighter and a Texas Ranger. Colonel Hall was married to Mary Minerva King in Gonzales County. He spent the last years of his life in La Salle County, living on the Nueces River. He died December 19, 1899, in Cotulla, Texas.

Born in Mexico in 1866, Gabriel Garza became a citizen at age 21. Gabriel Garza and Porfiria Sepulveda were married in 1889 and settled in La Salle County. They were the parents of eight children: Julia, Aurelia, Blaza, Tomas, Nazario, Juana, Rafael, and Jose, all pictured below with their father (far right). Gabriel and Porfiria both died in La Salle County and are buried in the Antigua Cemetery in Cotulla.

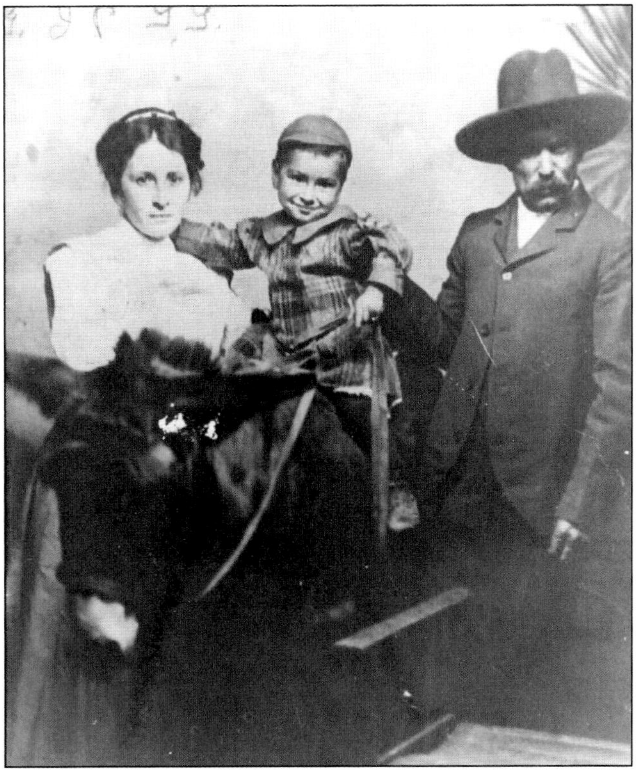

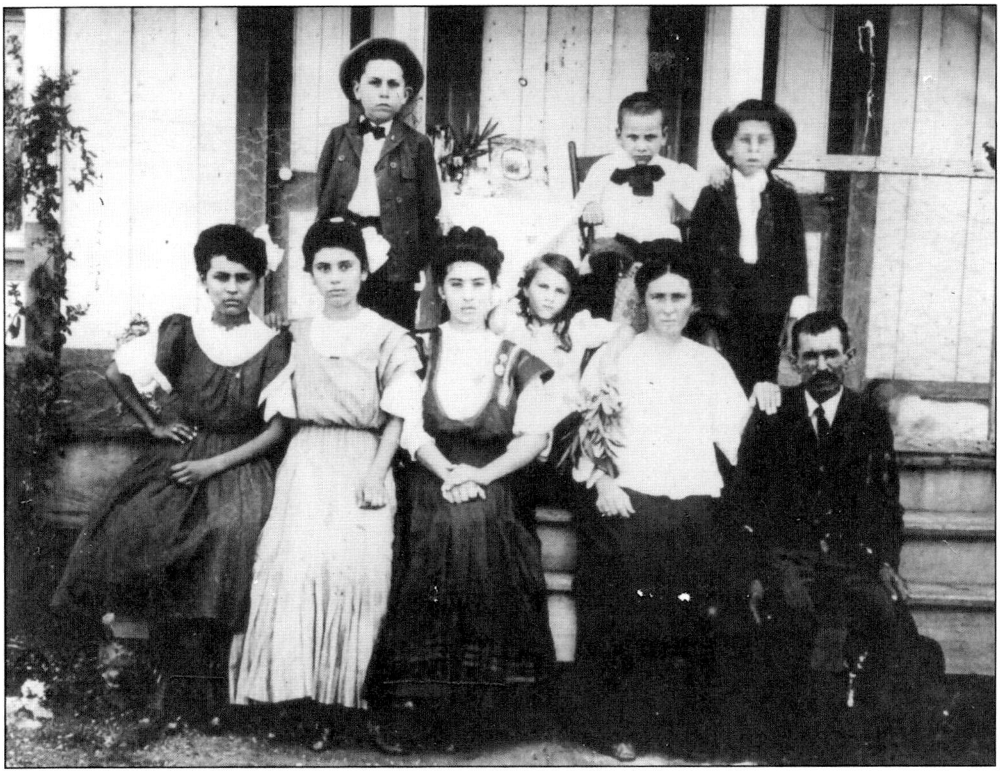

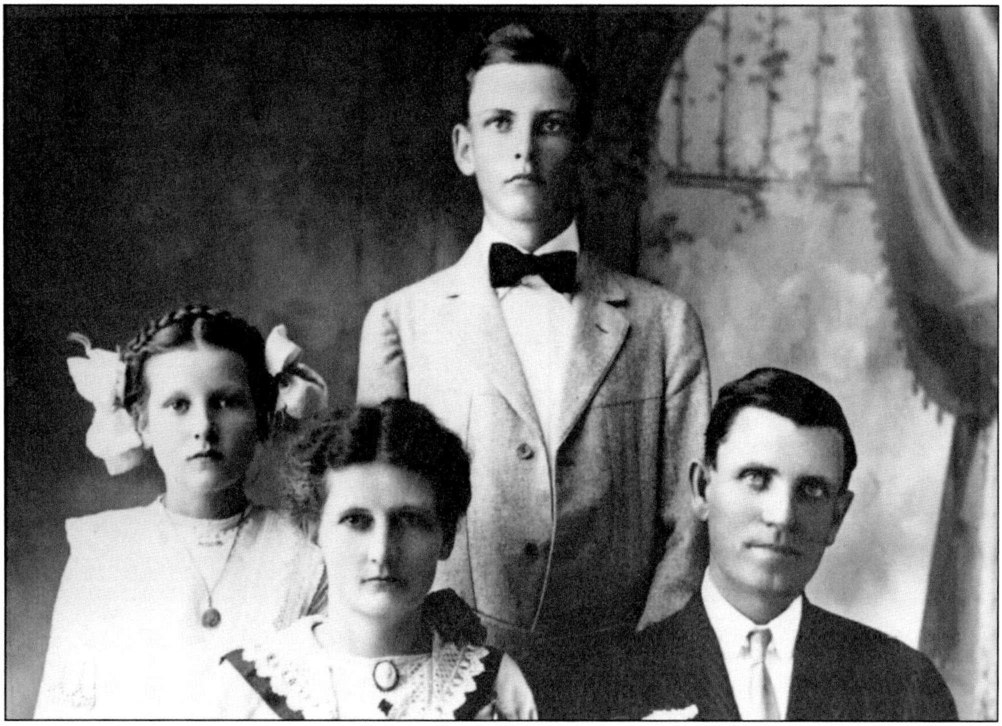

David L. and Delia Fullerton Neeley decided to move to Cotulla in 1901. David went into business with his father-in-law, who operated a small grocery store. He later expanded the business by buying the Cotulla Mercantile, which became known as the "Red and White." David and Delia were the parents of two children, Marion J. (farthest left) and Bernice. They are all shown above.

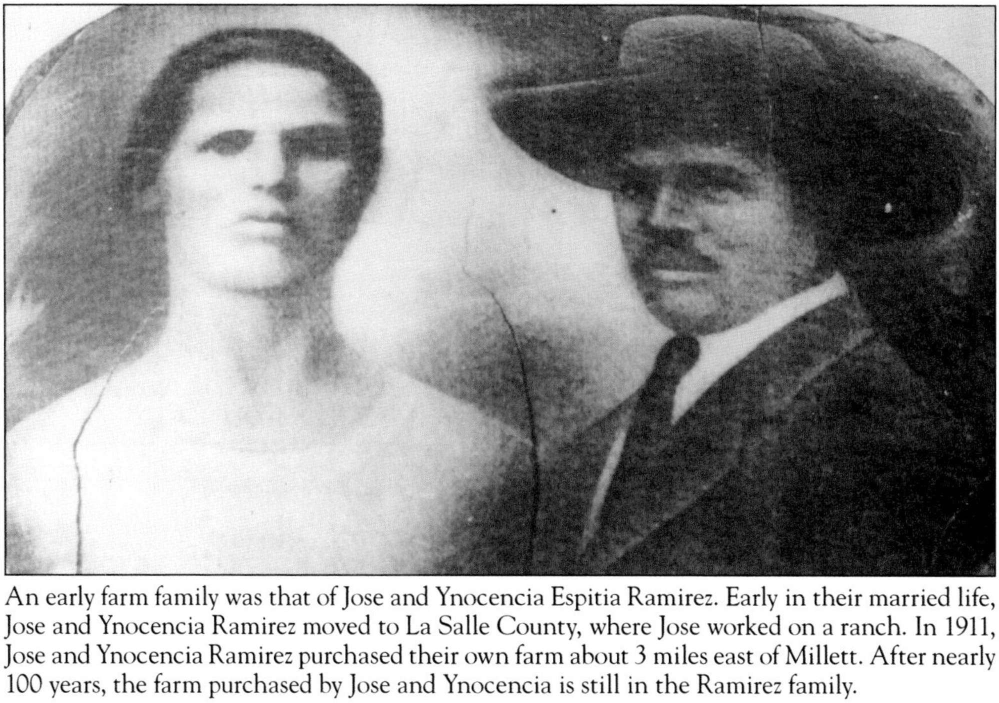

An early farm family was that of Jose and Ynocencia Espitia Ramirez. Early in their married life, Jose and Ynocencia Ramirez moved to La Salle County, where Jose worked on a ranch. In 1911, Jose and Ynocencia Ramirez purchased their own farm about 3 miles east of Millett. After nearly 100 years, the farm purchased by Jose and Ynocencia is still in the Ramirez family.

Two

LAW AND ORDER

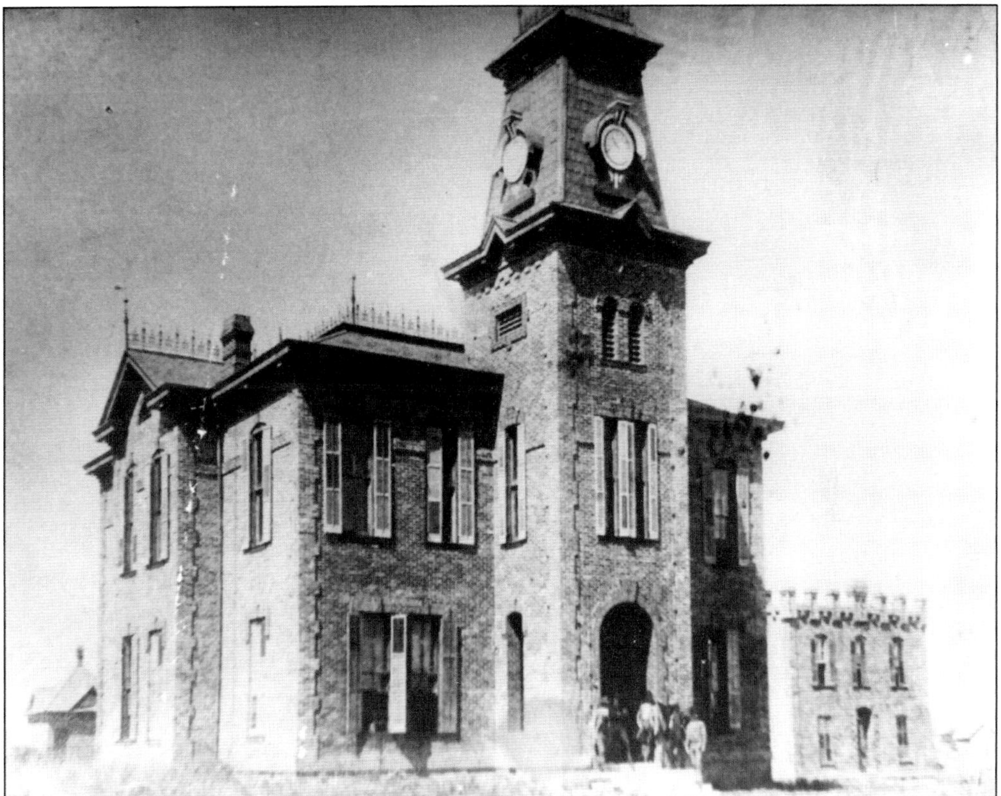

After an election in 1883, the town of Cotulla was officially designated the county seat, and plans to build a courthouse soon started. Architect J. C. Breeding submitted plans, and construction on the first courthouse began. The structure consisted of two stories and was constructed of Cotulla brick. A fireproof vault was installed to protect the county records. In 1895, the courthouse was destroyed by fire. Arson was suspected but never proven. Most of the county records were preserved in the fireproof vault. The building was insured for $9,500, which was used to erect another building on the courthouse square. The current courthouse is the fourth structure to be erected in the same location.

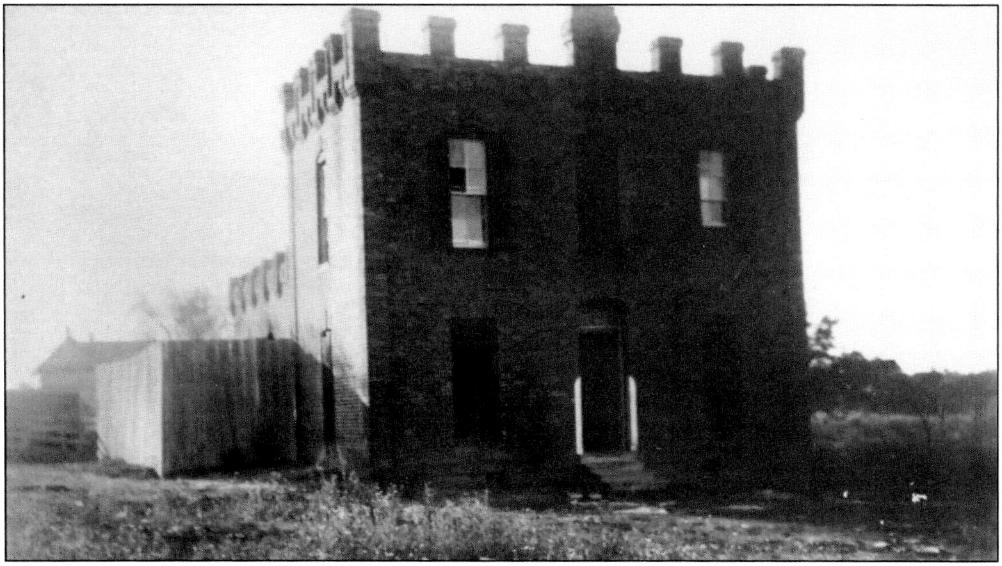

The first county jail was located on the courthouse square just to the north of the courthouse. The jail had six cells, each 5 feet squared with a 7 foot ceiling, made of five-ply wrought iron and steel bars. The cells' tops were made of five-ply welded iron and steel plate one-fourth of an inch thick. A 4-foot hall separated each section of cells. The iron and steel was saw- and file-proof and was tested by an expert. Soon after the jail opened, the citizens of Cotulla stormed it, overpowered the guard, took custody of Green McCullough, and hung him on a mesquite tree in back of the courthouse.

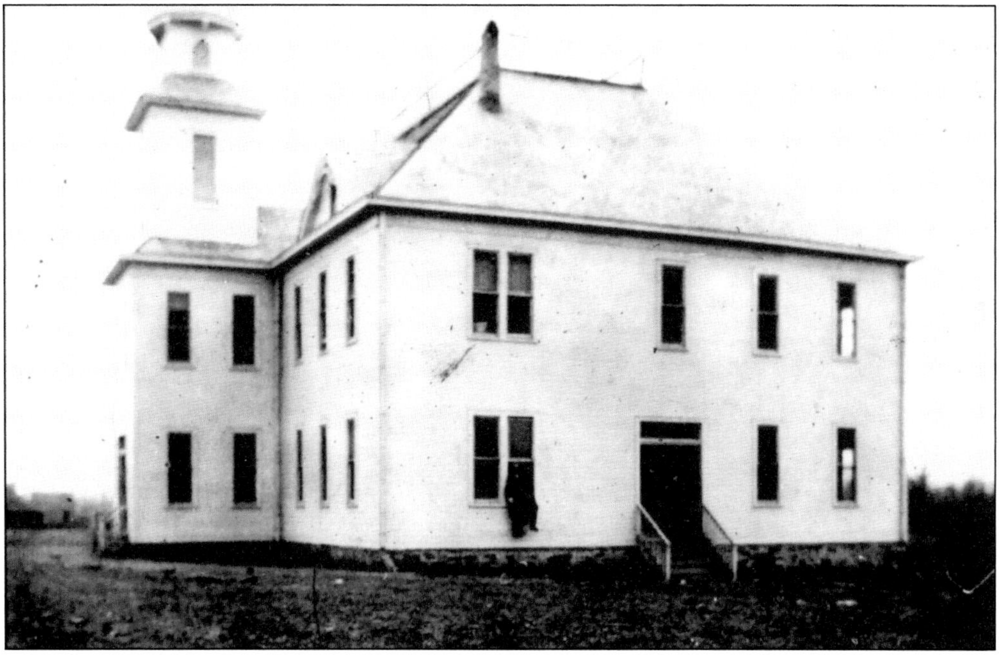

Shortly after the original courthouse burned, the citizens of the county met to discuss the construction of a new one. It was decided that due to the tense political situation in the county it would be wise not to invest much money in a new building. A two-story wooden building was constructed for $5,000. This was a wise decision, as the second courthouse burned in 1904.

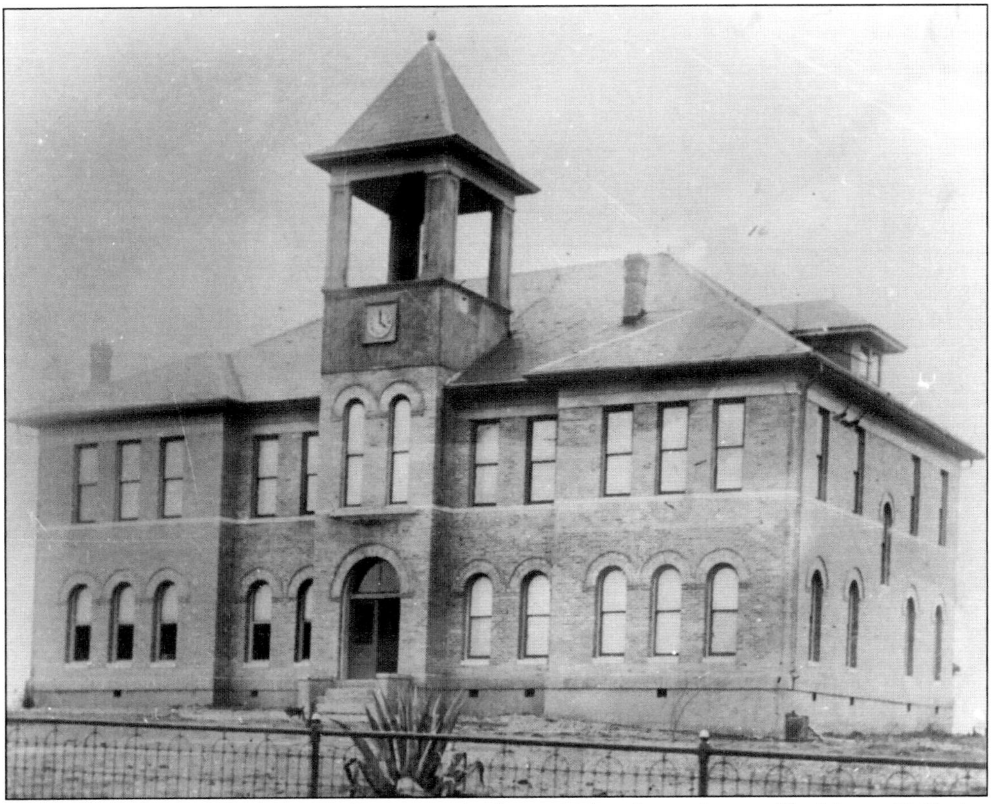

The third La Salle County Courthouse was built in 1905 and was designed by Henry T. Phelps of San Antonio. It was a two-story brick structure with a cupola and a slate roof. From the very beginning, there were problems with the construction of the building. The slate roof proved to be too heavy for the building, causing the walls to spread apart. The cupola and eventually the slate roof were removed, but the problem remained. In 1931, the courthouse was torn down and the present courthouse was erected.

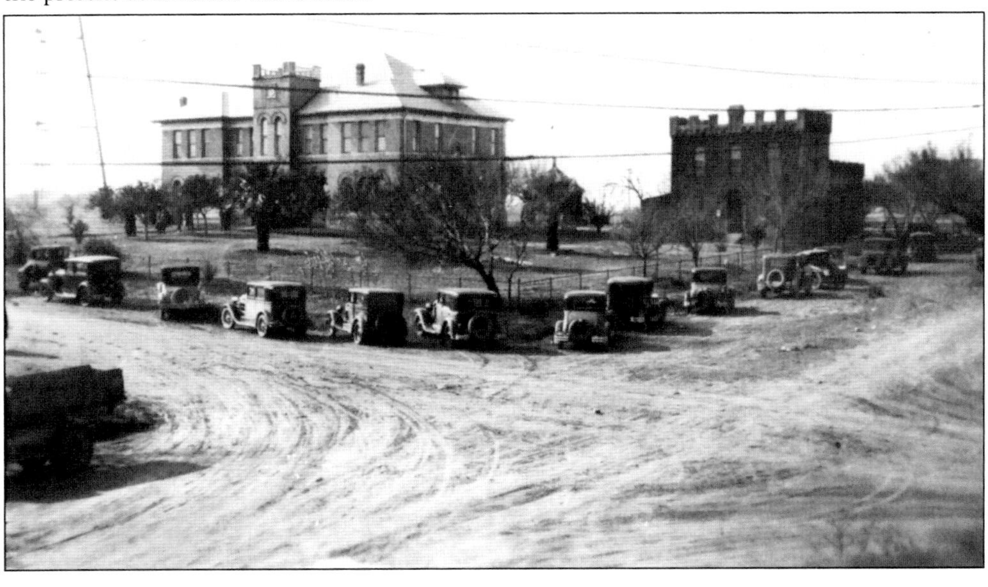

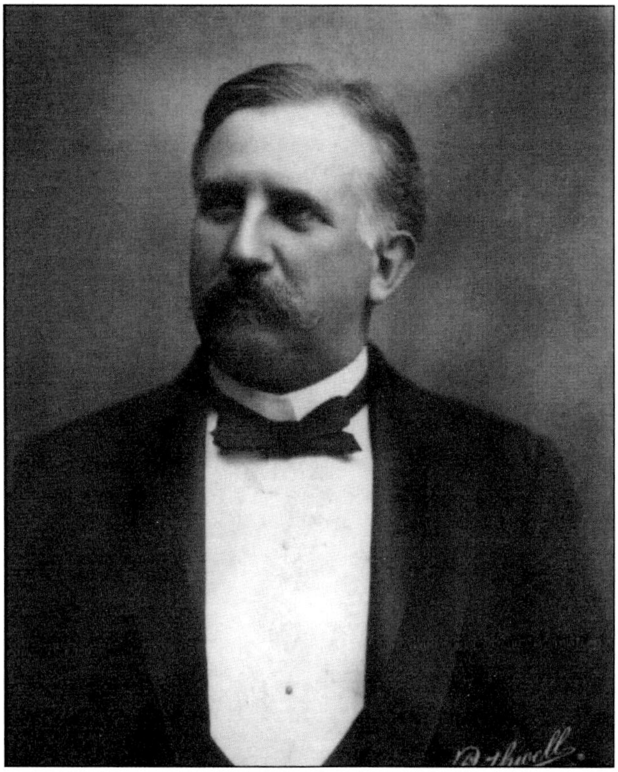

Frank B. Earnest, an attorney, began his career in 1881. His first job was not law, but tutoring young adults on the Dull and neighboring ranches, preparing them for college. Not long after, clients began seeking his legal advice, as he was the only attorney in La Salle County. In 1884, he was elected county judge. The first courthouse and jail were built during his tenure in office.

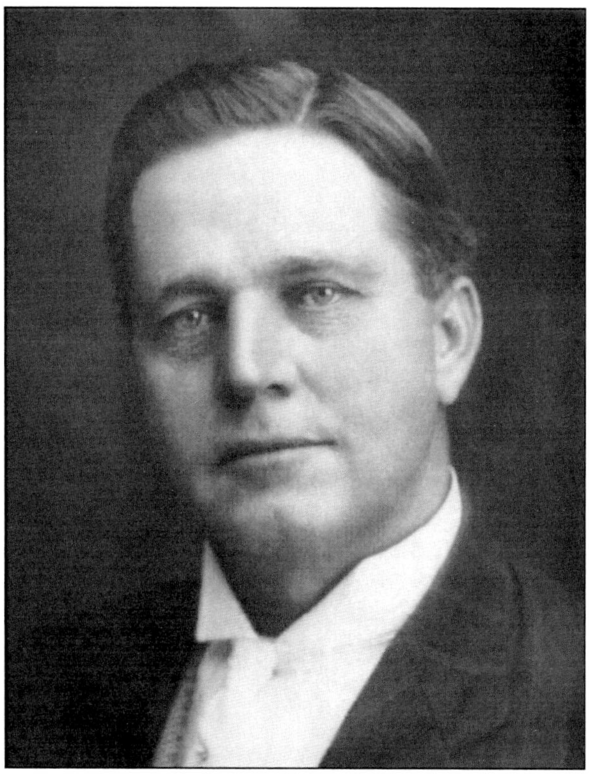

After graduating from the University of Texas Law School in 1896, Covey C. Thomas returned to his hometown to practice law. Shortly after returning home, he was elected county attorney. Four years later, he was elected county judge and served as judge for 16 years. When the 81st Judicial District was created, the governor appointed him district judge. After serving as district judge for years, he ran for chief justice of the Texas Supreme Court, but was defeated.

Gustav A. Welhausen was a rancher when he became county judge in 1916. Having served earlier as a school trustee in Encinal, he was a firm believer in educating the young people of La Salle County. During his time in office, Judge Welhausen was instrumental in replacing all the wooden school buildings in the county with modern brick ones. He resigned in 1943 after 27 years in office.

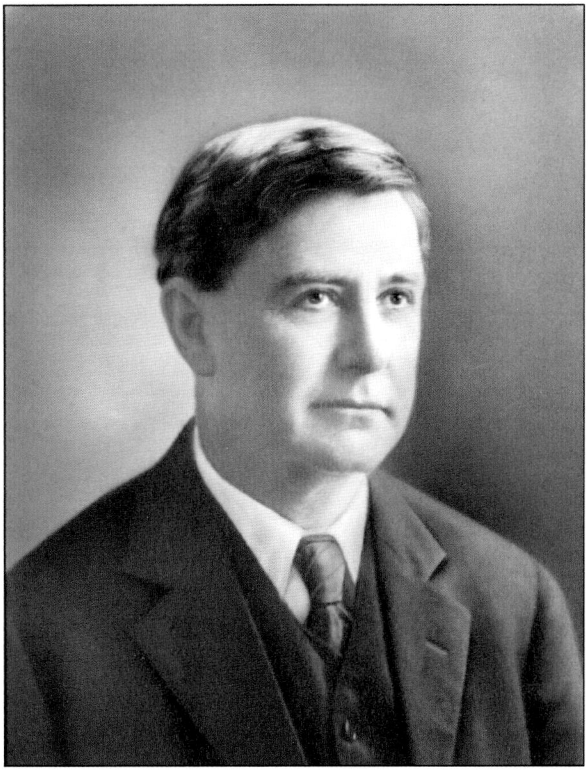

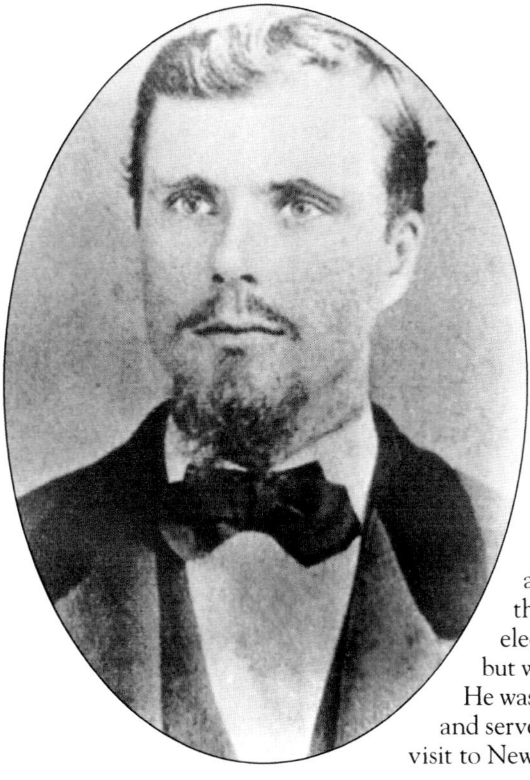

Patrick Dargan Hickey was a native of Ireland who made his way to La Salle County to be appointed county judge in 1882. Hickey held this position until November 1882 when he was elected county clerk. He served a two-year term, but was defeated in November 1884 by J. H. Reese. He was again elected county clerk in November 1886 and served until dying on August 18, 1896, while on a visit to New Orleans.

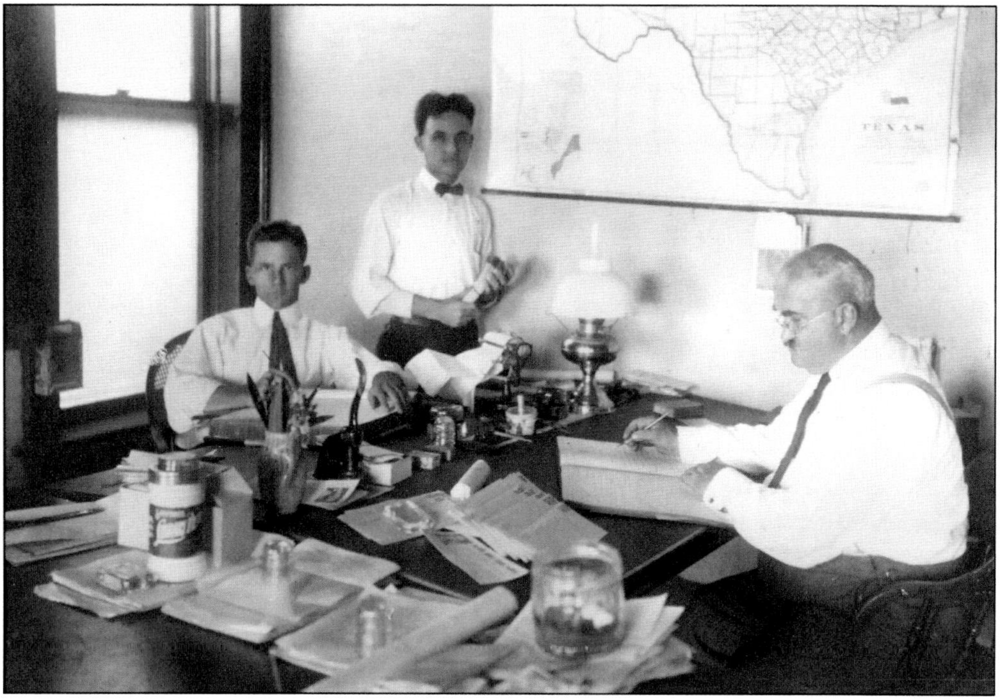

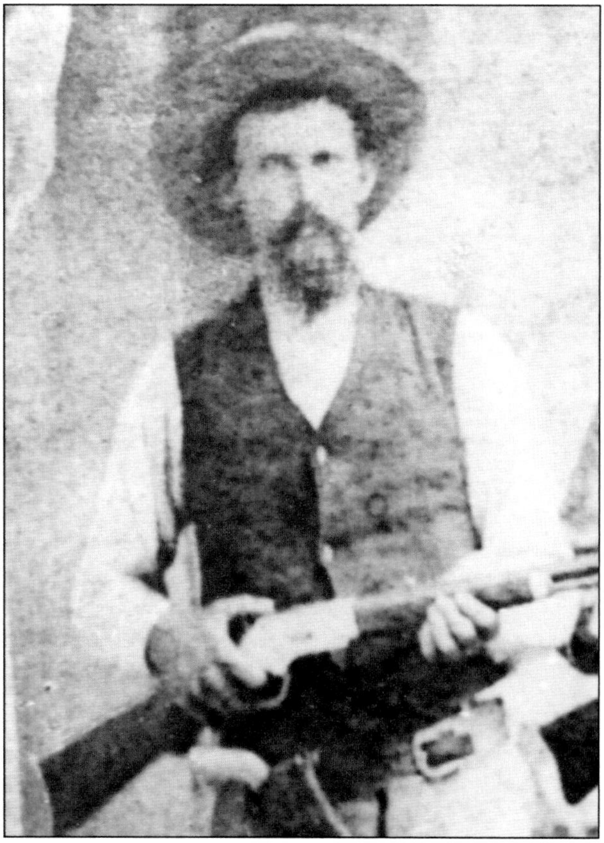

After the sudden death of county clerk P. D. Hickey, George H. Knaggs (above, right) was appointed to fill out his unexpired term of office. Knaggs was elected county clerk in November 1896, and he continued to serve the people of La Salle County for the following 23 years. At his death, the commissioners' court adopted a resolution of respect stating that "this court loses a faithful member and the county a most worthy member."

James Madison Buck was the first sheriff of La Salle County, taking the oath of office and posting bond in January 1881. Sheriff Buck's tenure of office was very short. He resigned in May 1881 after serving only five months in office.

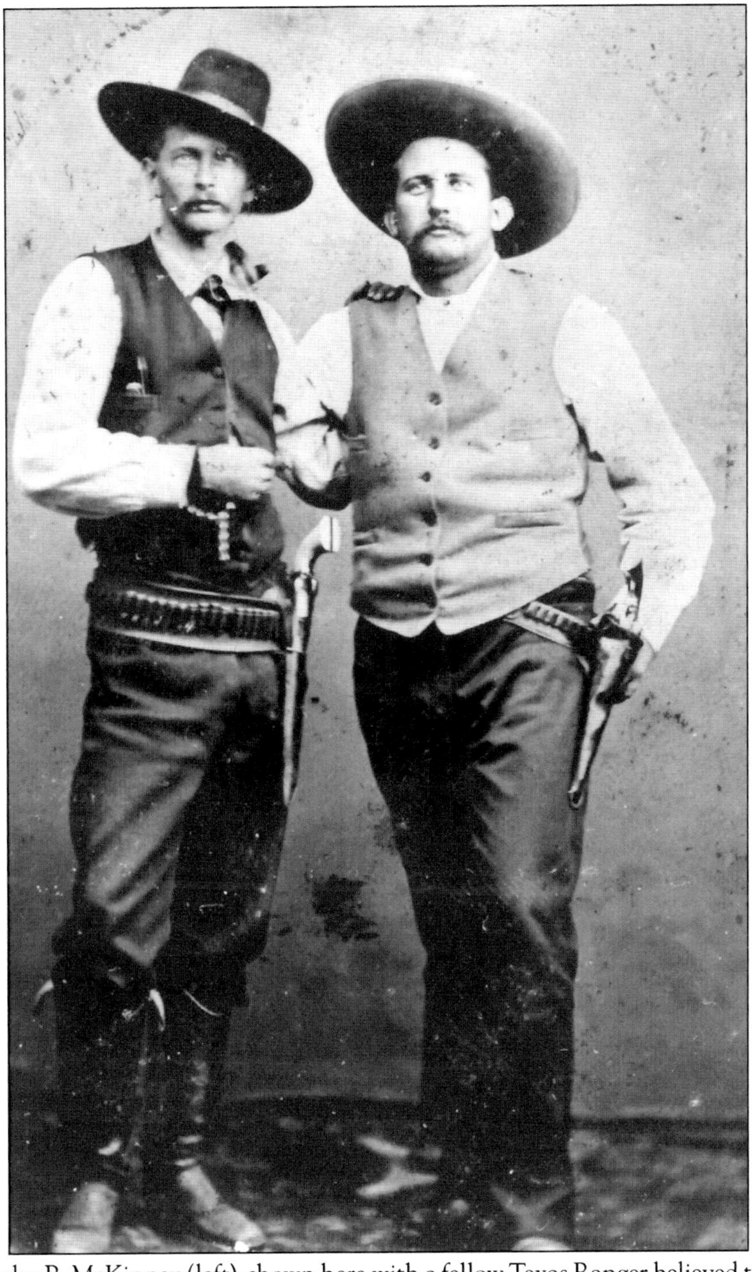

Sheriff Charles B. McKinney (left), shown here with a fellow Texas Ranger believed to be George W. Farrow, was only 29 years old when he was shot and killed by Bud Crenshaw and Jim McCoy on December 26, 1886. Sheriff McKinney was on his way to investigate the alleged rape of Mary Galloway, a 10-year-old girl, when he encountered Crenshaw and McCoy, and a gunfight ensued. On January 2, 1887, McKinney's father-in-law, Silas Hay, came to town seeking revenge for the death of his son-in-law. Hay lay in wait and shot and killed George Hill, a brother-in-law of Crenshaw, who he felt was responsible for the death of McKinney. Bud Crenshaw was shot and killed by the Texas Rangers. Jim McCoy later turned himself in to the sheriff. McCoy's trial was transferred to Bexar County on a change of venue. A jury found him guilty of murder. He was hanged for his crime.

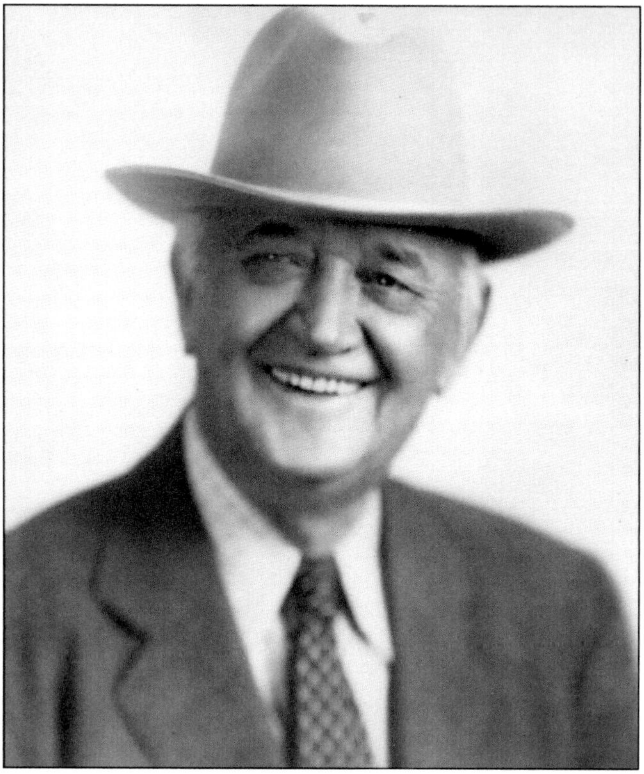

At the age of 19, Travis Hogue Poole entered law enforcement as a Texas Ranger. After leaving the Rangers, he served as a deputy sheriff in La Salle County. "Chub," as his friends knew him, became sheriff of La Salle County in 1908. He was an outstanding law enforcement officer, holding the position until his death on October 6, 1943.

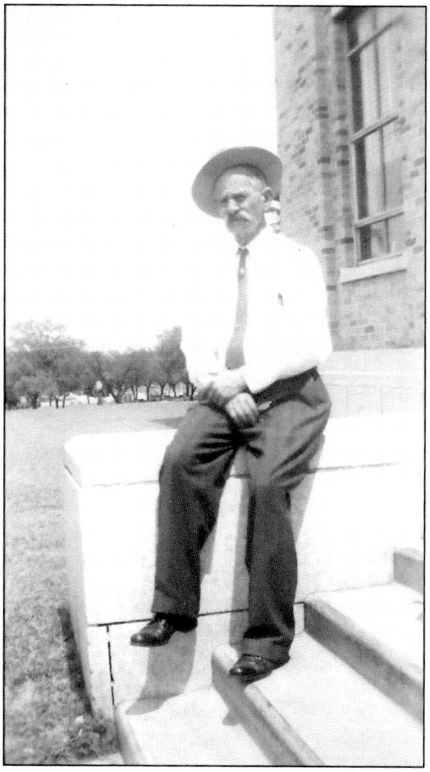

William Augustus Kerr spent many years of his life as a public servant. Kerr served the citizens of La Salle County as a commissioner, justice of the peace, and at the time of his death he was serving as district clerk. He always participated in the political process of the county and state. He took time out from his busy life to attend the Democratic county and state conventions. The photograph at right shows Judge Kerr taking a break on the steps of the La Salle County Courthouse.

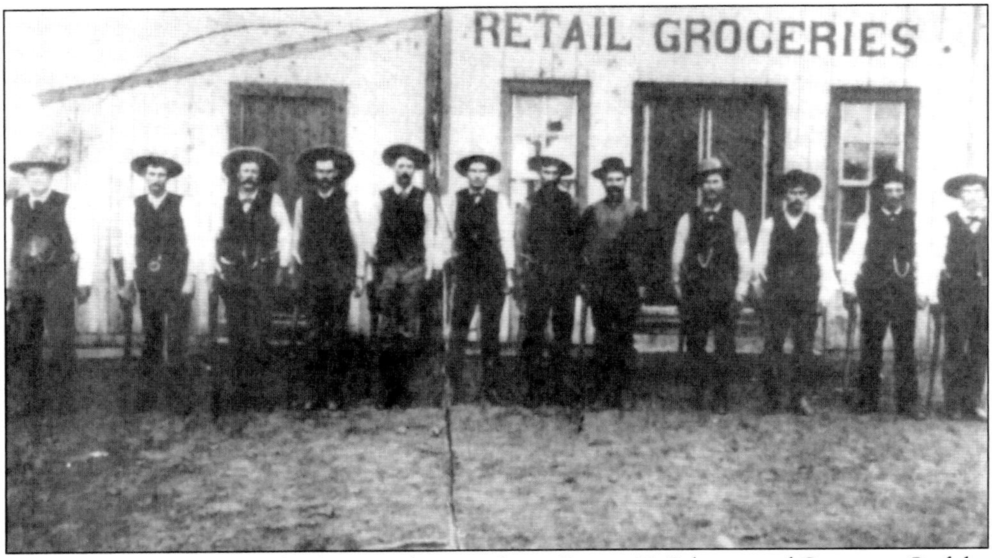

After the death of sheriff Charles B. Mckinney, Capt. George H. Schmitt and Company C of the Frontier Battalion were sent to Cotulla to not only solve the murder, but to keep peace among the unruly citizens. Company C is pictured in front of a Cotulla grocery store.

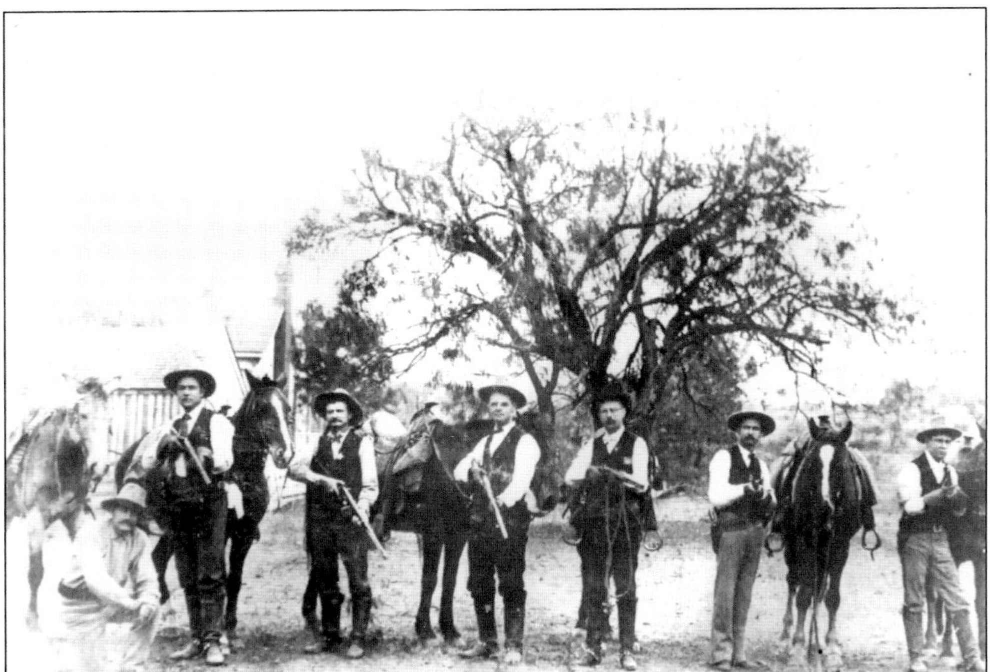
Company B of the Texas Rangers was stationed at Cotulla, sent there to keep law and order. Members of Company B were, from left to right, the company cook (kneeling), Jim Moore, W. A. Olds, Sgt. H. G. Dubose, Will L. Wright, and T. C. "Creed" Taylor.

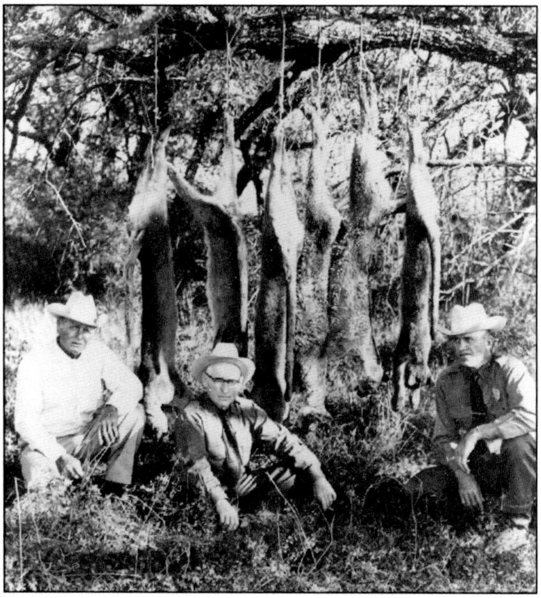

State game warden John E. Hearn (center) did more than enforce the game laws; he helped rid La Salle County and South Texas of predators. *The Texas Lion Hunter*, by John R. Vossbourgh, is a book written about John Hearn and his lifetime of hunting and trapping in La Salle County and South Texas. John Hearn spent much of his life studying the habits of wild animals. In his younger days, he trapped skunks, raccoons, opossum, and ringtail cats.

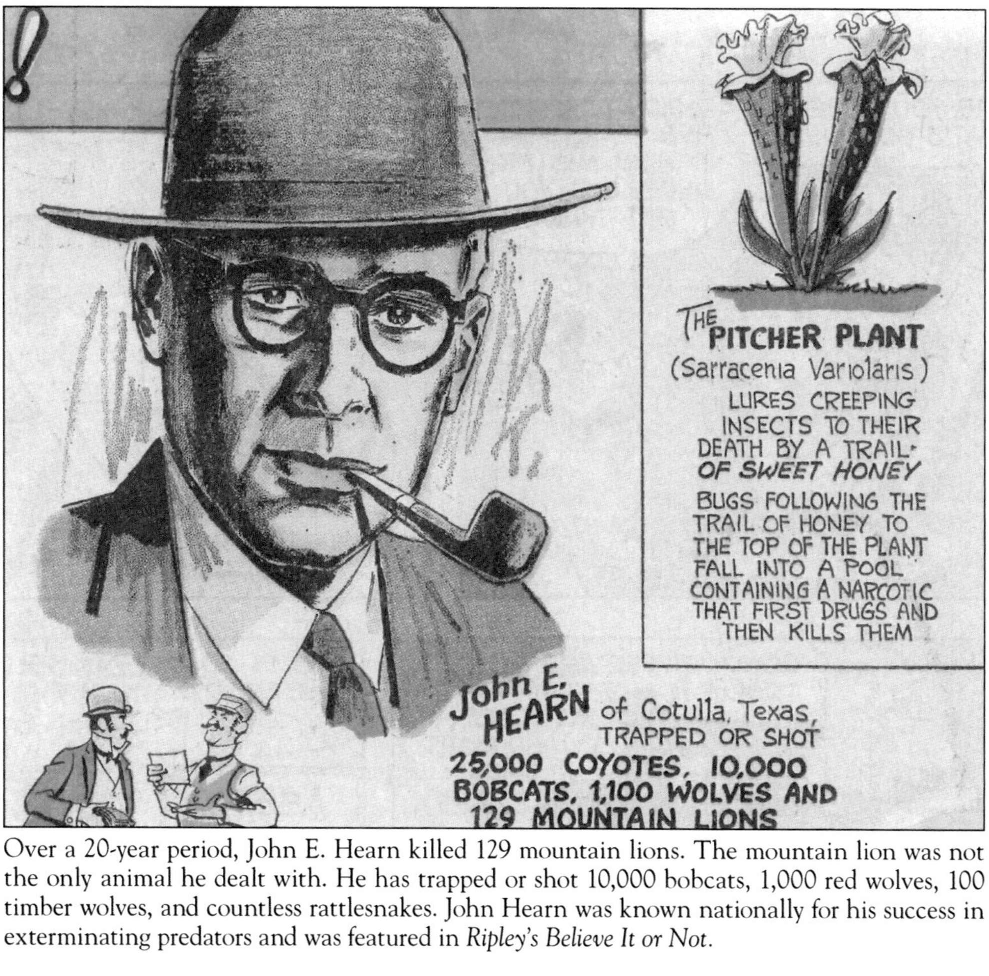

Over a 20-year period, John E. Hearn killed 129 mountain lions. The mountain lion was not the only animal he dealt with. He has trapped or shot 10,000 bobcats, 1,000 red wolves, 100 timber wolves, and countless rattlesnakes. John Hearn was known nationally for his success in exterminating predators and was featured in *Ripley's Believe It or Not*.

Three
COTULLA

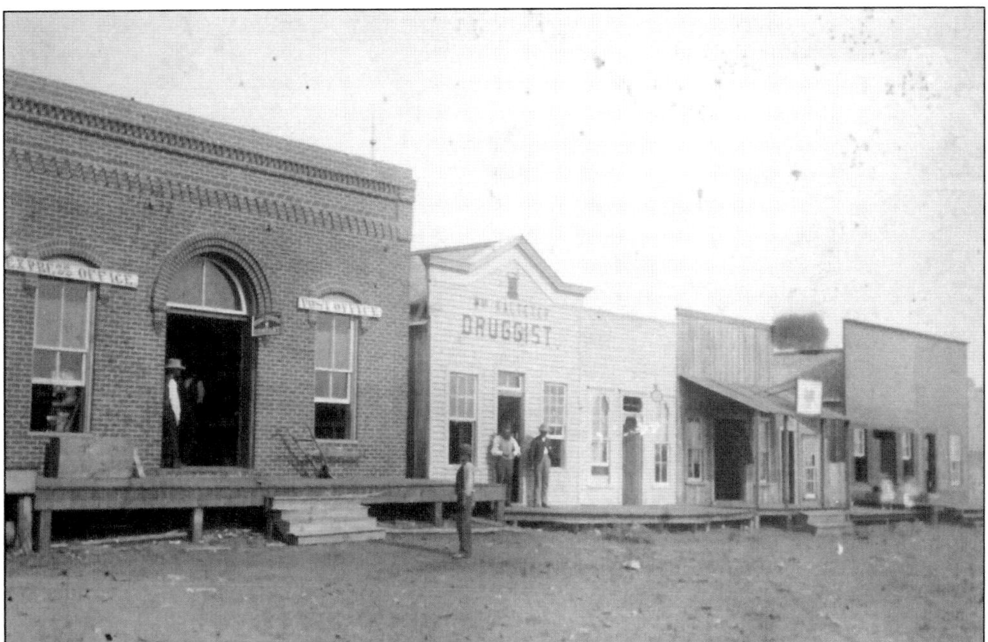

Front Street in downtown Cotulla runs parallel to the International and Great Northern Railroad. It soon became the business district. The first brick building was located on the corner of Front and Center Streets and was constructed by Monroe P. Kerr. Other businesses pictured on Front Street in 1885 were Kalteyer's Drug Store, a watchmaker, a saddle shop, and the Butler Brothers' Saloon. Two other saloons, The Senate Bar and Copp's Saloon, were located on Front Street farther south. (Courtesy of Nora M. Tyler.)

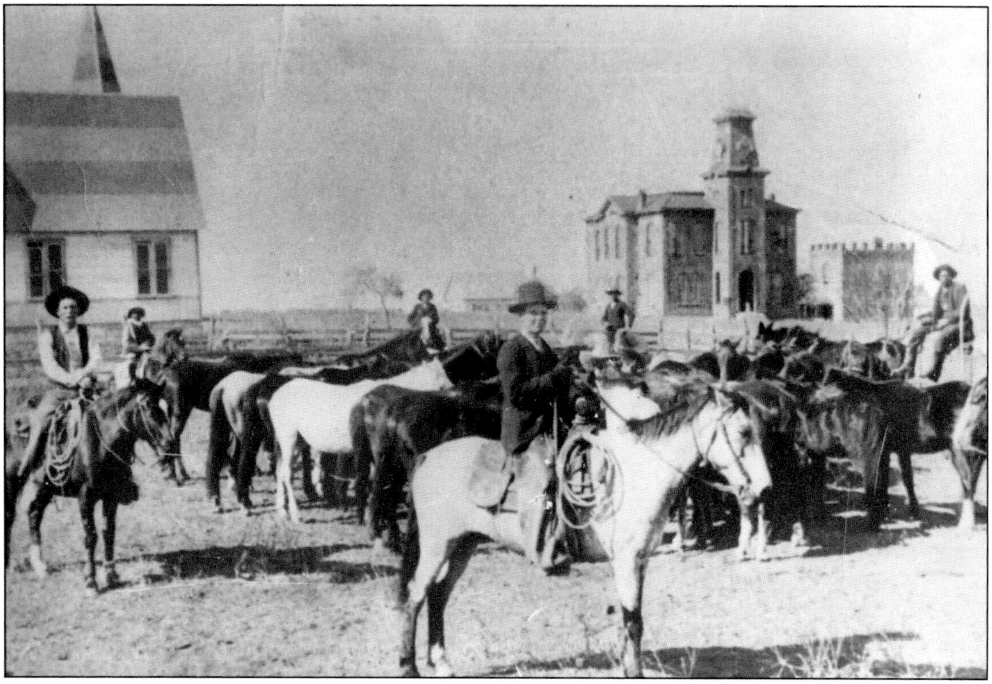

When Joseph Cotulla was planning his town, he designated a block in the middle of town as a public park. During the early days, the park was used as a gathering place for wagons and horses when the farmers and ranchers visited town. Notice the Presbyterian church and courthouse in the background.

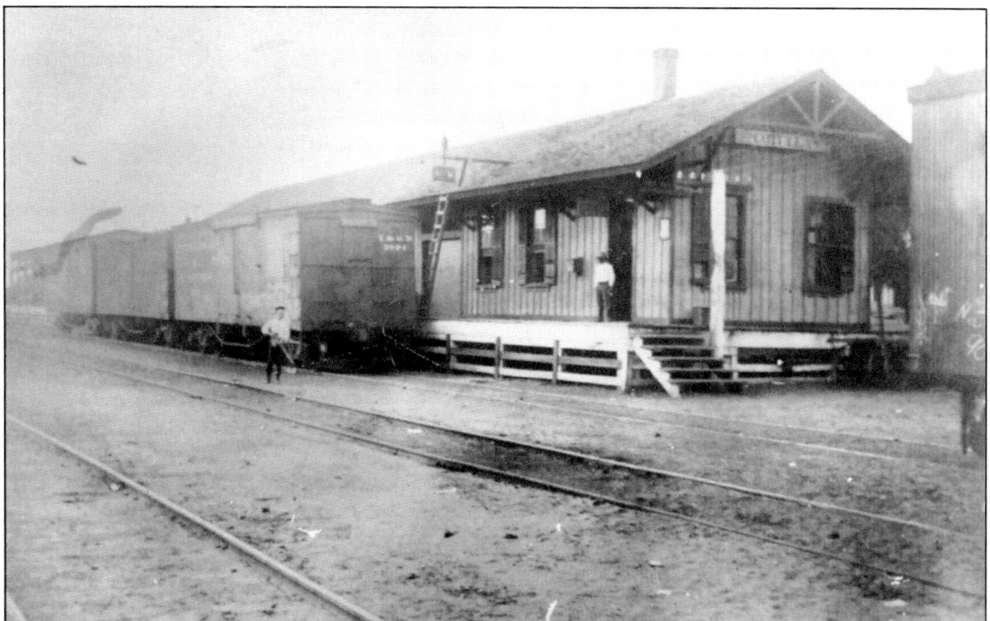

A depot was soon built to handle the influx of people to the fast growing town of Cotulla. On January 10, 1882, Joseph Cotulla's family arrived on the first train. The fare for a round-trip ticket from Cotulla to San Antonio was $4.30.

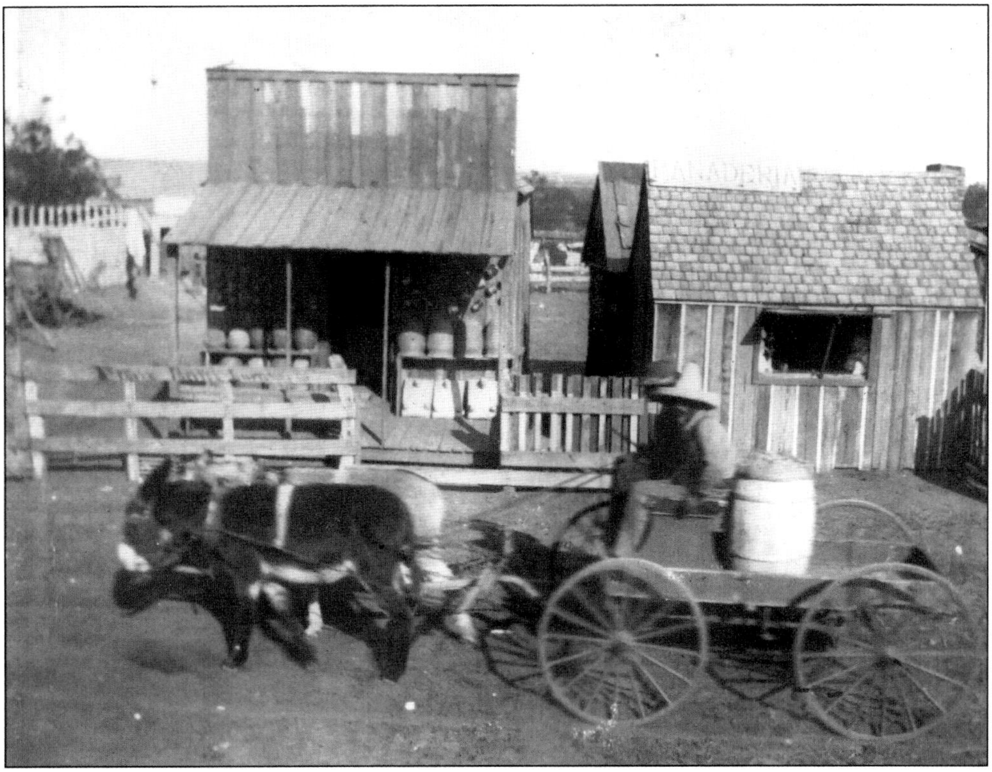

The first water for Cotulla residents came from the Nueces River. It was a common sight to see a wagon pulled by a team of mules along the streets of Cotulla. In the wagon bed would be a wooden barrel full of water from the river headed for someone's home.

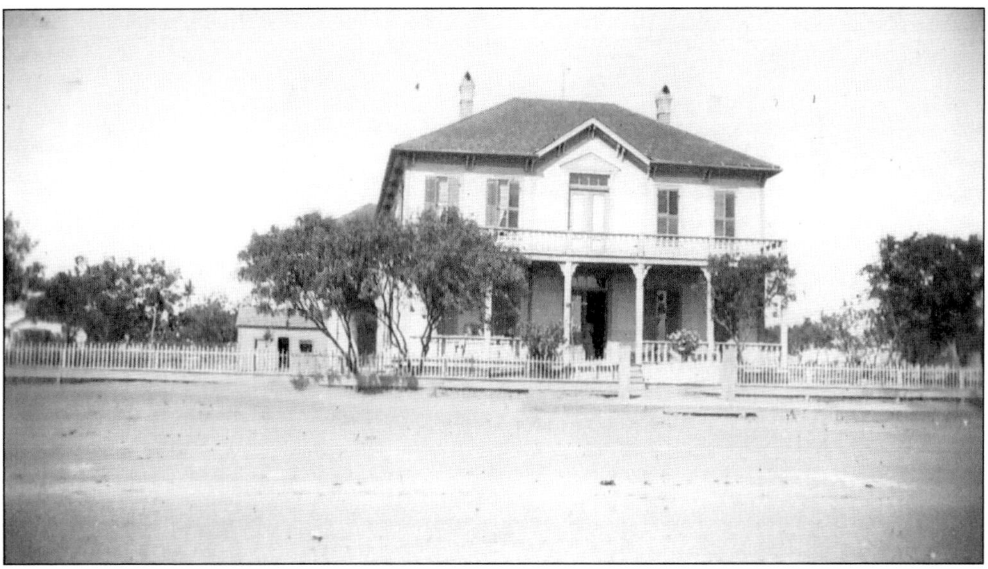

The Burke Hotel was built in the late 1880s. Jerry Gilmer and his wife, Emma, began operating the hotel in 1890. Shortly after, Mr. Gilmer died, and Emma continued to operate the hotel. She later purchased the business and changed the name to The Gilmer. The hotel was known far and wide for the delicious meals served there.

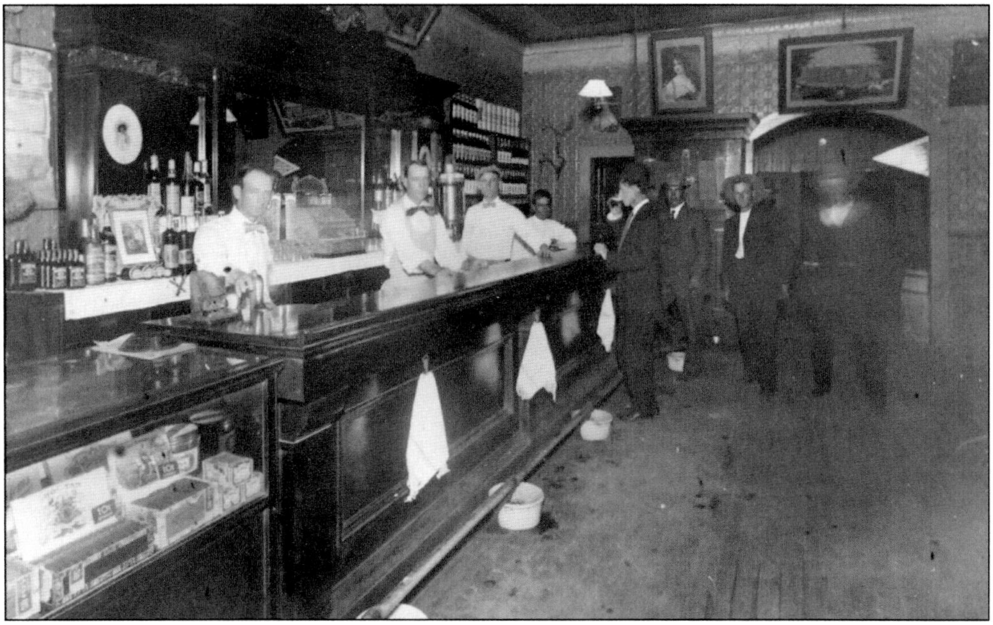

Saloons seemed to be very popular in the early days of Cotulla and played an important part in the early economy of the town. By 1883, Cotulla had three saloons along Front Street. J. Arthur Reed, Will Cotulla, and Green Boyd wait to be served in an early saloon in the image above.

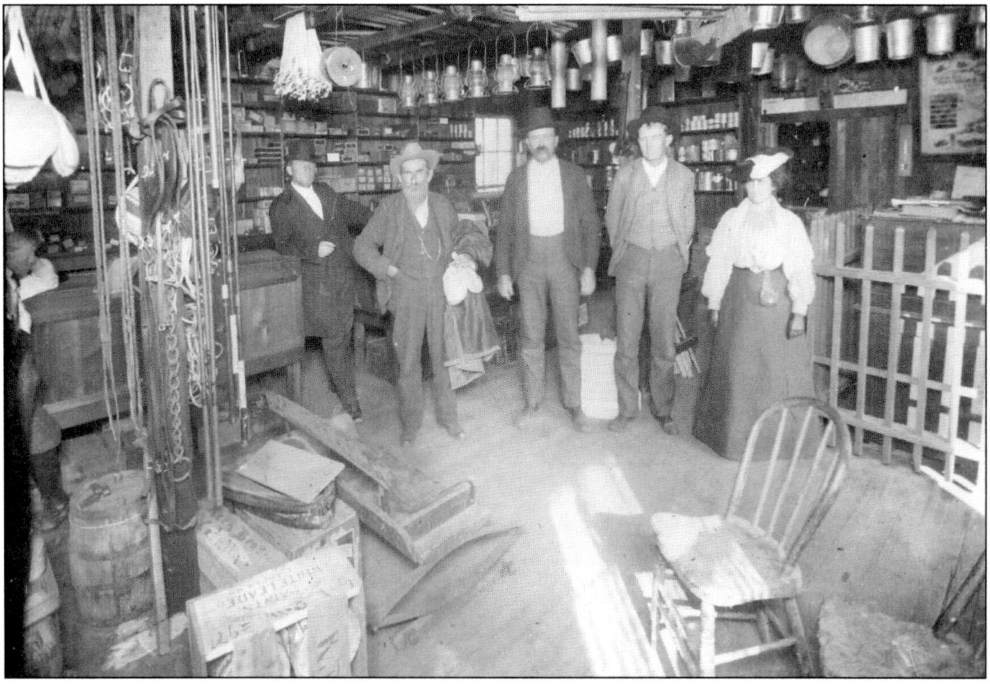

Thomas Randall Keck and his brother Edgar A. Keck purchased a lumber business in 1893 and operated it under the name Keck Brothers. Edgar A. sold his interest to his brother in 1903, and the business became known as T. R. Keck Lumber and Hardware. Later T. R. took his two sons into the business, and the business became known as T. R. Keck and Sons, which carried a complete line of lumber, hardware, and ranch supplies.

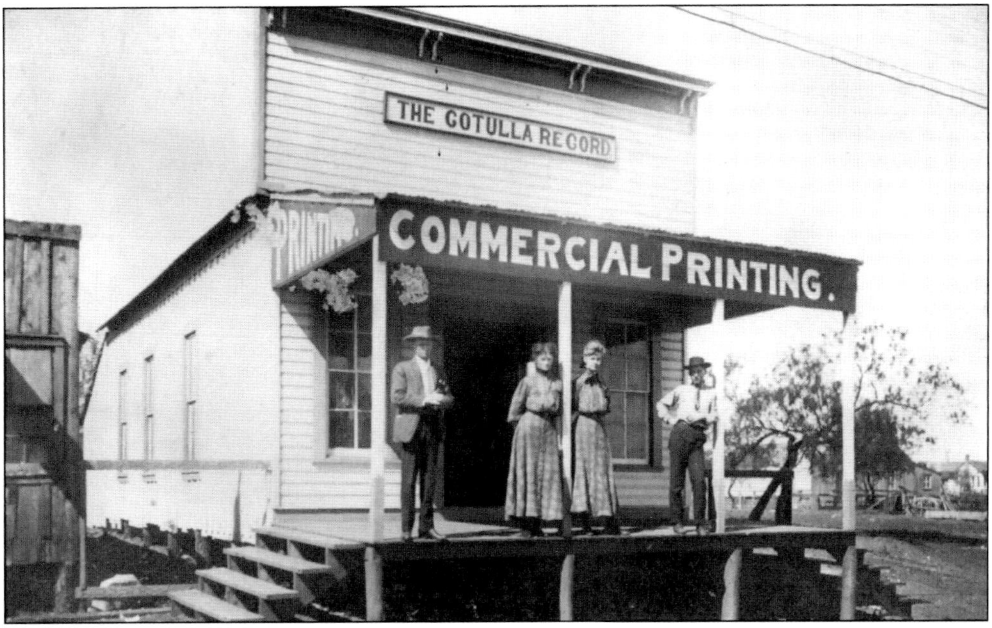

In 1898, Clarence E. Manly and J. M. Daniel bought the *Cotulla Ledger* and renamed their newly purchased newspaper the *Cotulla Record*. The *Cotulla Record* was published weekly. Daniel soon sold out his interest, and in 1919, Walter M. Manly acquired one-half interest in the newspaper. In 1923, a fire on Front Street destroyed most of the wooden buildings, including the *Cotulla Record* building. A new brick building was erected on North Center Street with much-improved equipment. The *Cotulla Record* kept the citizens of La Salle County informed for over 50 years.

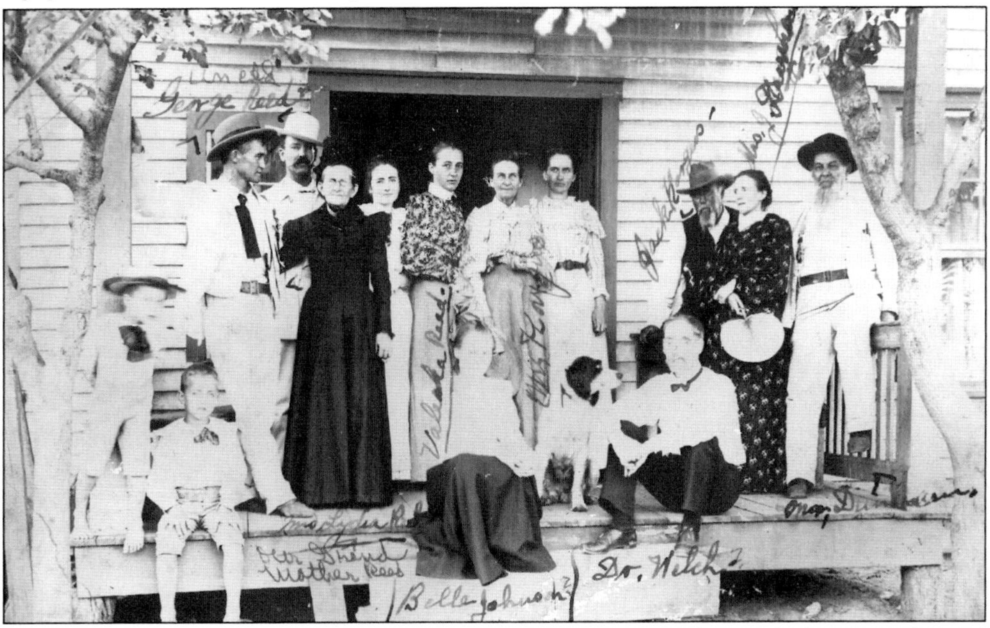

The Dunham Hotel was owned and operated by Mortimer T. Dunham. The hotel was located on the south side of Center Street. S. T. Dunham was also a justice of the peace. In September 1898, the Dunham Hotel was sold. Judge Dunham resigned his position, and he and his family moved to Laredo.

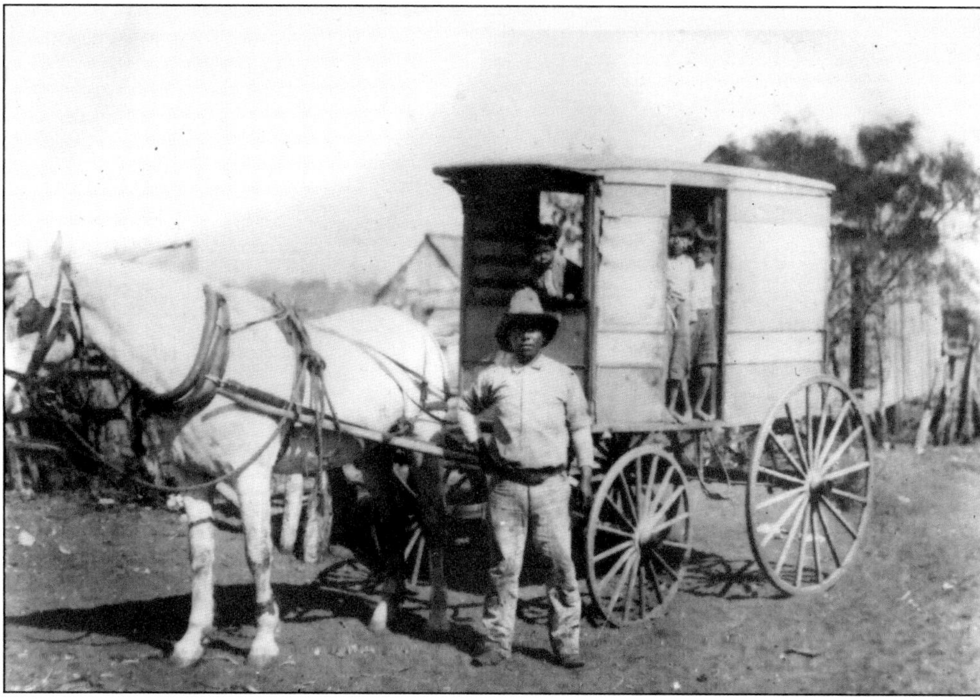

A horse-drawn wagon that delivered ice door to door was common in the early days. George Copp owned the first ice wagon in Cotulla and delivered ice to the homes along the streets of Cotulla. Pictured is George Copp's first ice wagon and driver.

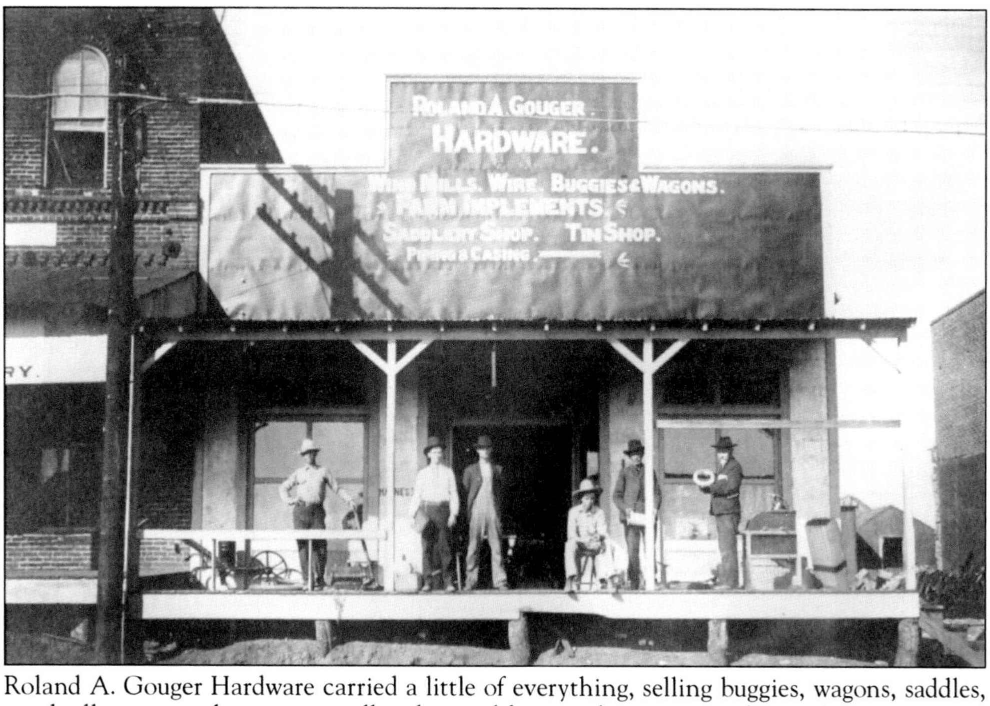

Roland A. Gouger Hardware carried a little of everything, selling buggies, wagons, saddles, windmills, pipes, and casings, as well as the usual farm implements. Standing in front of the store are Bud Neal, Bob Gouger, Jody Boyd, Joseph Cotulla, and two unidentified.

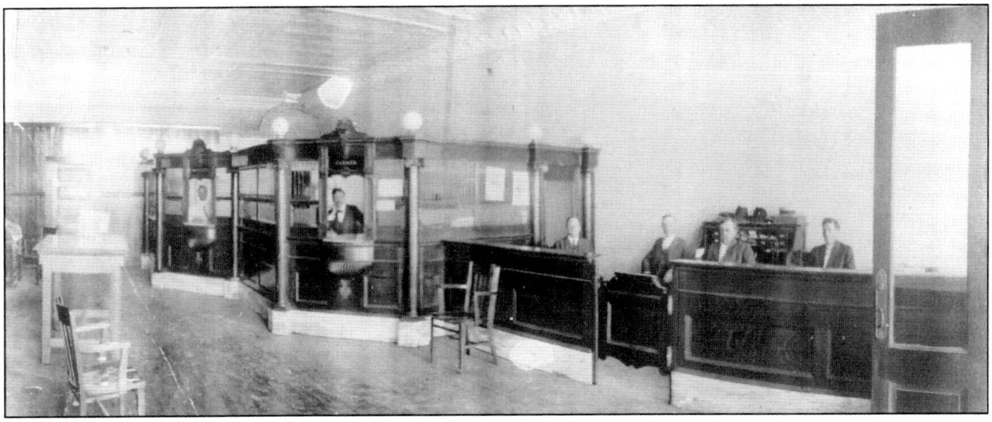

In 1904, Stockmens National Bank in Cotulla was chartered. L. A. Kerr, Covey C. Thomas, G. W. Henrichson, George Copp, and Thomas Randall Keck founded the bank. In 1934, the bank was reorganized and renamed Stockmens National Bank of Cotulla. The first bank was located on the corner of Center and Front Streets. In 1913, a new building was constructed on Front Street.

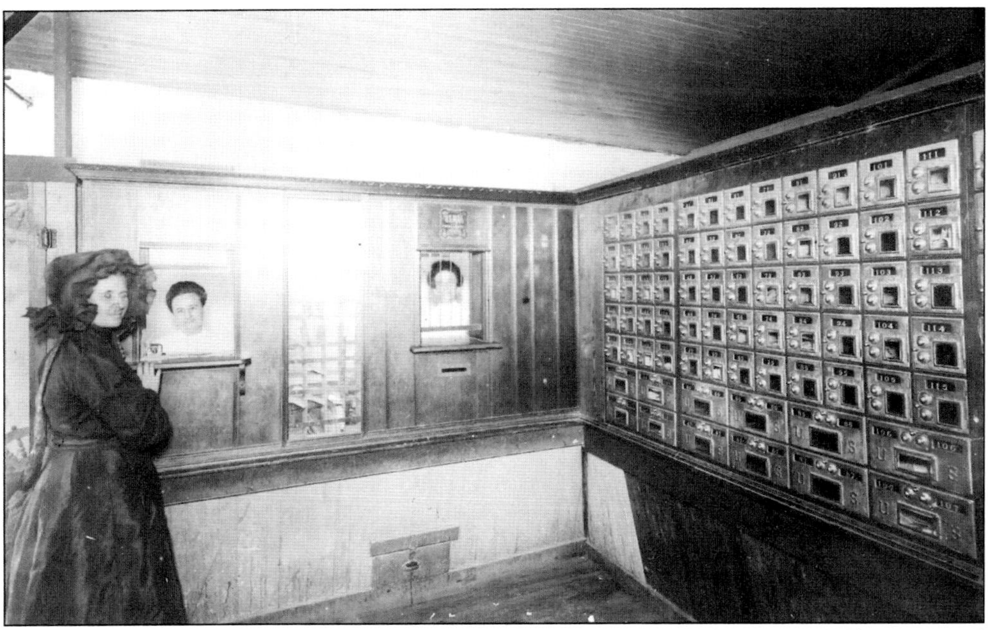

Caroline Cotulla attended a meeting of Texas postmasters in Waco in August 1909. She presented a paper titled, "The Duties of the Postmaster to the Public and the Duties of the Public to the Postmaster," which was ordered printed in the official proceedings. Cotulla is pictured at the left window.

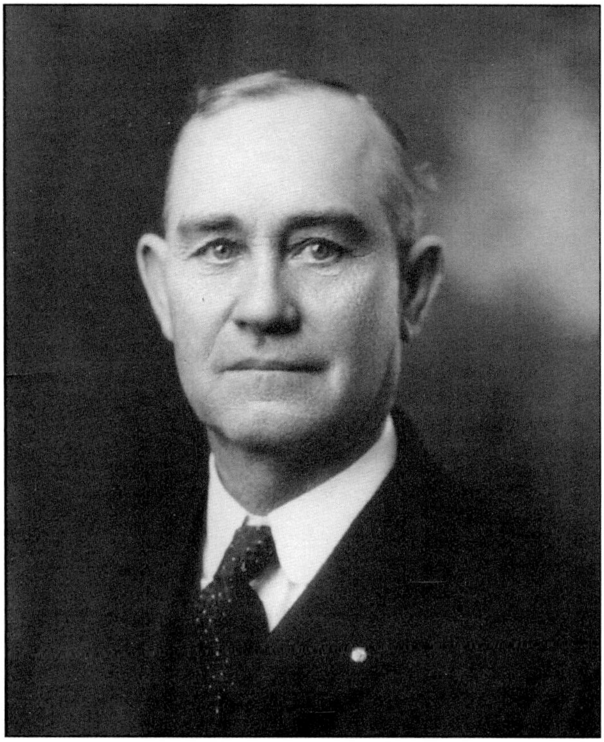

In December 1909, an election was held to incorporate the town of Cotulla. The move to incorporate was successful, and in early 1910, an election was held to elect a mayor and city councilmen. Charles Fredrick Binkley was elected the first mayor of the city of Cotulla.

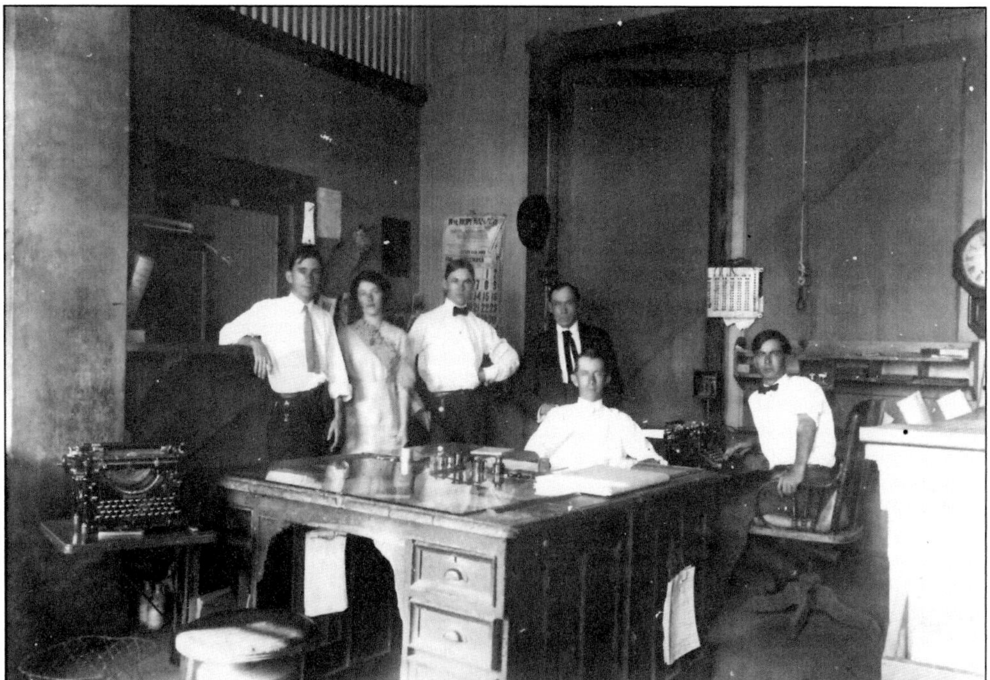

In 1912, John W. Lacey (seated second from right) came to Cotulla as a station agent for the railroad, a position he would hold for 56 years. Cotulla was one of the busiest stations in South Texas, with many cars of onions, spinach, and plants being shipped daily. (Courtesy of John H. Keck.)

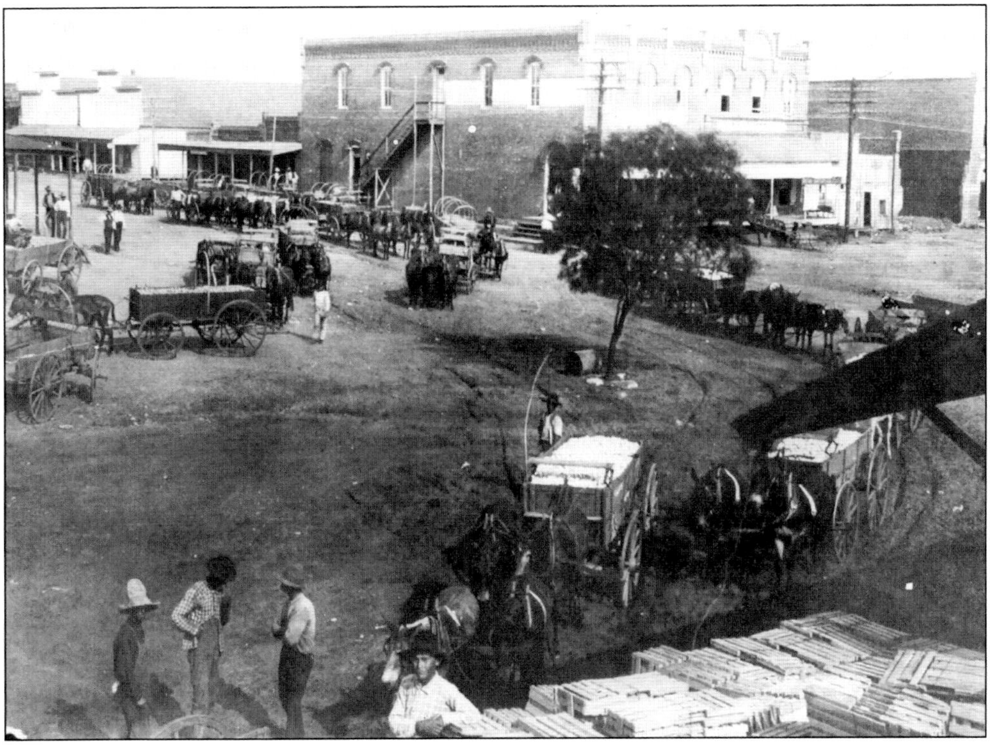

It was a busy day on the streets of Cotulla, when the onion farmers lined up along Center Street with their wagons. Each wagon was piled high with onions waiting to be put in crates and shipped by rail all over the United States.

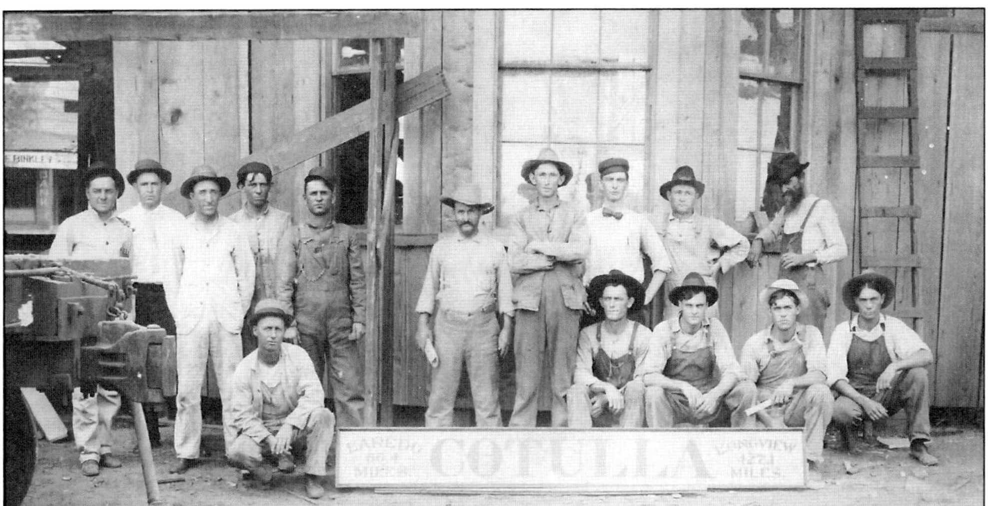

Employees of the International and Great Northern Railroad, which later became Missouri Pacific, are standing in front of the Cotulla depot. The sign at center displays the distance from Cotulla to Laredo to be 66.4 miles and the distance from Cotulla to Longview to be 427.1 miles.

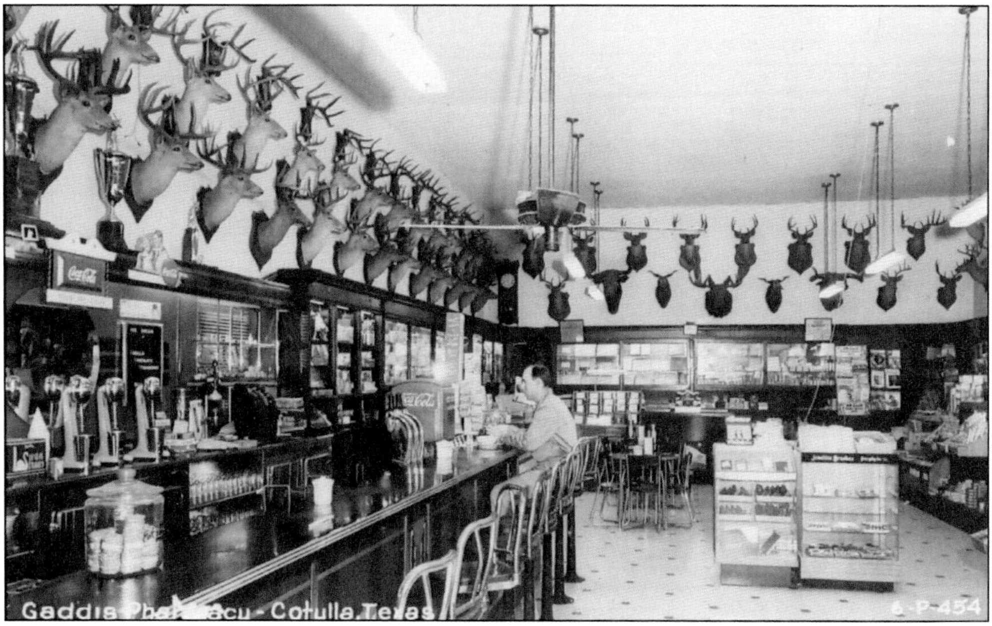

Gaddis Pharmacy, owned by Lewis W. Gaddis, carried an extensive and complete stock that would be found in a large city pharmacy. Besides a large stock of drugs and medicines, Gaddis Pharmacy carried a large stock of perfumes, toilet articles, and fine soaps. The cold drink and ice cream department was the pride of the young people of Cotulla.

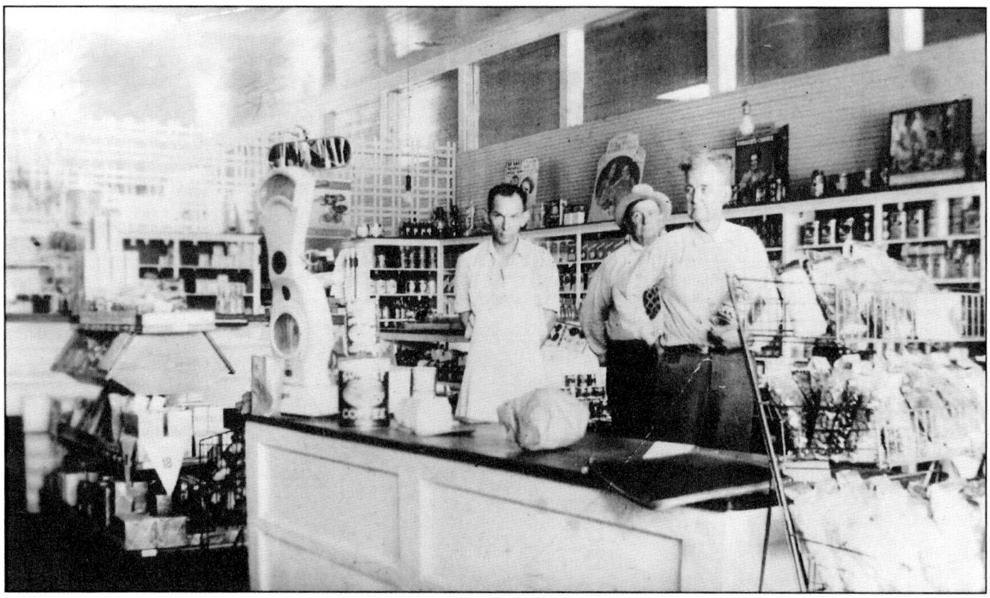

The Fullerton's Hardware was a small store when David L. Neeley married the owner's daughter Delia and entered the business. David Neeley soon expanded the business by buying the Cotulla Mercantile. The Cotulla Mercantile carried a complete line of groceries, hardware, stoves, furniture, men's furnishings, ranch and farm supplies, as well as everything needed for the home. Pictured above are Glenn Soles, Jonatan Lopez, and an unidentified man outside the prosperous business.

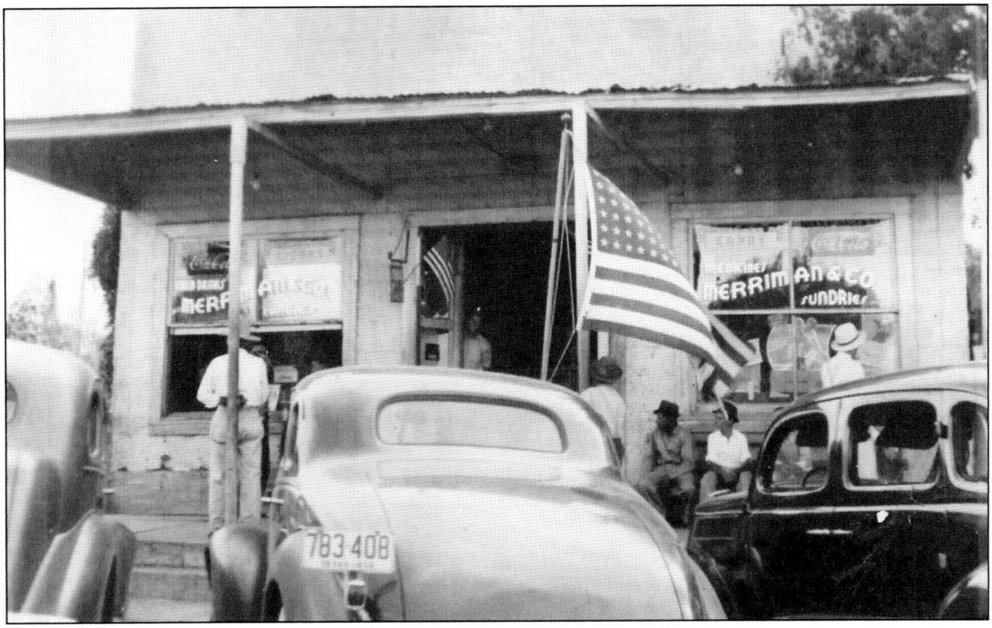

Merriman's Drug Store was located on Front Street in downtown Cotulla. Not only could medicine and other sundry items be purchased, but the drugstore also had a soda fountain. Customers could drive up, honk their horns, and get curb service. A soda would be delivered for a nickel.

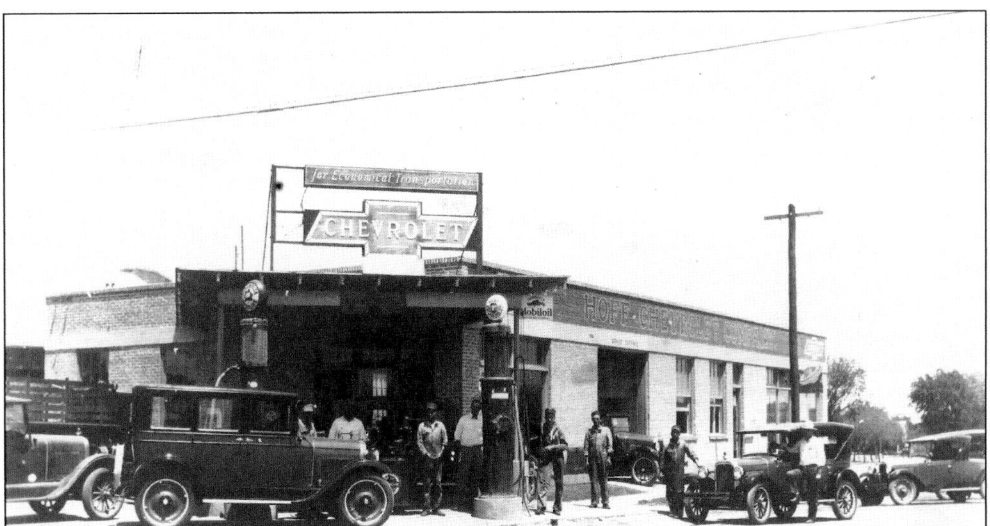

Hoff Chevrolet Company, located on Tilden Street, moved into new and sumptuous quarters on January 27, 1927. The business, run in connection with an oil and gas station, was thoroughly modern and up to date, with a comfortable women's restroom. A complete line of tires and accessories was also sold. The business was managed by Gus R. Hoff.

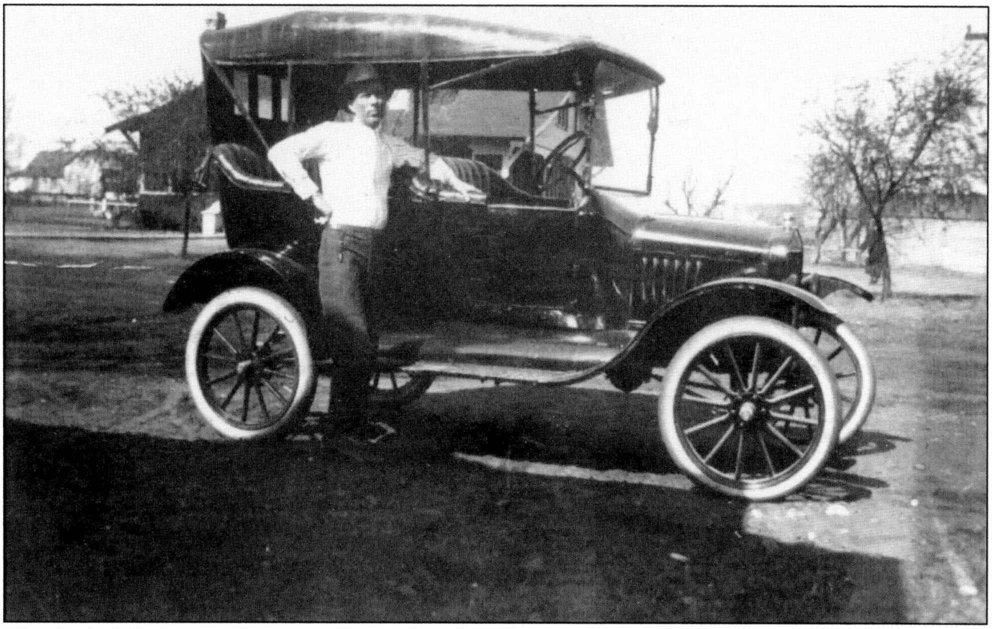

Charles E. Neal Auto Company, located in Cotulla, was one of the best-known Ford agencies in the state of Texas. In 1912, Charles Neal decided Cotulla needed a garage to service the up-and-coming automobile business. Neal rented a shed and hired one mechanic. From that humble beginning, the garage grew into a Ford dealership. The first year, he contracted for 24 cars and sold all 24. He expanded his business and contracted for 54 cars the next year. That year a hurricane hit and nearly devastated his business, but, undismayed, Charlie Neal sold all 54 cars. Charles E. Neal Auto Company continued to grow, and in 1926, the company sold 250 cars.

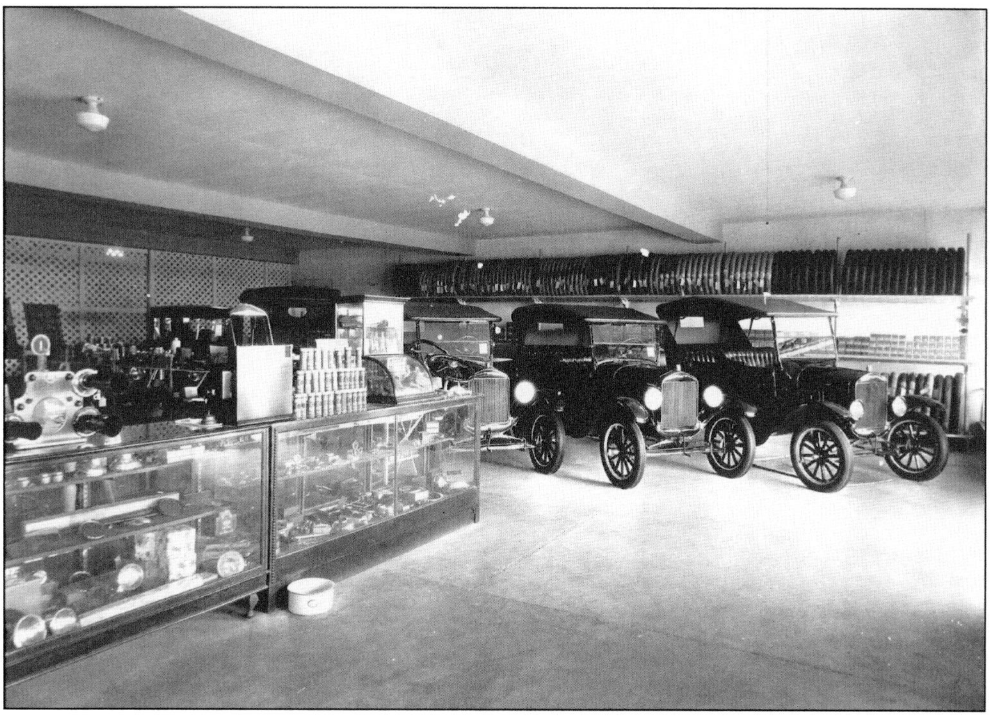

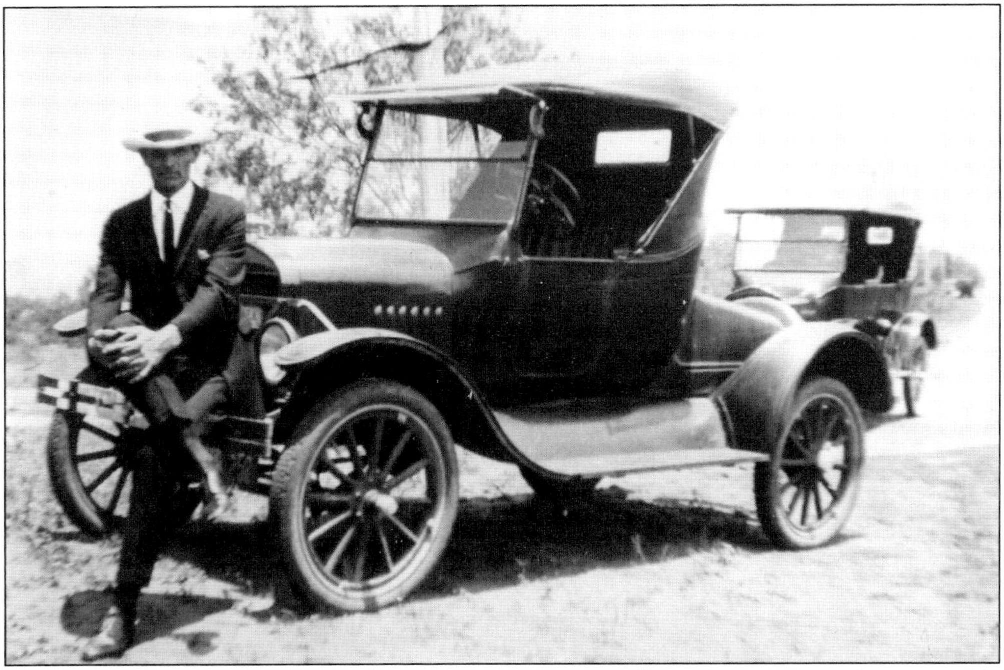

Lee Peters was a prominent building contractor in Cotulla and the surrounding area. He constructed many of the brick buildings in Cotulla. Peters was the contractor for the high school in Cotulla and the school buildings in Millett, Los Angeles, and Artesia Wells, all constructed in 1927 and 1928.

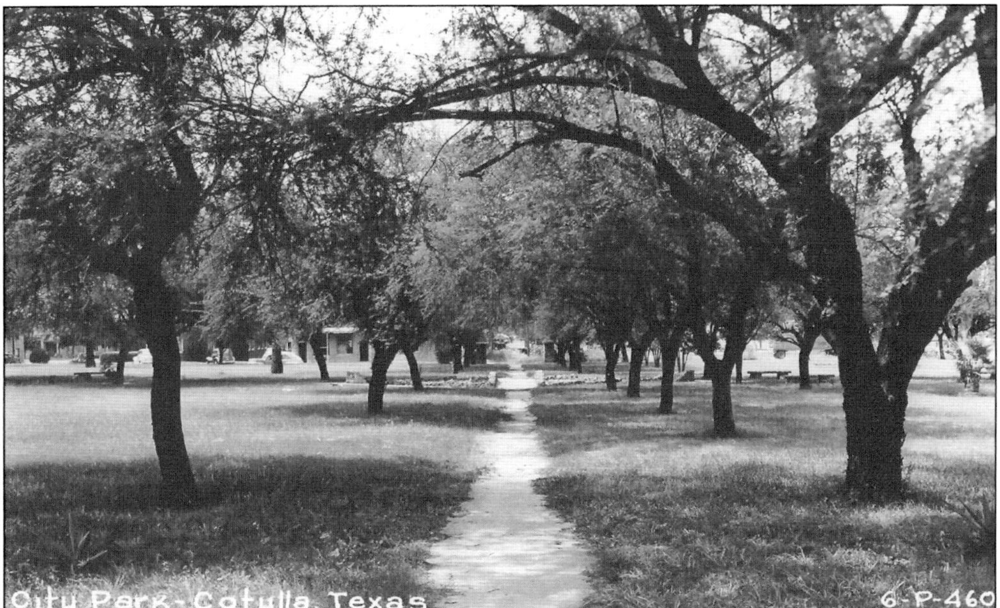

Huisache trees were planted in the public park donated by Joseph Cotulla. Sidewalks, benches, a gazebo, a bandstand, and a goldfish pond were built. A merry-go-round and other playground equipment were installed for the enjoyment of the children of Cotulla.

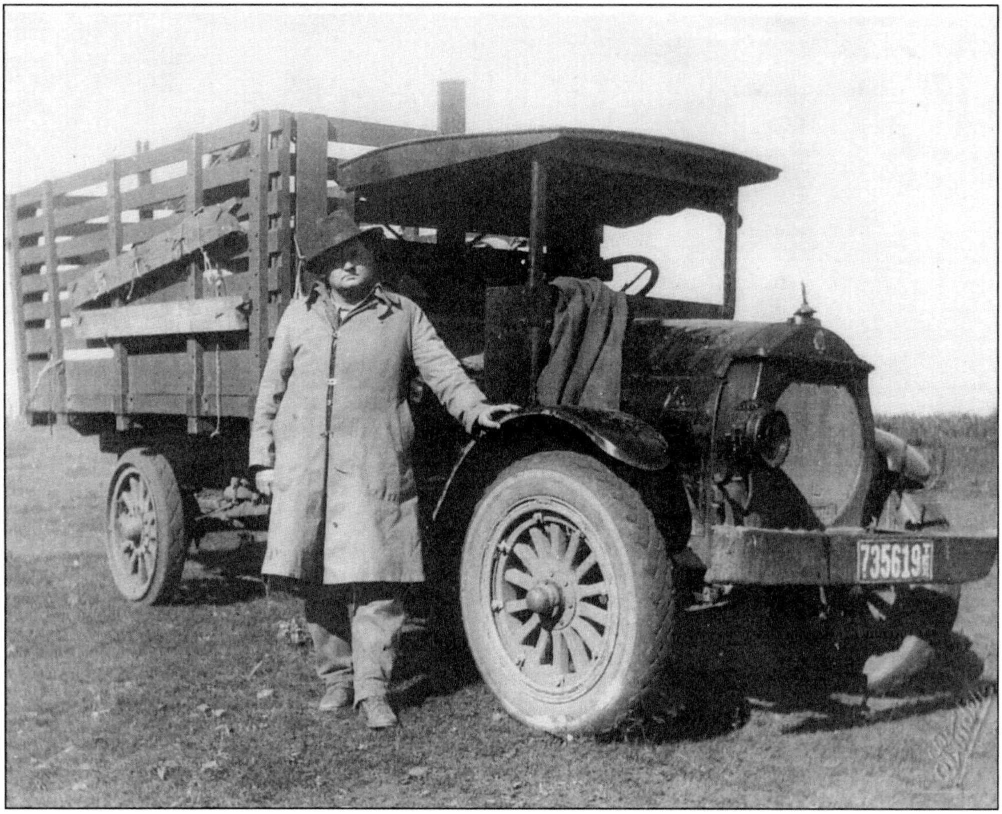

In 1930, Roy Gilbert started out with one used truck that he used to haul freight from Cotulla to San Antonio. It was a 1922 Fulton with a top speed of 18 miles per hour. A trip to San Antonio took a long time.

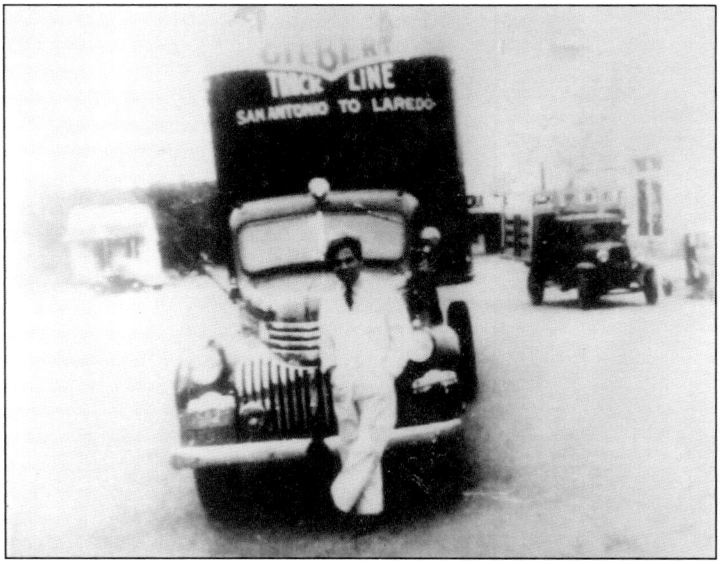

By 1940, the Gilbert Truck Line had a fleet of trucks, 40 employees, and had extended their territory to serve Laredo and the Mexican border. At this time, the headquarters moved from Cotulla to Laredo. From its humble beginning in Cotulla, Gilbert Truck Line evolved into Southern Motor Transport, traveling all of the United States.

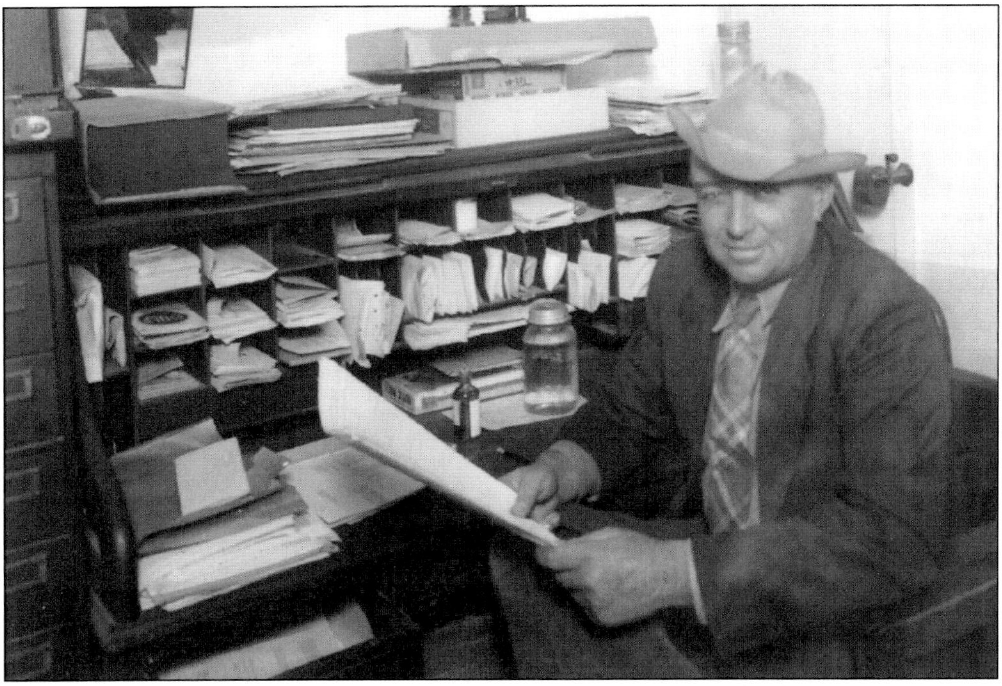

The Federal Farm Loan Act was passed to provide money for agricultural development. Dee Stewart was secretary-treasurer of the Cotulla National Farm Loan Association. Stewart is pictured at his roll-top desk ready to make a loan to a local farmer.

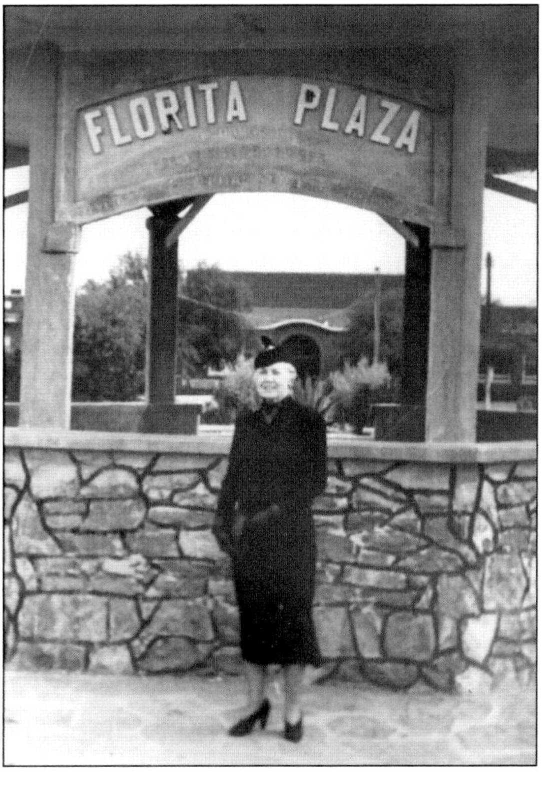

Florita Plaza was built especially for the Mexican citizens of Cotulla. The plaza was named for Flora Maltsberger in recognition of her work among the Mexican people of Cotulla. For over 20 years, Florita Plaza was a pet project of Flora Maltsberger. Florita Plaza had rock gardens, walks, landscaping, fountains, and natural rock benches, as well as the bandstand. Many dances, Cinco de Mayo celebrations, *jamaicas*, and political rallies have taken place in Florita Plaza.

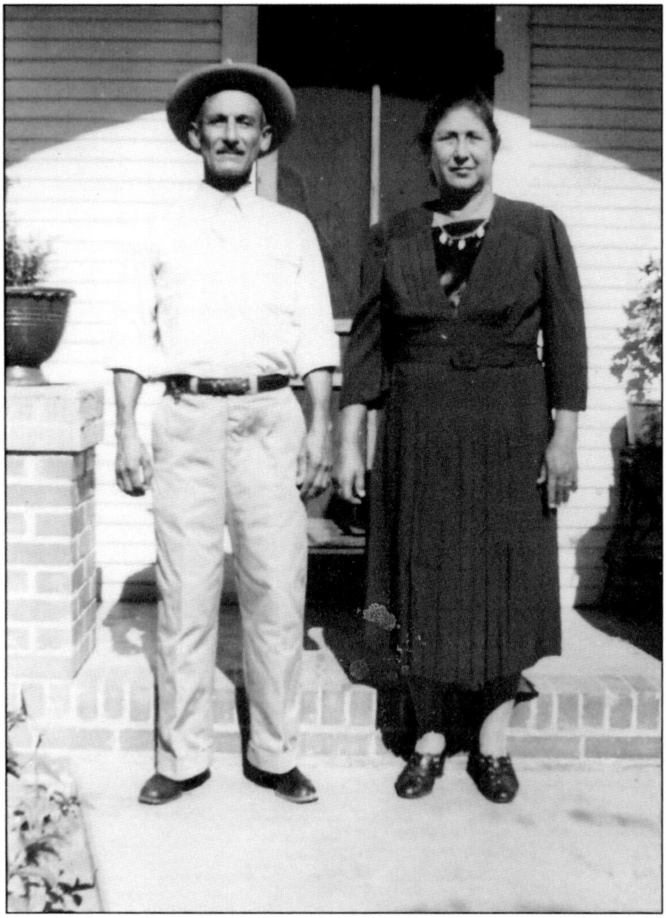

Francisco and Juanita Garcia and their family settled in La Salle County in the 1920s. Francisco soon opened a small meat market located on Thornton Street. In 1937, he built a new store one block east of the original location. It was named La Tienda Colorado because of its red color. The new business thrived, and he soon added on to the building. At some point the business became known as the "Red Store," its English name. After more than 70 years, there remains a Red Store in business on Thornton Street.

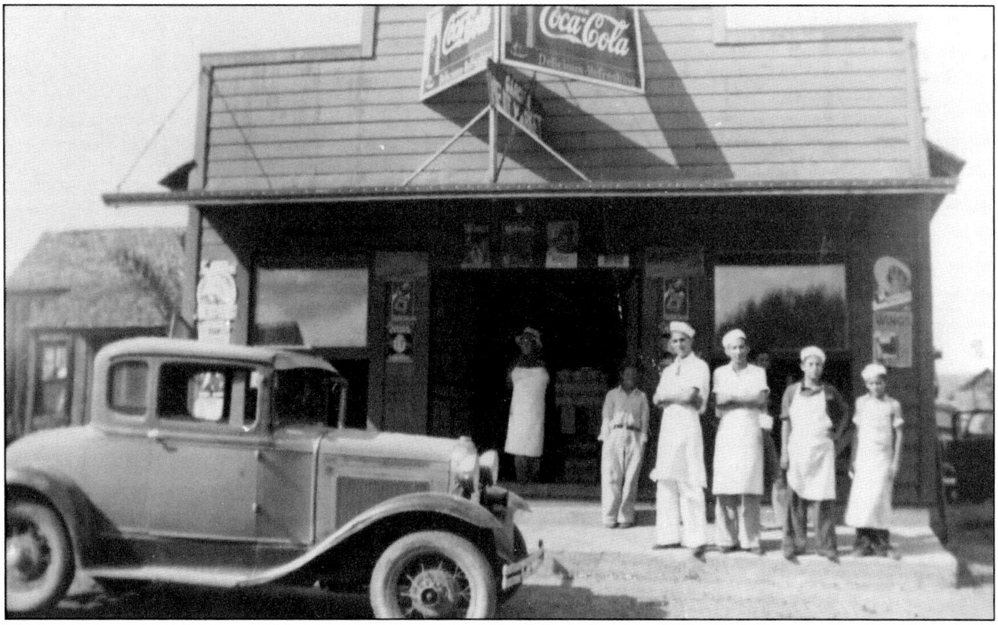

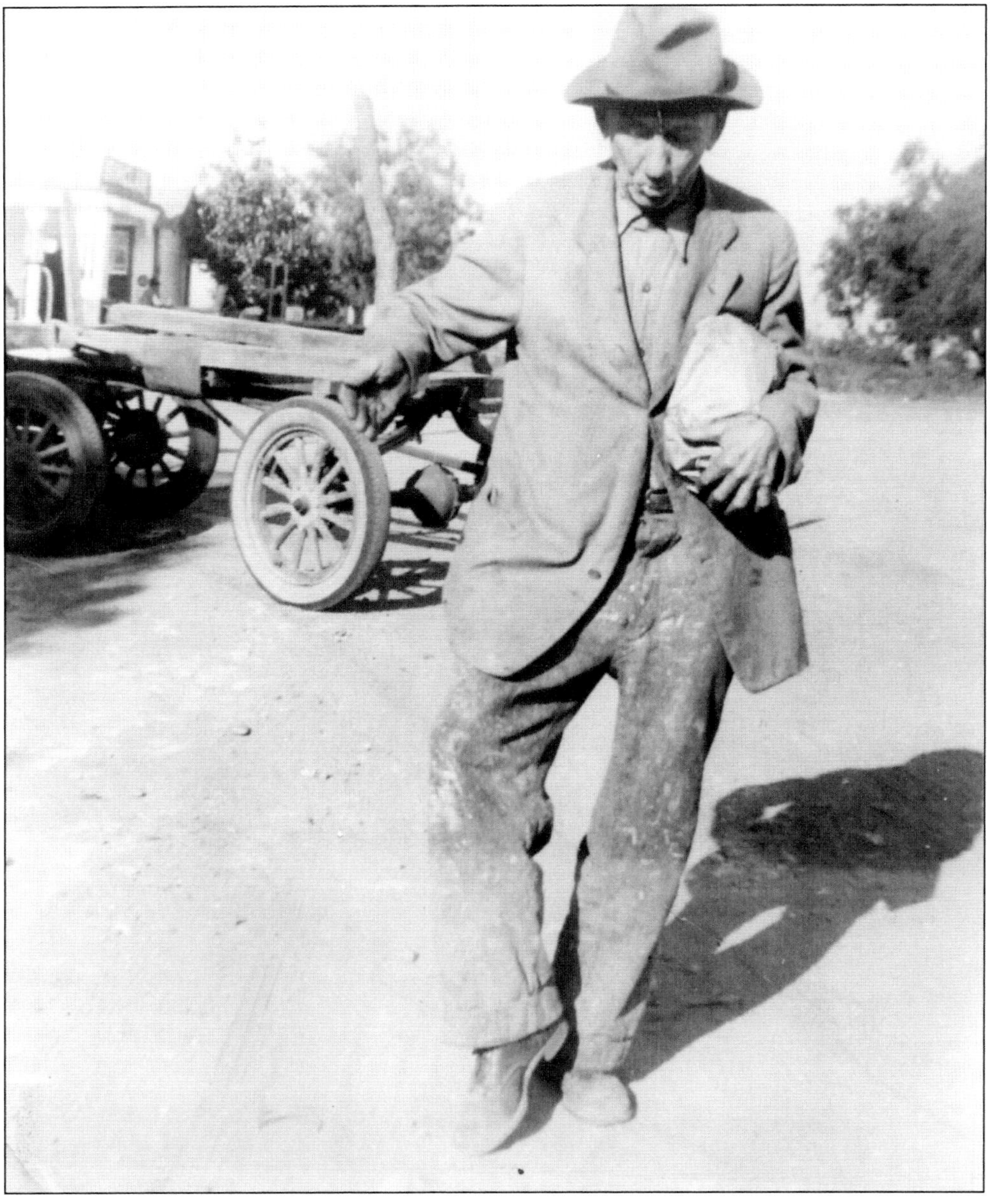

Frank Gerdes was a local paper hanger. He was better known in Cotulla as "Happy Jack" because of his love of alcoholic beverages. Happy Jack is credited as having invented the first pear burner. He used an old kerosene can as the air tank and a vaginal syringe as the air pump. The contraption somehow worked. He never patented his invention and supposedly sold his idea for $30. Happy Jack immediately headed for a liquor store and used the money to buy whiskey. He had several versions of this story and was always ready to share one of them with anyone that would listen. Frank Gerdes died November 29, 1952, and is buried in an unmarked grave in the Cotulla cemetery.

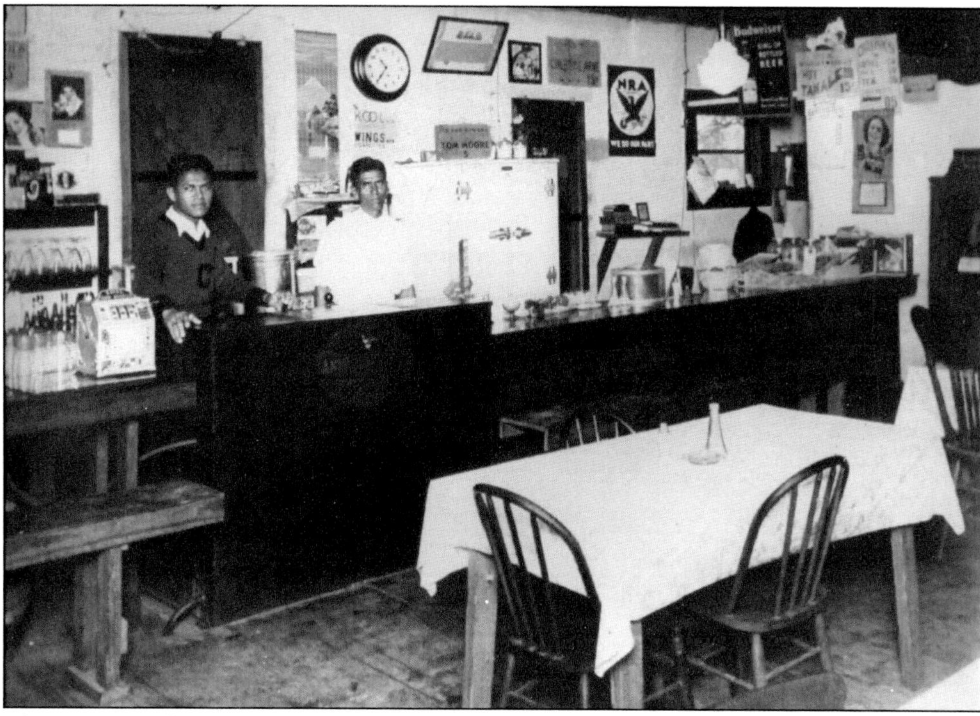

There was no place like Trine's Café for Mexican food. Trine's was located on Main Street in Cotulla. The café was owned by Trinidad Abrego and later operated by his wife, Catarina, and daughter, Concha. Beer was sold on tap or by the bottle. A cold Budweiser could be purchased for 15¢.

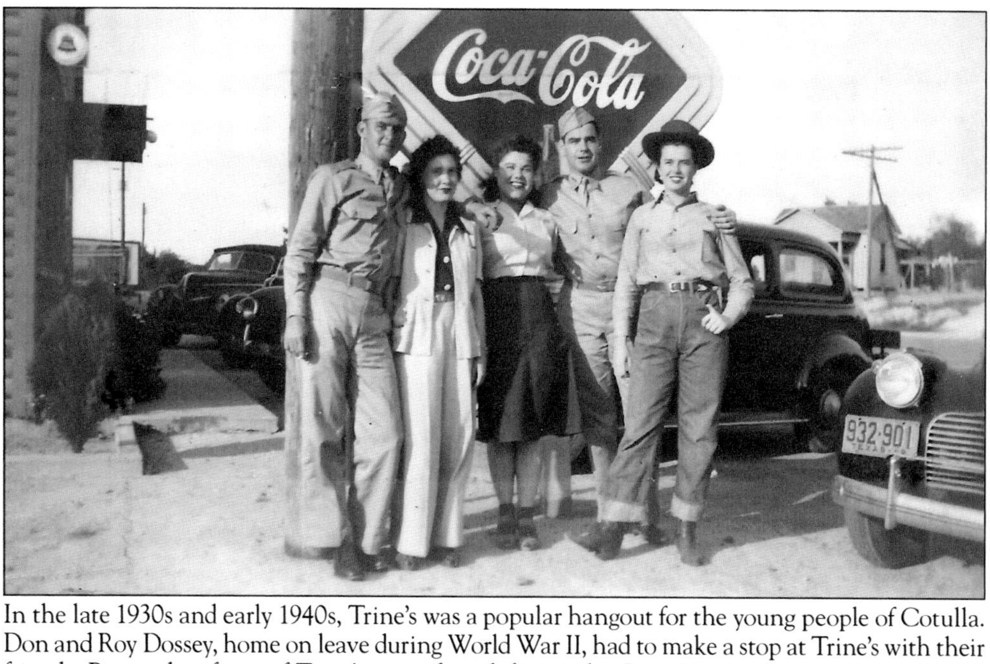

In the late 1930s and early 1940s, Trine's was a popular hangout for the young people of Cotulla. Don and Roy Dossey, home on leave during World War II, had to make a stop at Trine's with their friends. Pictured in front of Trine's were, from left to right, Don Dossey, Norma Reese, Fredna Knaggs, Roy Dossey, and Kassie Keithley.

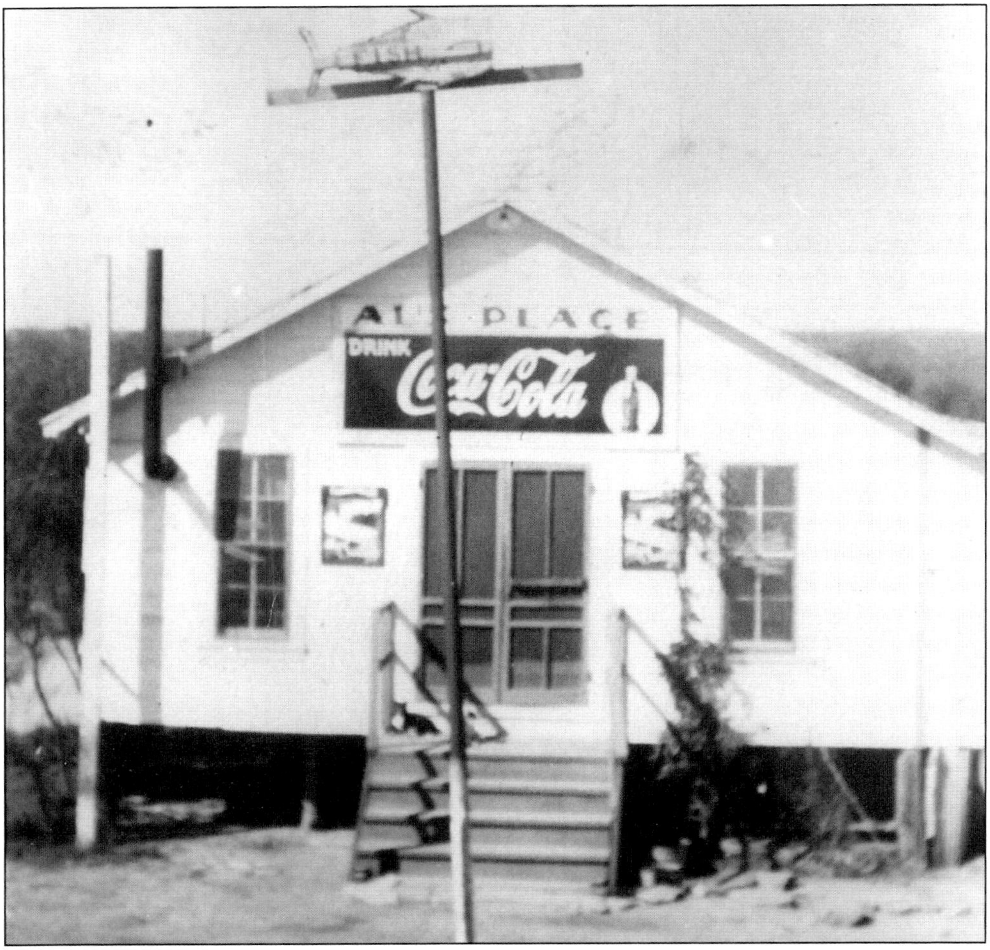

Al's Place was located on the south side of the Nueces River. It was owned and operated by Newton W. "Al" and Thelma Jennings. Al's was a popular place for the locals to meet and drink a few beers or play a game of pool on a Saturday night.

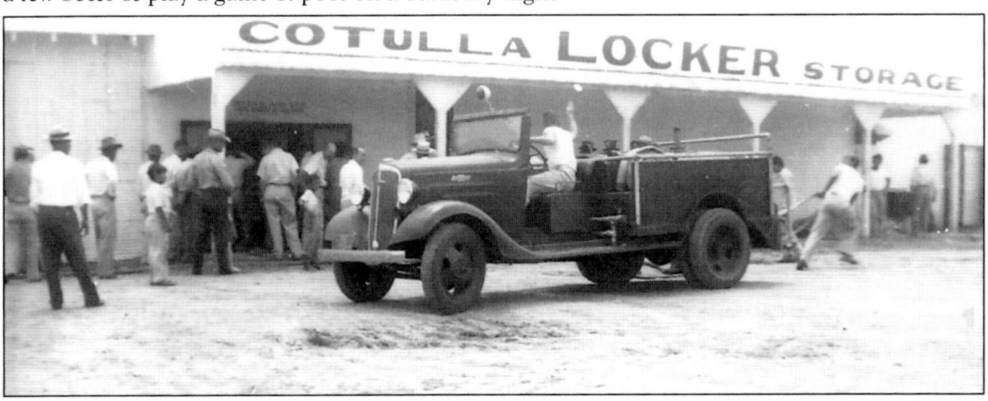

Bernard Wildenthal Jr.'s Cotulla Locker and Storage Plant was located on the west side of Texas U.S. Highway 81, just north of the Nueces River bridge. Farmers, ranchers, and other individuals lacking access to electricity could rent frozen food compartments so that they could preserve their meat until needed.

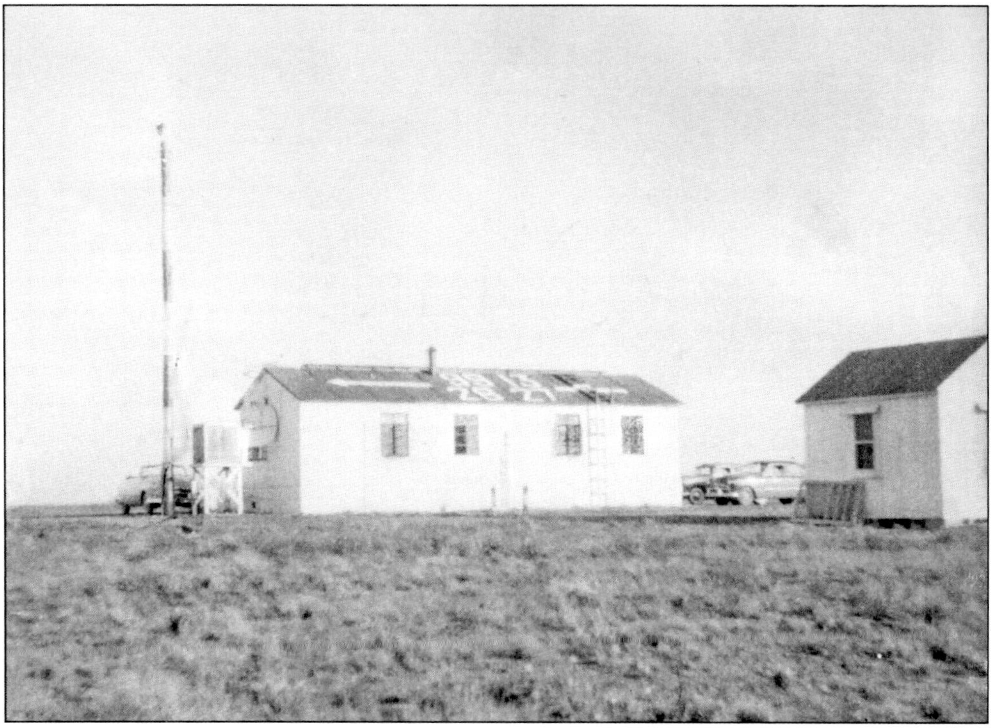

The airport, located 2 miles west of Cotulla, started full-time operation on August 1, 1949. The City of Cotulla furnished the land. The Civil Aeronautics Administration (CAA) installed the weather station and communications system. The airport had two 4,000-foot dirt runways and a green and white beacon visible at night. The airport was open 24 hours a day with six employees.

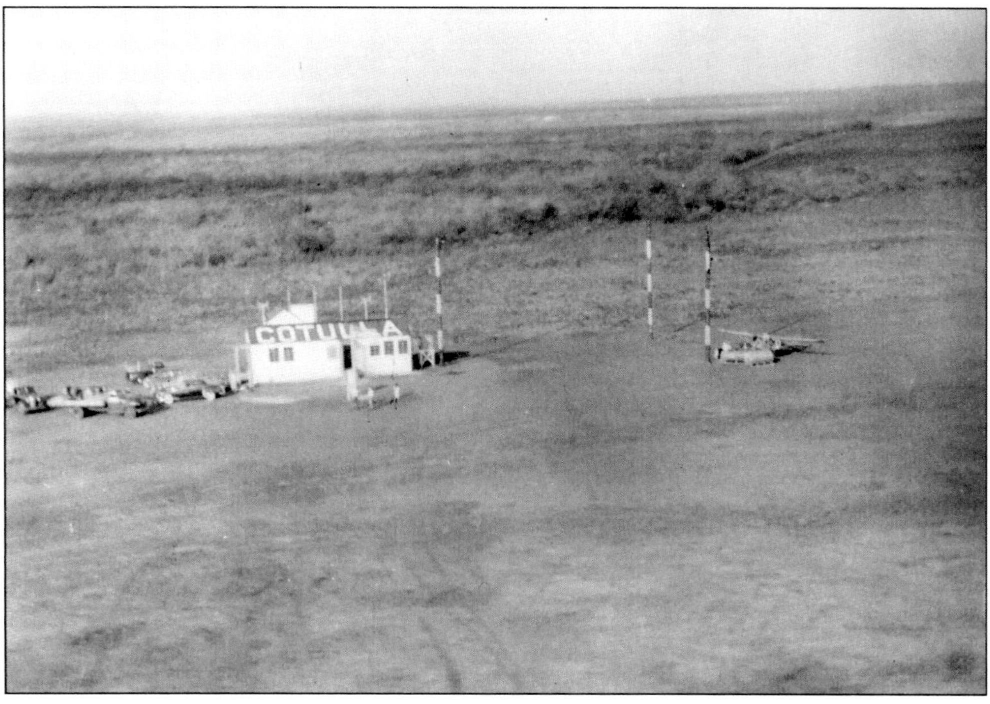

Four

RAMBLING ABOUT THE COUNTY

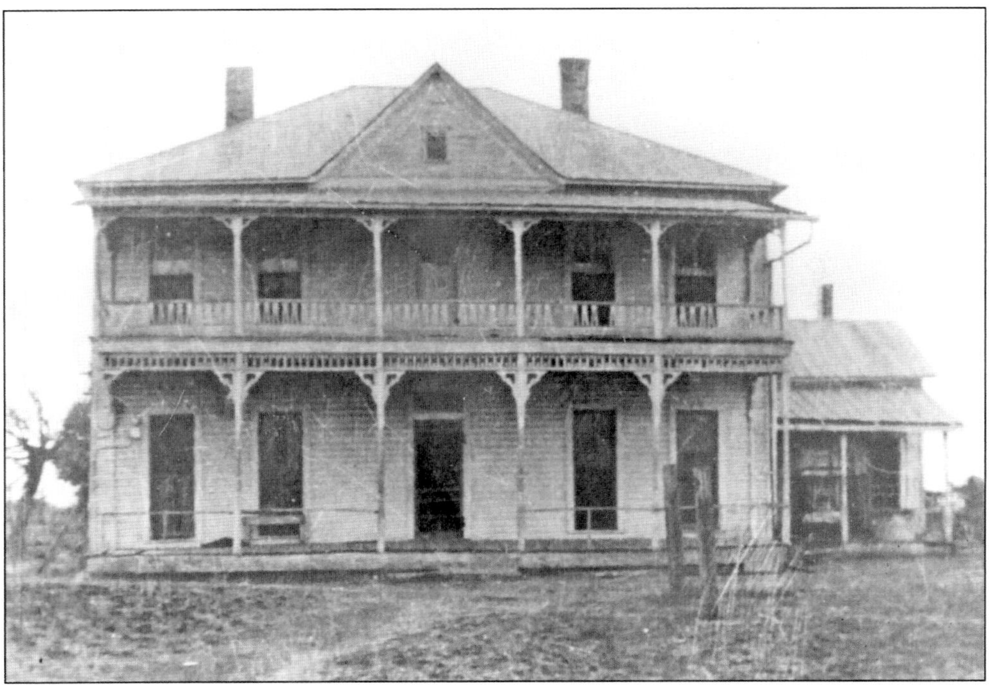

In the early 1900s, Millett was a bustling community with people coming and going. Florence Yeager opened the Buena Vista in 1907. At the time it was the most up-to-date hotel south of San Antonio. The Buena Vista had two floors with 17 gas-lit rooms and hot and cold baths on each floor. In conjunction with the hotel was the Buena Vista Stables. Carriages met each passenger train to carry visitors back to the hotel.

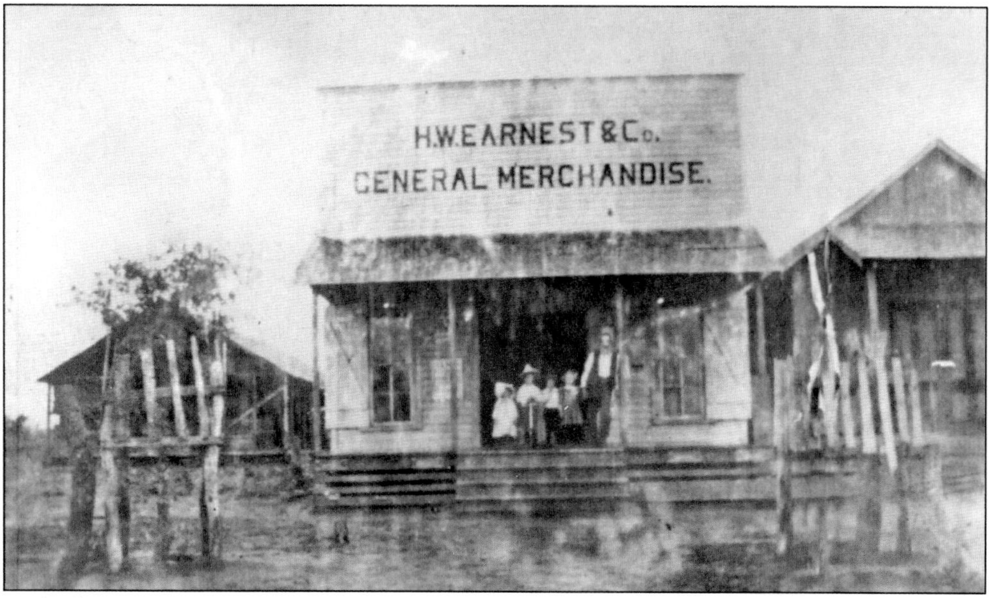

In the late 1890s, H. W. Earnest and Company opened a general merchandise store in the town of Millett. Henry W. Earnest and William A. Waugh were senior partners. The company soon expanded and began operating a cotton gin. Apparently they overextended; the company filed for bankruptcy in 1904.

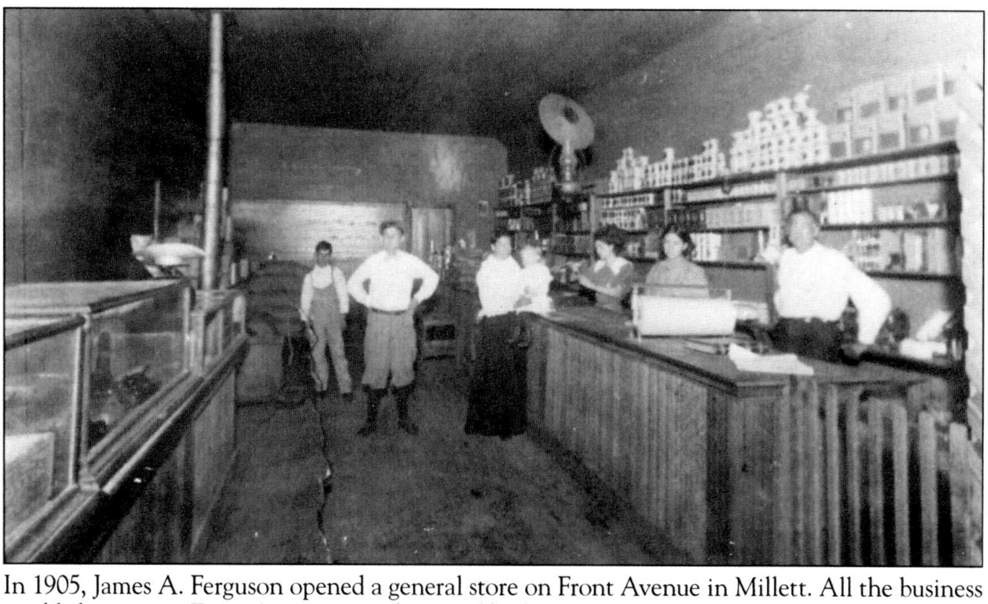

In 1905, James A. Ferguson opened a general store on Front Avenue in Millett. All the business establishments on Front Avenue were destroyed by fire on November 23, 1913. Four general stores and one big store were destroyed at an estimated cost of $60,000. Ferguson's was one of the general stores destroyed by fire. Ferguson rebuilt, and his store remained in business until 1960.

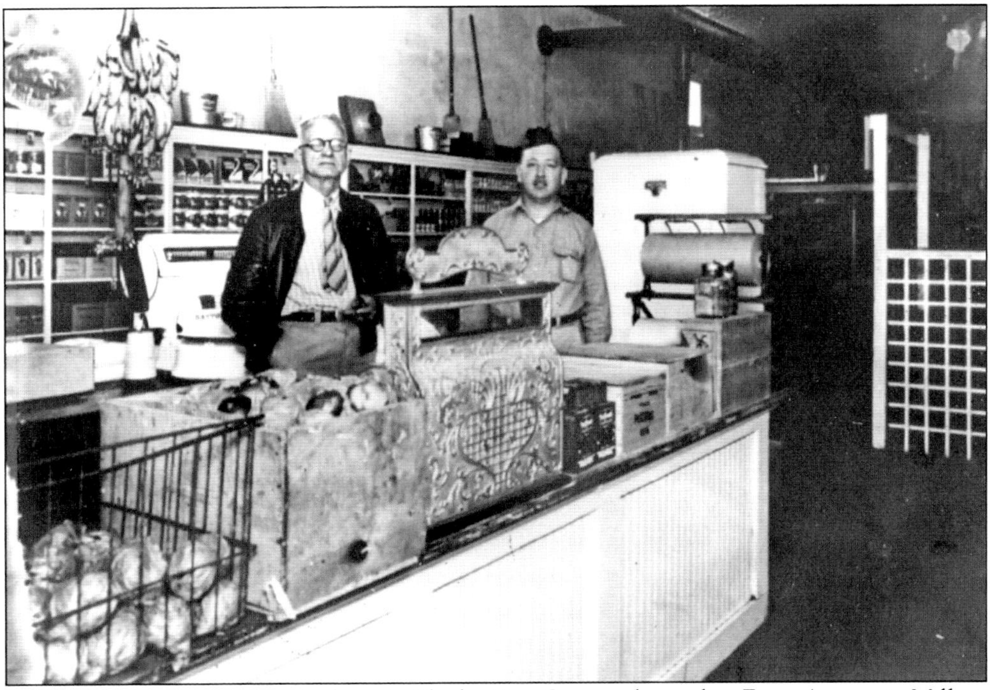

Lee Andrew Harr and his son Jack are inside the Harr Grocery, located on Front Avenue in Millett. The store carried a complete line of groceries and other sundry items. The post office was also located inside the store. Stevie Ray, wife of Lee Andrew, served as postmistress for many years.

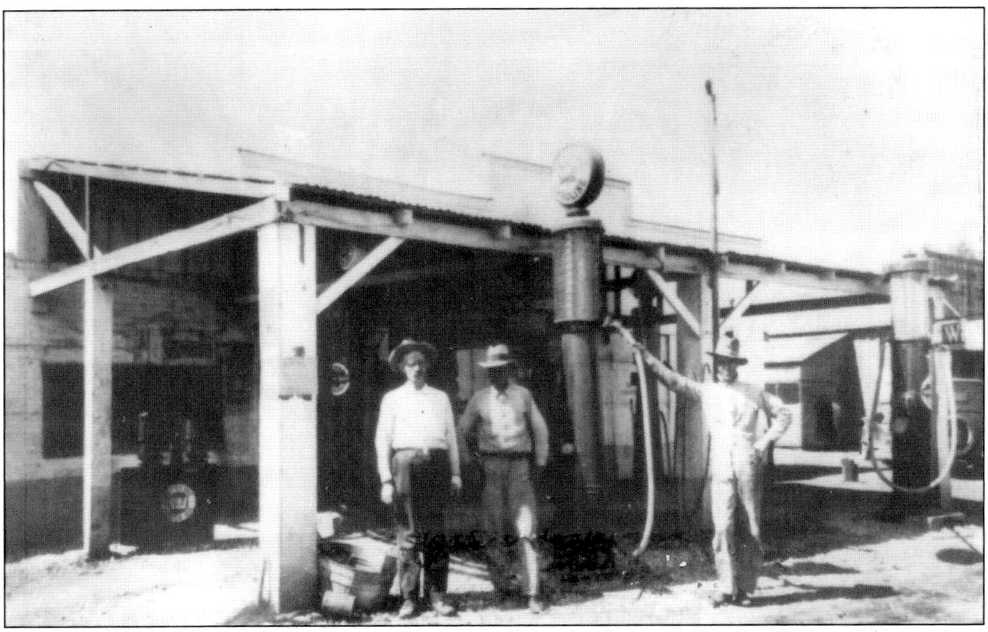

Vaughn and Shull opened a garage on Front Avenue in Millett in 1920. By 1928, gasoline pumps had been added to serve the local residents and travelers along U.S. Highway 81. Pictured from left to right are Silas F. Riddell, Harvey Shull, and Charles Shull.

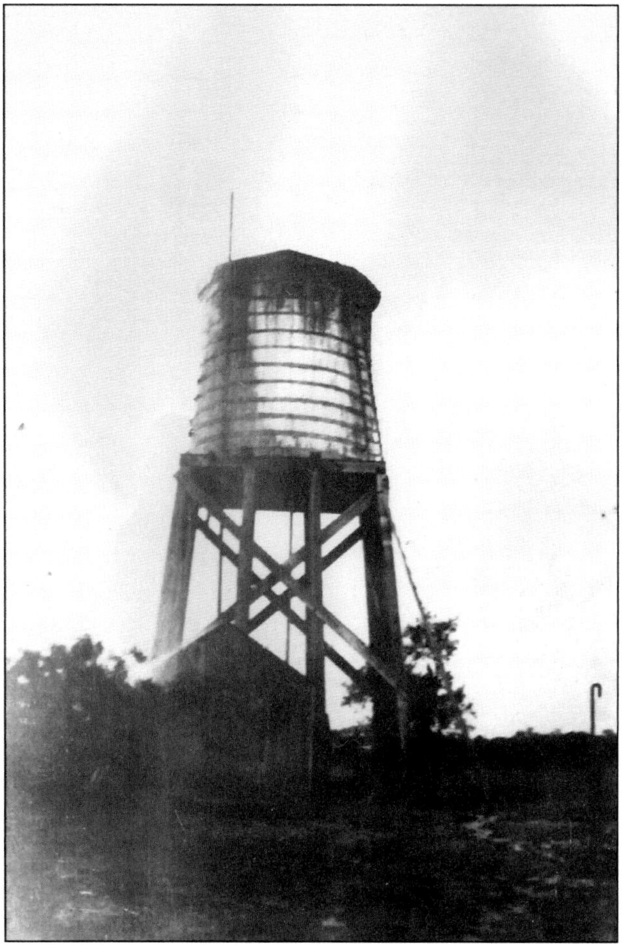

Gardendale was a new town in 1908, built on the International and Great Northern Railroad. The town sits in the middle of 16,000 acres cut up into 20-acre tracts and sold to settlers. One of the first items of business was drilling a well and erecting a water tower to accommodate the residents of the new town.

By 1914, the San Antonio, Uvalde, and Gulf Railroad had intersected with the International and Great Northern at the town of Gardendale. The two railroads had eight passenger trains running daily. The town had a roomy plaza with a fountain and wide, graded streets. Gardendale also boasted a school, a 24-room hotel, a print shop, and three stores.

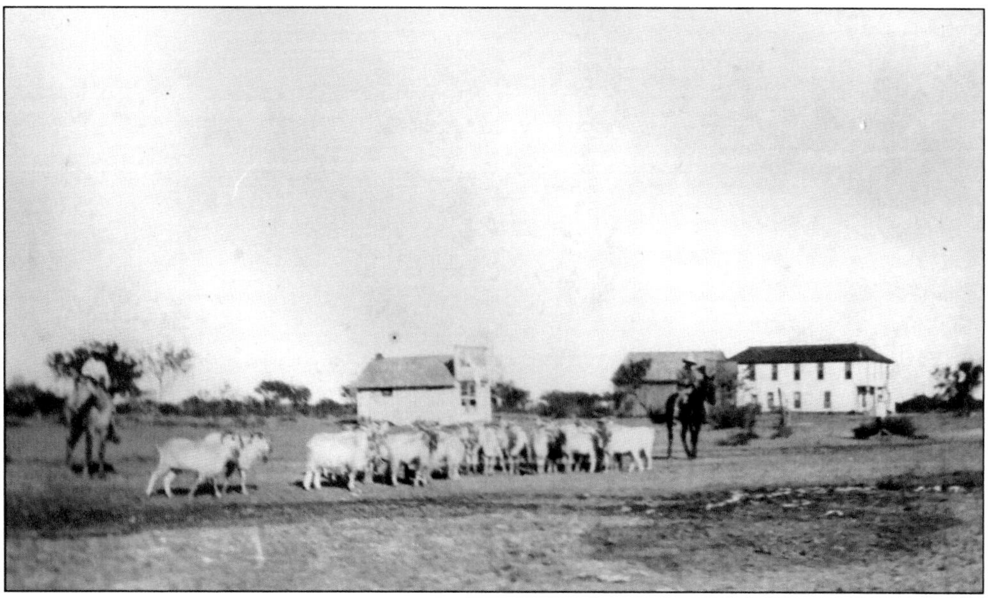

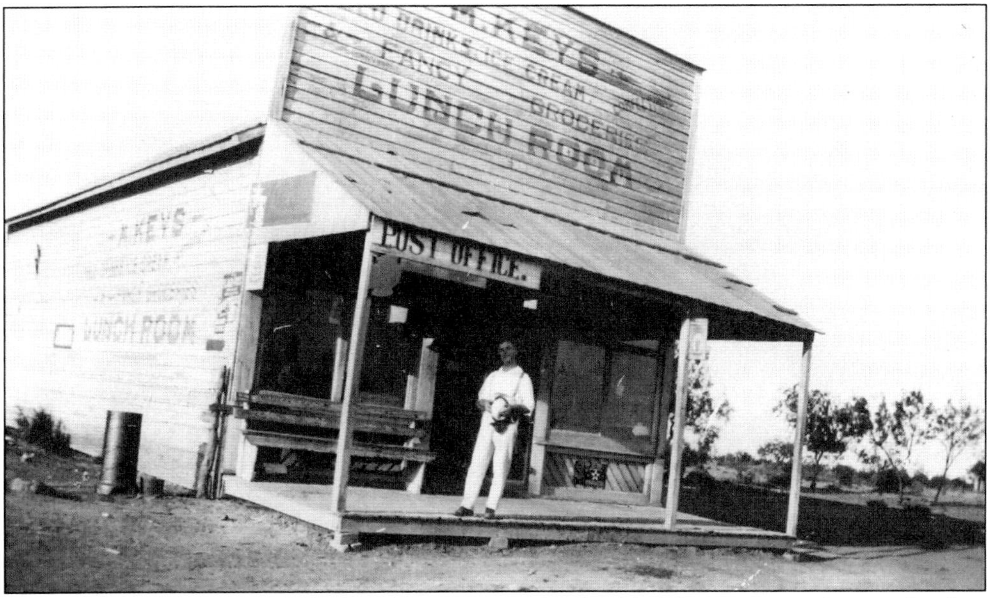

Whatever one needed, it could be found at M. Keys in Gardendale. The store carried a complete line of fancy groceries and confectioneries. The post office was also located there. After checking their mail and shopping, patrons could enjoy a cold drink, ice cream, or a snack in the lunchroom.

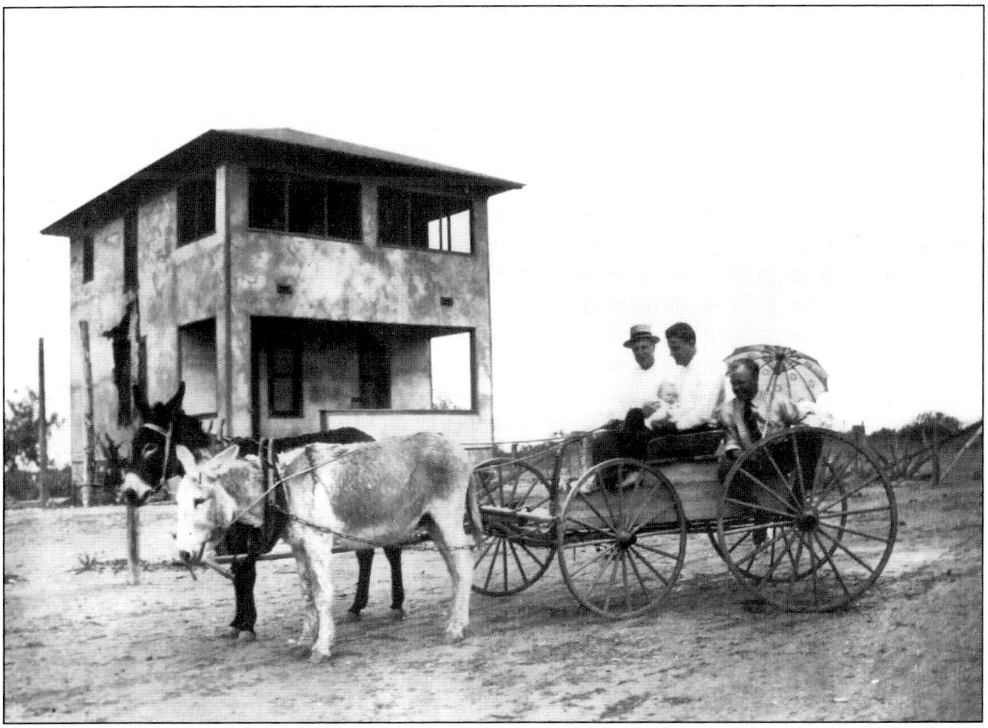

The Wine residence was one of the early homes in Gardendale. The residence of John and Eula Wine was located at the intersection of the International and Great Northern Railroad and the San Antonio, Ulvalde, and Gulf Railroad. By 1916, the Wine House was being used as a rooming house.

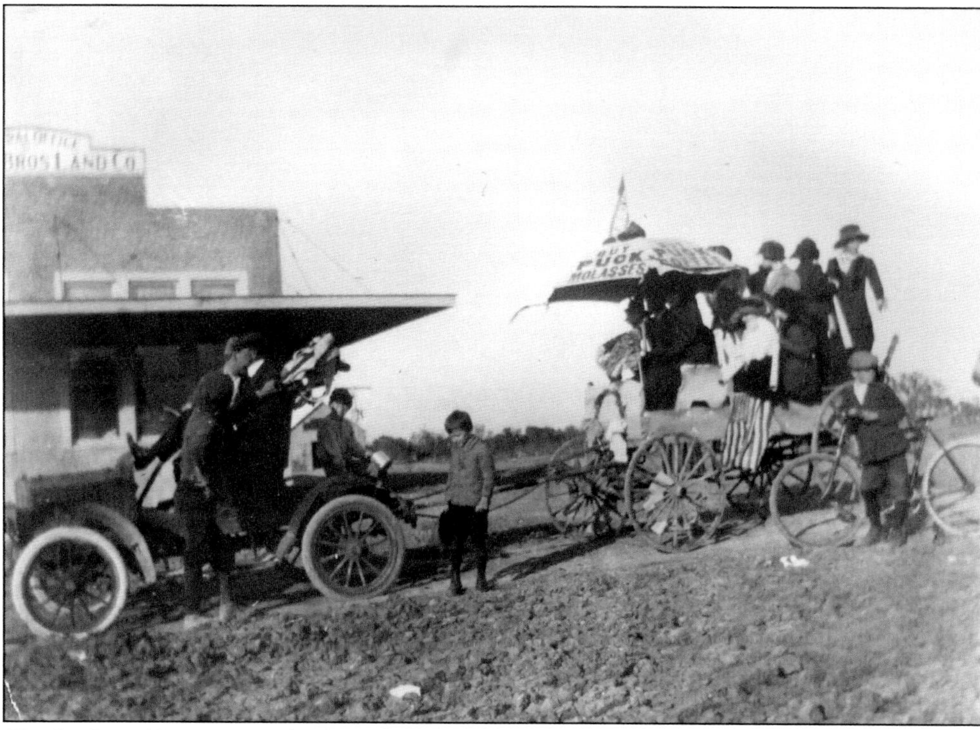

Charles S. and James G. Fowler formed the Fowler Brothers Land Company in 1911 and opened an office in the new town of Fowlerton. The brothers set out to sell 100,000 acres of land that had been subdivided into 10-acre tracts. Pictured is a 1911 float of the Fowlerton Brothers Land Company.

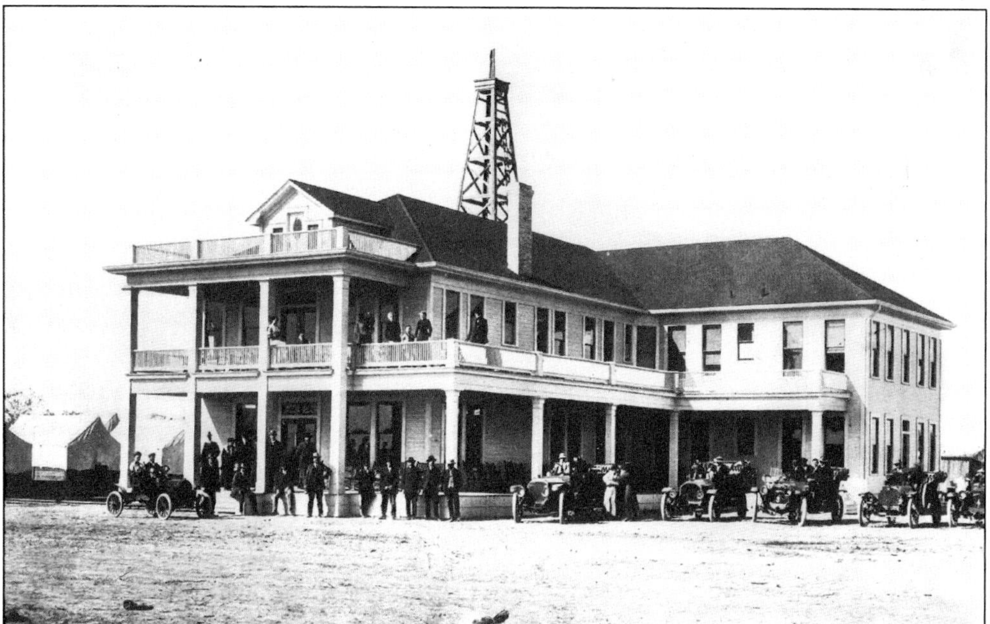

The Fowlerton Hotel was erected by the Fowler Brothers Land Company and cost $20,000. The hotel was a two-story frame building with 25 rooms. Baths with hot and cold running water were located between every two rooms. The hotel was always filled to overflowing.

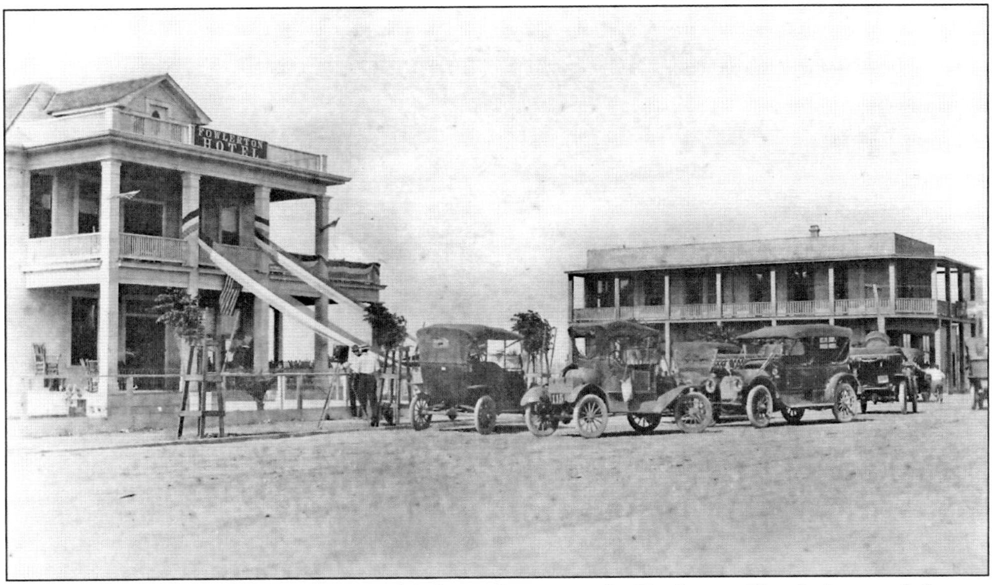

An early Fowlerton street scene is visible here, featuring the Fowlerton Hotel. Automobiles are parked in front of the hotel ready to take a group of prospective land buyers to view the 10-acre tract they were planning to purchase from the Fowler Brothers Land Company.

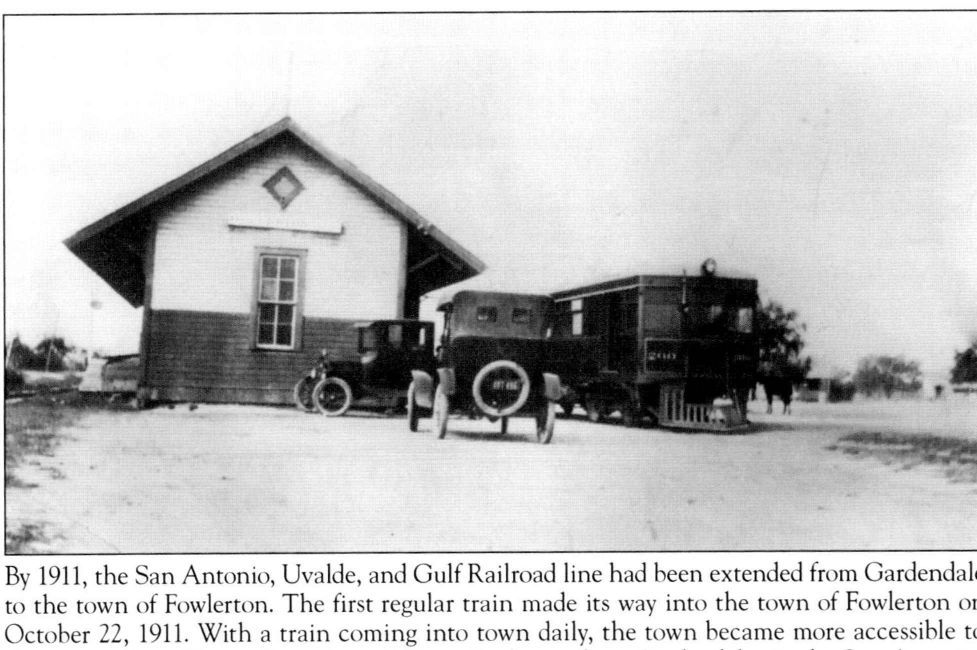

By 1911, the San Antonio, Uvalde, and Gulf Railroad line had been extended from Gardendale to the town of Fowlerton. The first regular train made its way into the town of Fowlerton on October 22, 1911. With a train coming into town daily, the town became more accessible to the new settlers. The mail was brought into Fowlerton from Gardendale via the San Antonio, Uvalde, and Gulf Railroad.

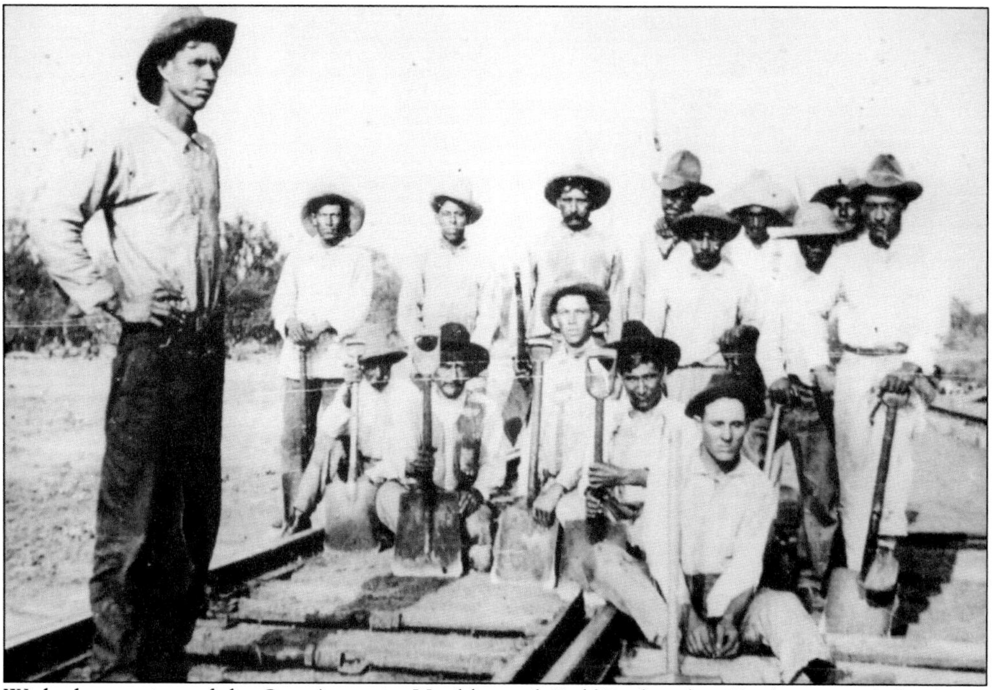

With the coming of the San Antonio, Uvalde, and Gulf Railroad to Fowlerton and the depot being built, the next order of business was hiring a section crew to keep the tracks in top condition. Pictured is the section crew stationed at Fowlerton.

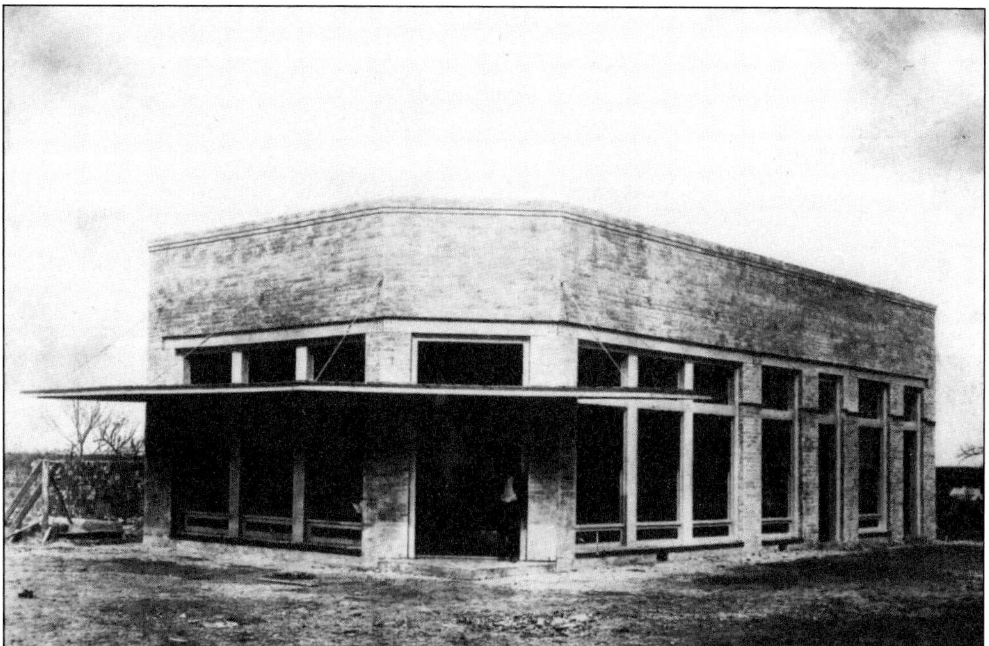

On January 17, 1914, the stockholders of the First State of Fowlerton met and elected W. H. Patton president, Robert C. Sutton vice president, and H. M. Patton cashier. The directors were W. H. Patton, Robert C. Sutton, H. M. Patton, C. J. Bain, and James G. Fowler.

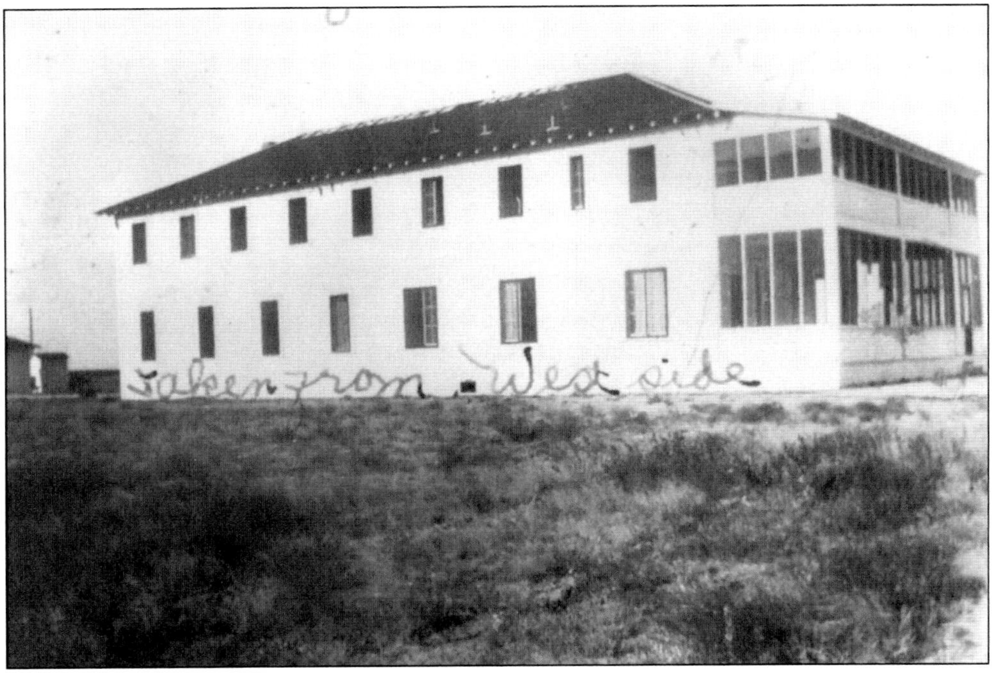

F. Z. Bishop, founder of the town of Los Angeles, built the Los Angeles Hotel near the San Antonio, Uvalde, and Gulf Railroad to accommodate the passengers arriving on the train. The hotel had 20 rooms and was operated by the Johnsons. Meals were served at noon and four in the afternoon.

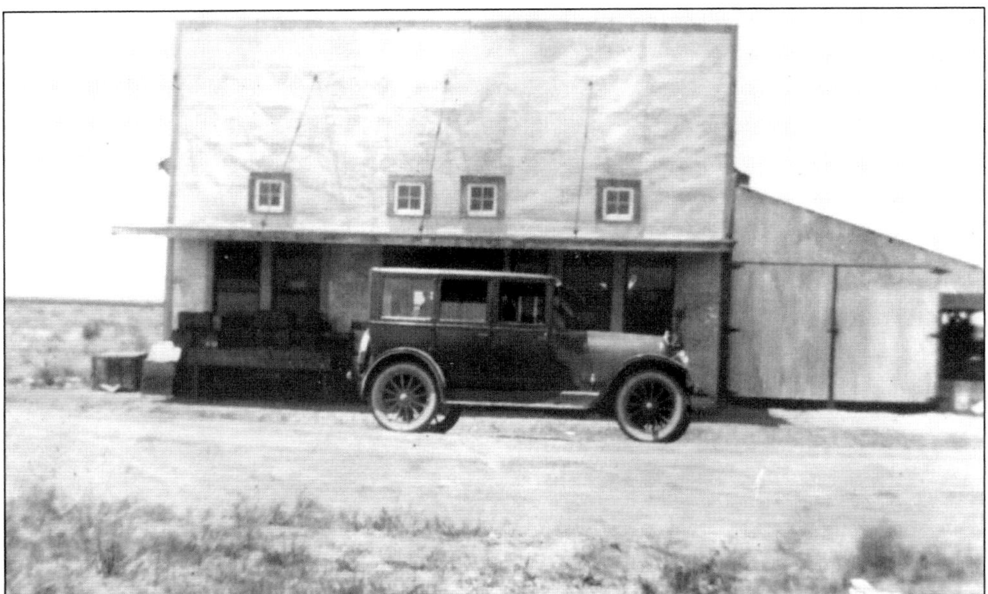

Elmer and William Fuchs owned a hardware store in Los Angeles. They later added other merchandise and the store became known as Fuchs Hardware and Mercantile and was one of the two stores built in Los Angeles. Klattenhoff and Sladek operated the other general store in Los Angeles.

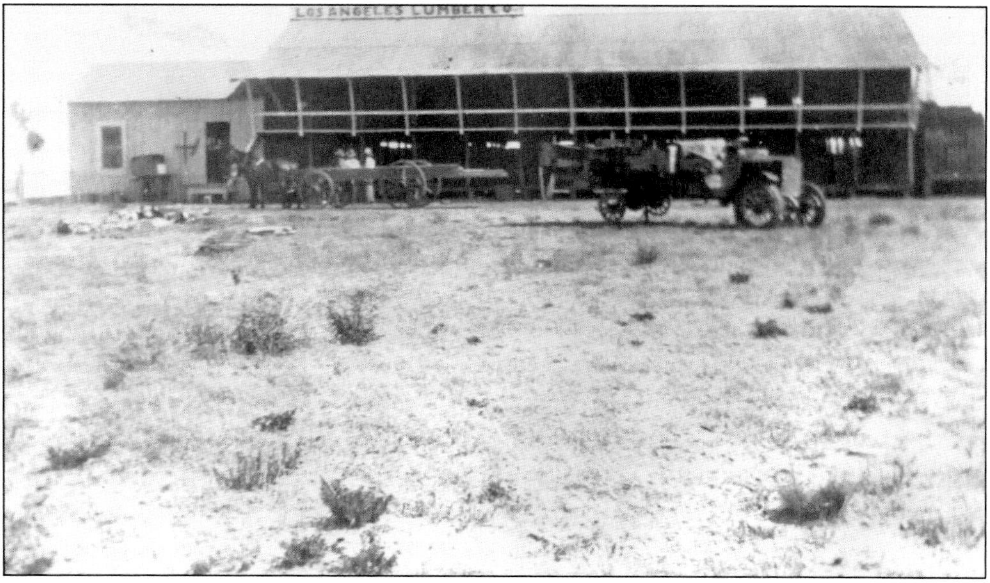

Edward Gustafson managed and had an interest in the Los Angeles Lumber Company. The lumber company furnished much of the lumber and other supplies needed to construct the businesses and homes in the Los Angeles area. A wagon is loaded with lumber headed for a building site.

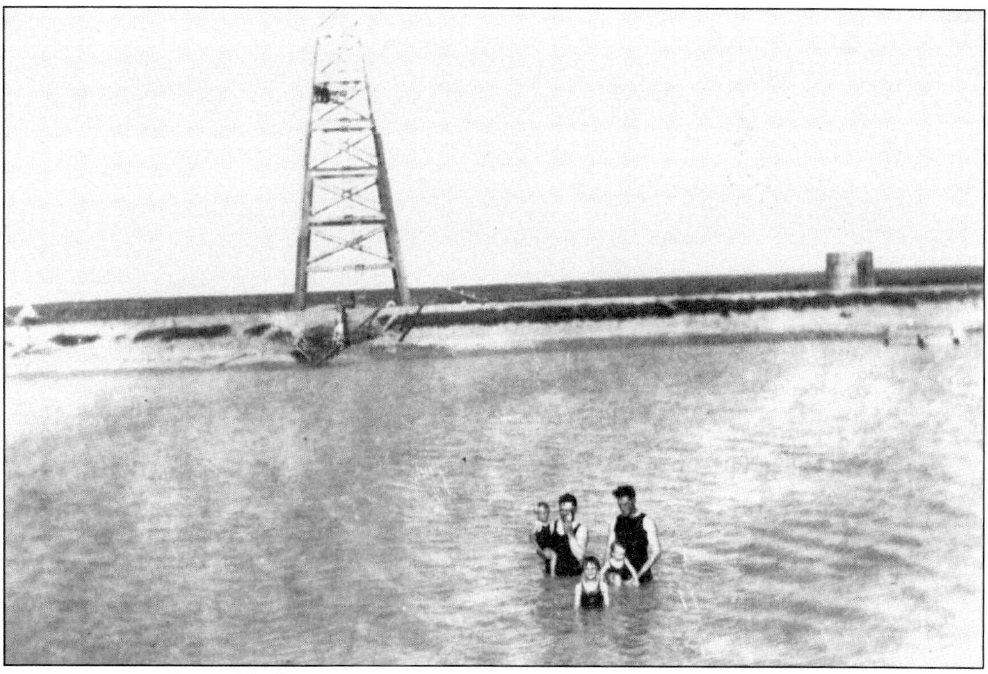

In 1923, an inexhaustible flow of pure artesian water flowed from the well at Los Angeles. The well furnished the town with excellent water. The reservoir soon became the local swimming hole and many children of Los Angeles and the surrounding area learned to swim there.

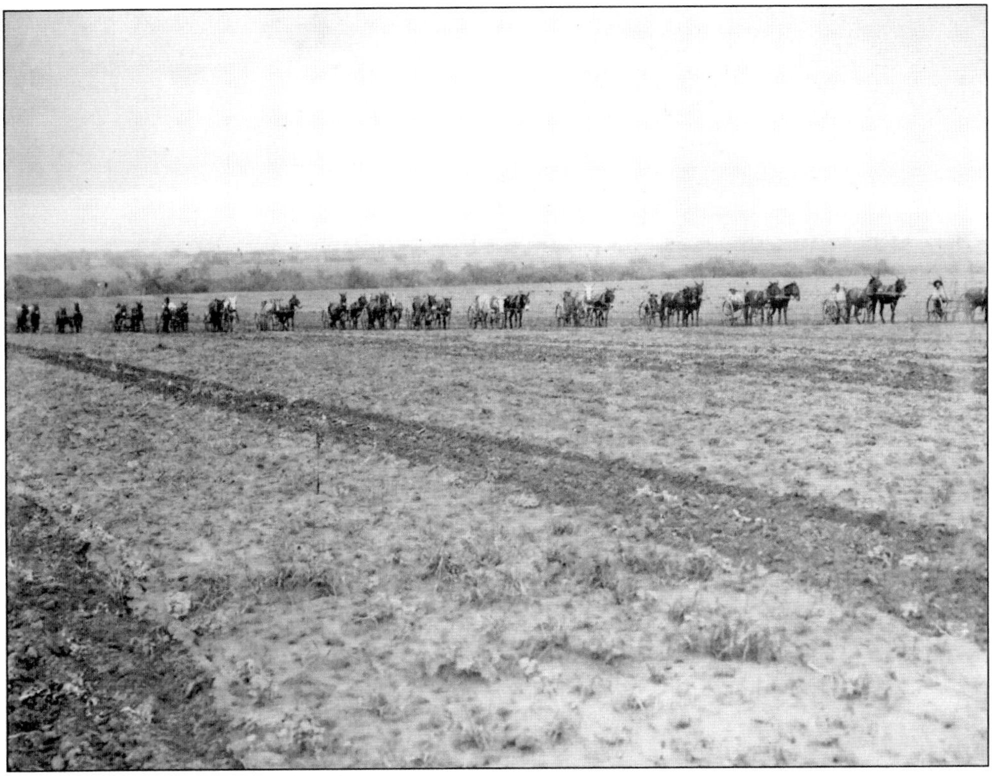

In January 1907, D. J. Woodward secured 35 Japanese workers at low wages to clear the brush from his property. Before the year was out he was expecting to have 5,000 acres ready for cultivation and sale. The land was advertised for $7 per acre.

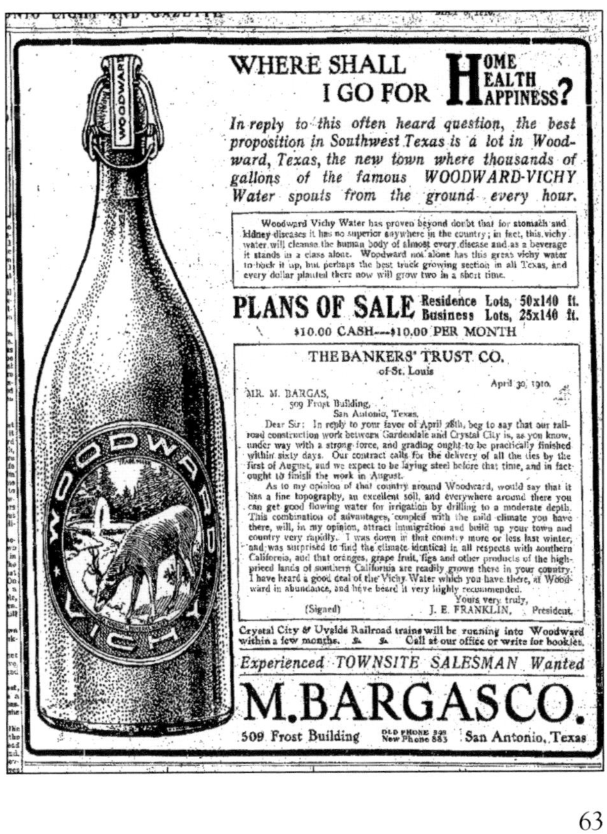

Thousands of gallons of the famous Woodward Vichy water flowed from the ground hourly. The water was bottled by the Woodward Vichy Water Company and drinking it was advertised as curing almost any disease. Bathing in the water was also advertised as a cure to aches and pains.

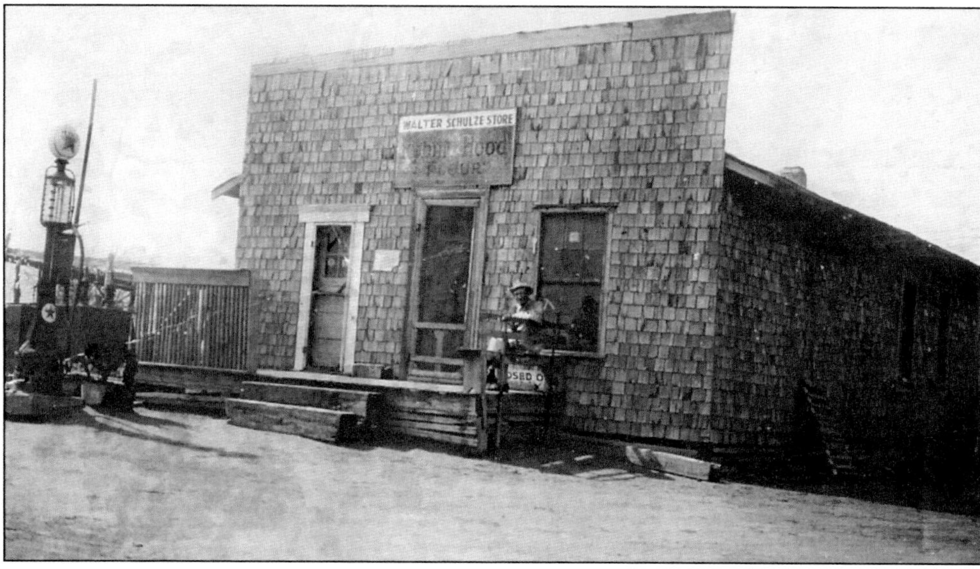

Growth in Woodward was slow. Pictured is Adolf Garmes sitting on the porch of the Walter Schulze Store located in Woodward. Other businesses in Woodward included a 13-room hotel and cotton gin. The flowing artesian well furnished water for the residents. Notice the Texaco gas pump.

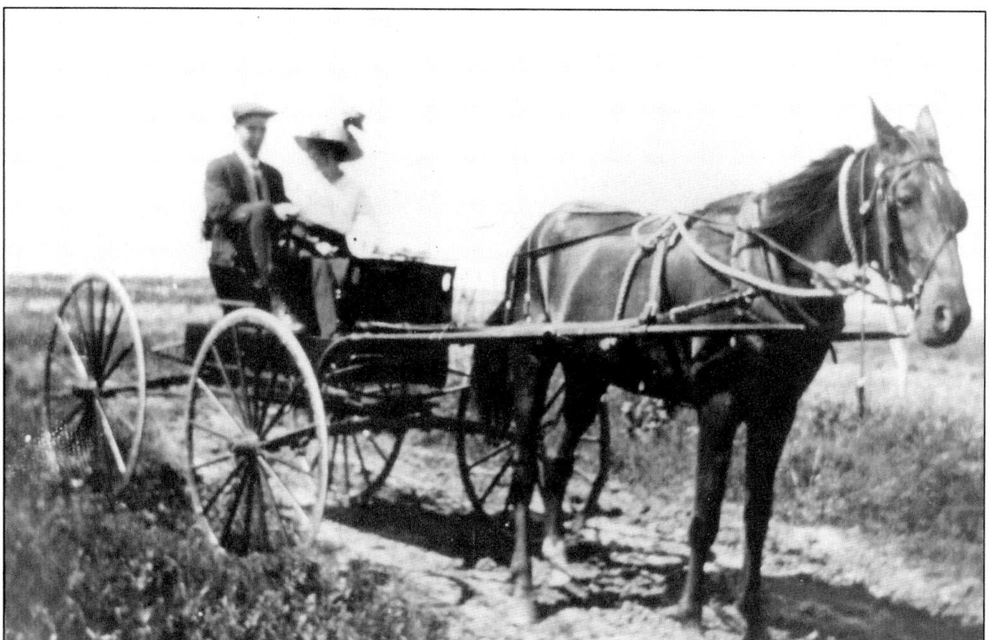

Shown on their way to town in their buggy are Henry A. and Cora Harrell Arnold. The Arnolds settled on Stringtown Road just north of Woodward in the early 1920s. Henry Arnold was a farmer, rancher, and a beekeeper.

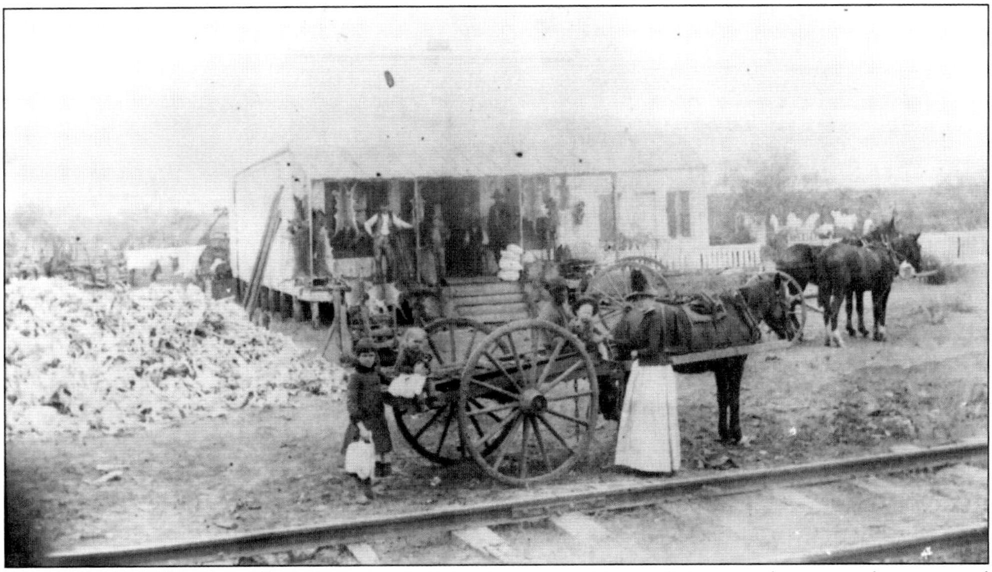

Moses Baine's Store in Twohig was a thriving business. Moses Baine made money buying and selling deer hides. One day he bid on a load of hides and won. The other bidder, a Mr. Long, angered by being outbid, took out his gun and shot Baine in the temple. His widow continued to run the store after his death.

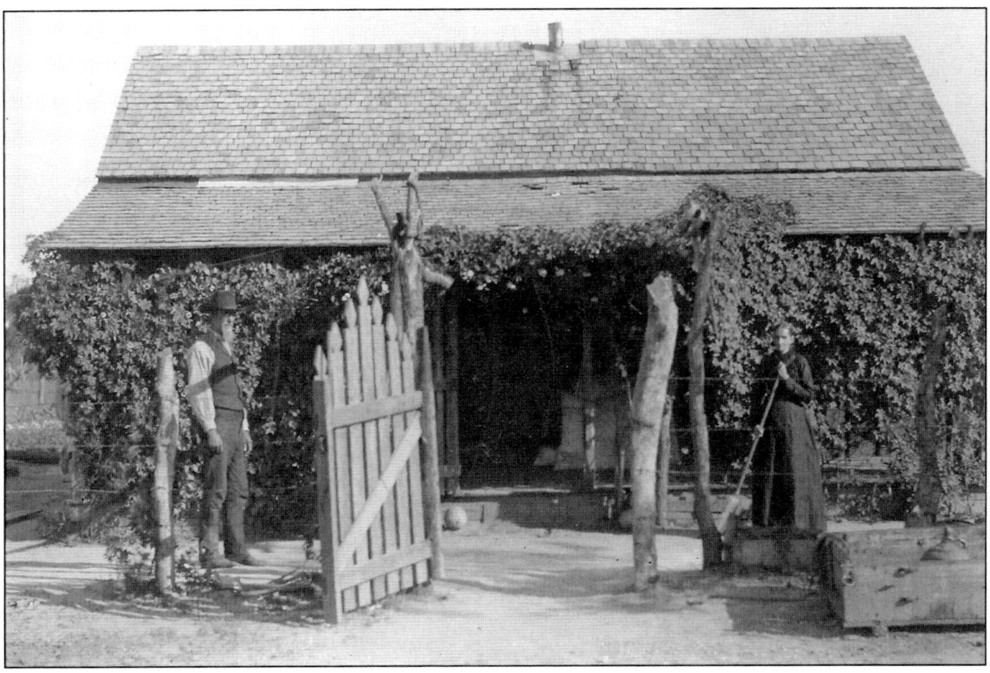

The developers of the town of Artesia Wells guaranteed to prospective buyers that they would make improvements to the town at their own expense. Each purchaser of a lot in Artesia Wells would receive an undivided interest in all of the improvements. The home of Henry Thomas and Elizabeth Lawson was among the early dwellings in the new town of Artesia Wells. Henry Thomas was a circuit Baptist preacher, traveling by foot to the nearby towns to preach.

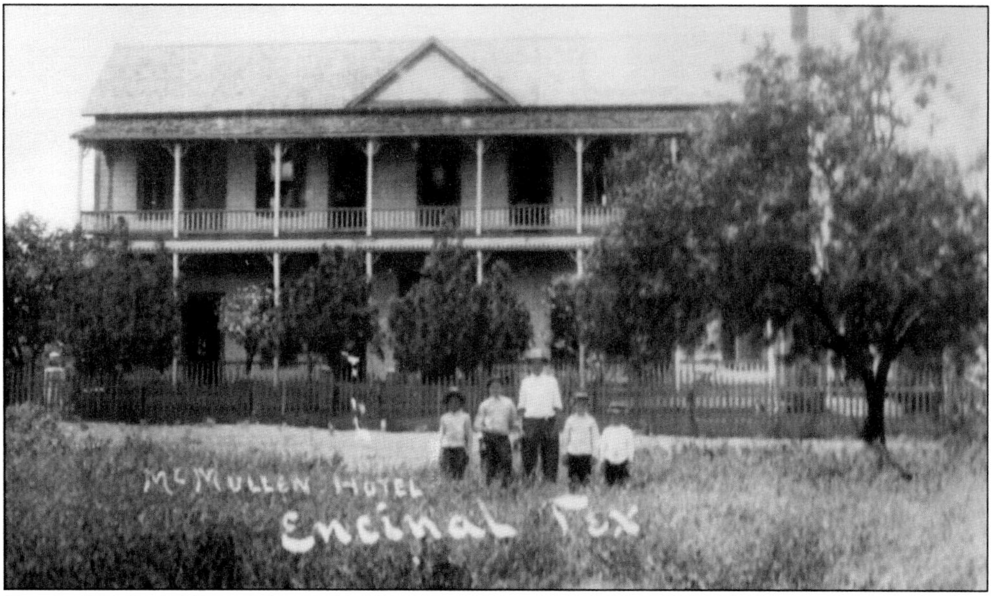

Joseph W. McMullin and his wife, Theresa, were among the early settlers in Encinal. They were the owners of the McMullin Hotel. The hotel was a favorite stopping place for the travelers, especially those on their way to San Antonio from Laredo.

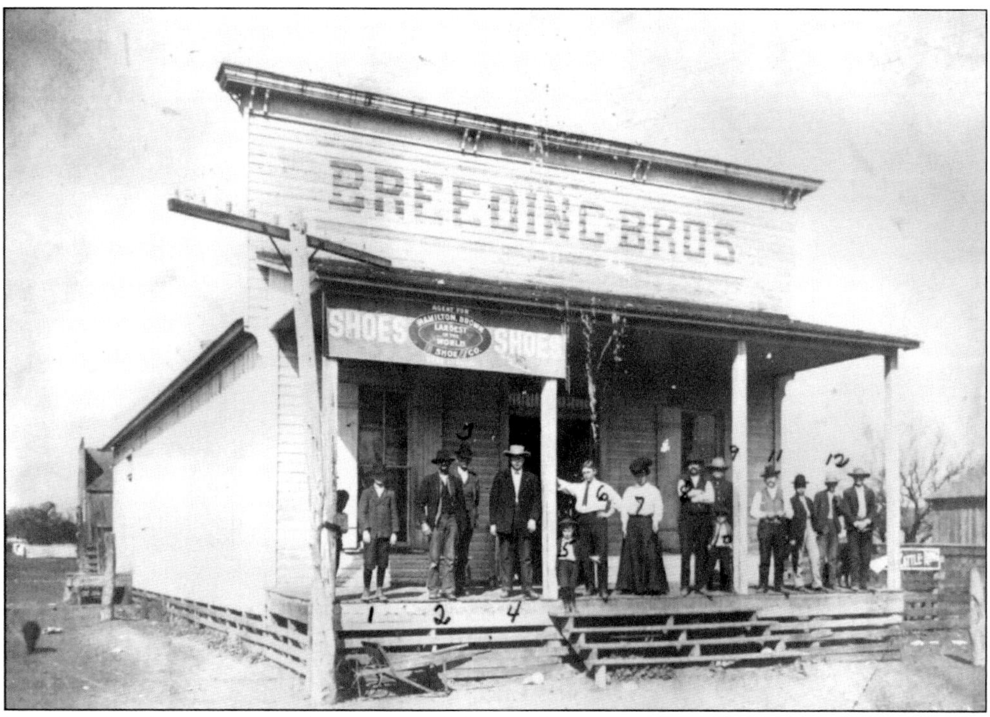

Breeding Brothers was an early grocery and dry goods store in Encinal. It was owned by Edward F. and James Breeding. One of the specialties of the store was shoes. The store was agent for the Hamilton Brown Shoe Company, which was advertised as being the largest in the world.

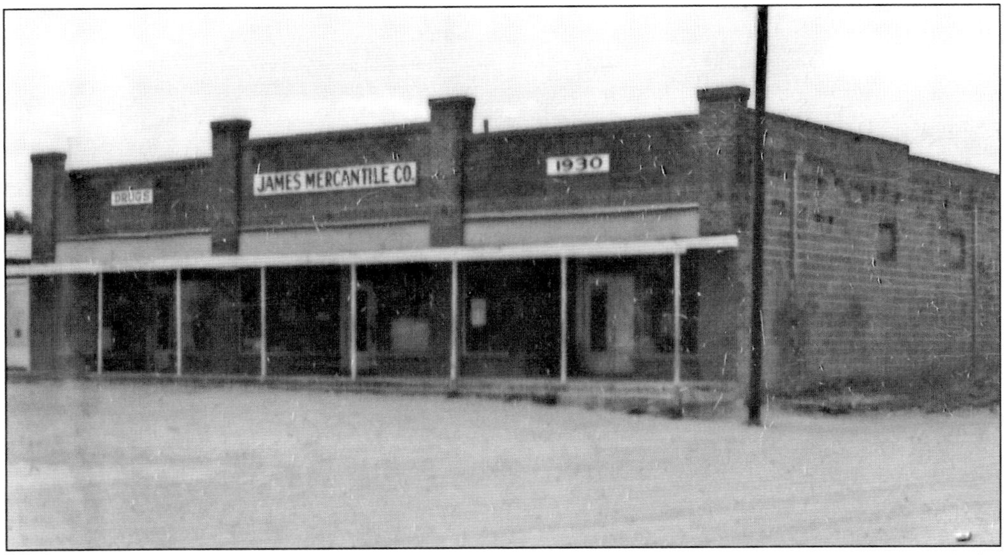

Sidney A. James was president of the James Mercantile firm. The business was one of the oldest mercantile firms in La Salle County. James Mercantile became the gathering place for Encinal residents and was laughingly called the "Encinal Country Club" because of its daily afternoon gatherings. The spacious store sold a little bit of everything, from dry goods and groceries to refrigerators.

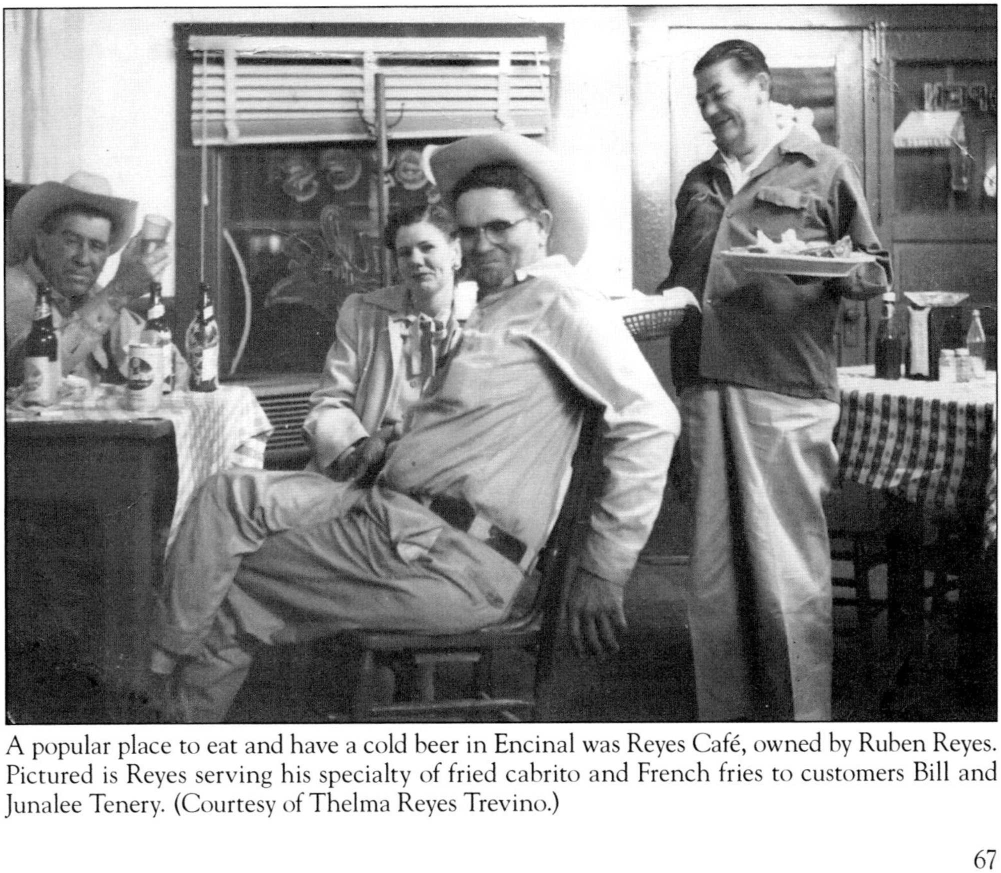
A popular place to eat and have a cold beer in Encinal was Reyes Café, owned by Ruben Reyes. Pictured is Reyes serving his specialty of fried cabrito and French fries to customers Bill and Junalee Tenery. (Courtesy of Thelma Reyes Trevino.)

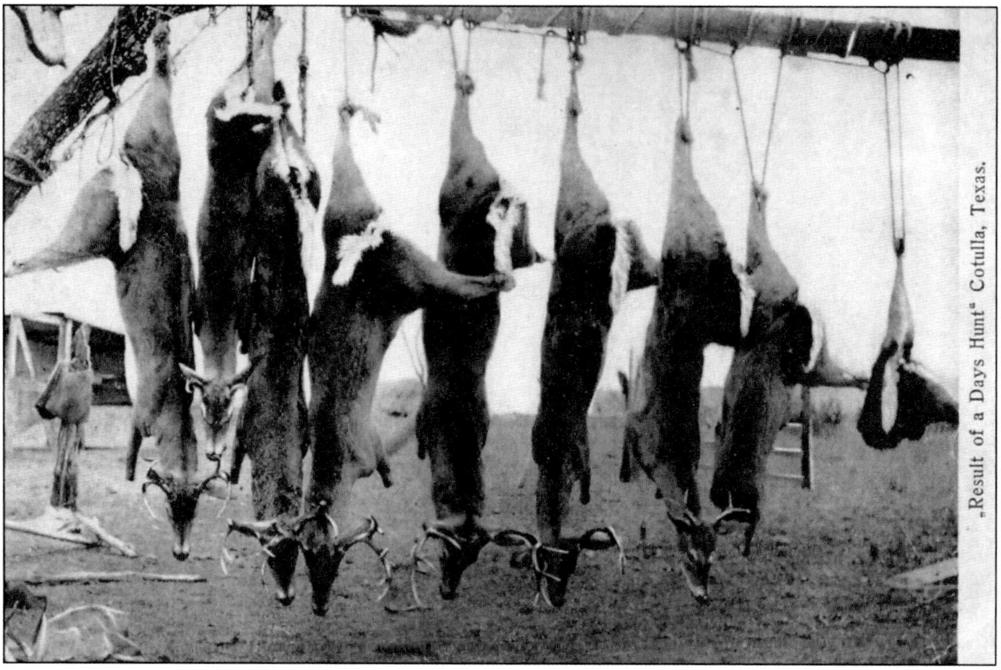

In the early days, hunters killed deer for their hides. Wagons piled high with deer hides were a common sight. The hunters left the deer meat for the coyotes and javelinas. In the 1890s, a market was found for the meat and the hunters shipped that also. During deer season, 25 to 75 deer carcasses were shipped daily from Cotulla. Finally a realization came that the deer were going the way of the buffalo, and the first stringent game laws were enacted.

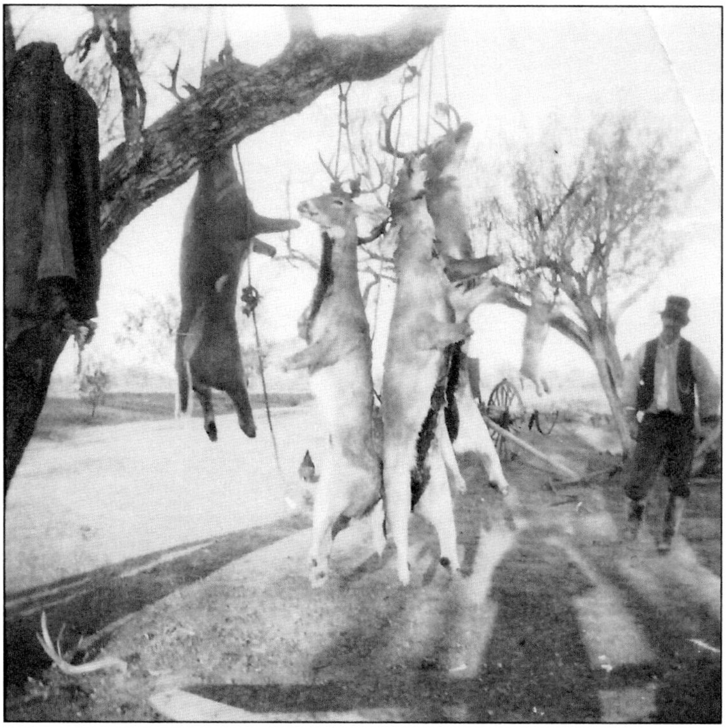

La Salle County has always been known for its big bucks. J. Frank Dobie in a 1946 *San Antonio Express* article said, "The biggest buck I ever saw I missed. It was on a high hill of black chaparral in La Salle County overlooking a vast country including wide sacahuista flats along the Nueces River."

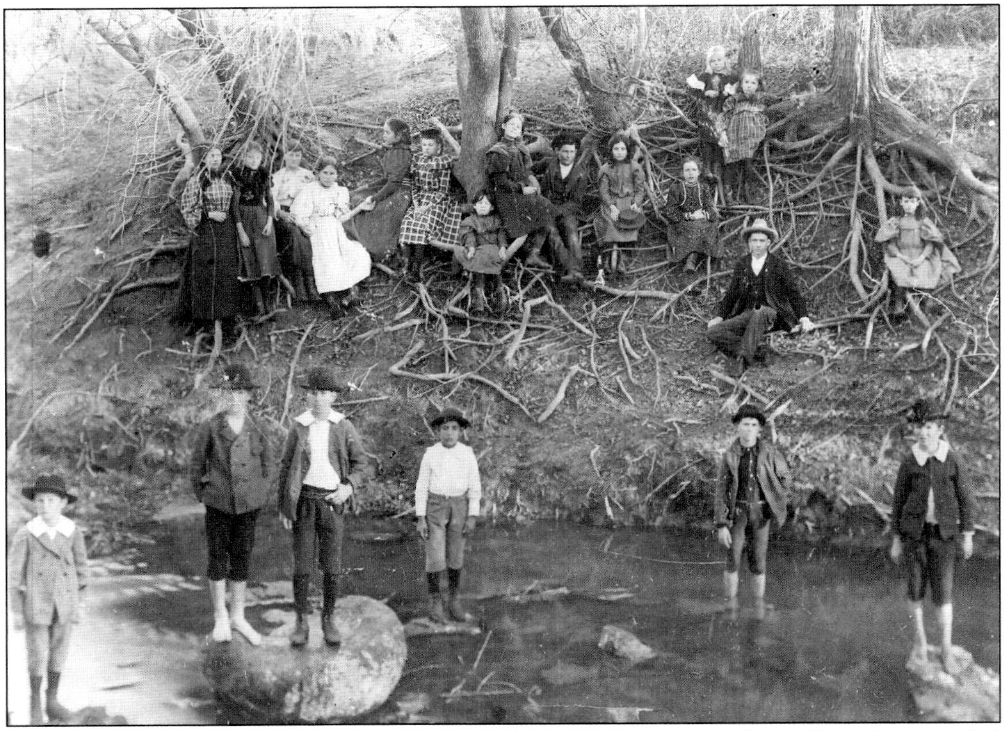

The Nueces River was not only a source of water for the early residents of Cotulla, it also provided a place to have fun. The river was also a popular place for picnics and other gatherings. A group of young people are pictured enjoying a picnic on the Nueces River.

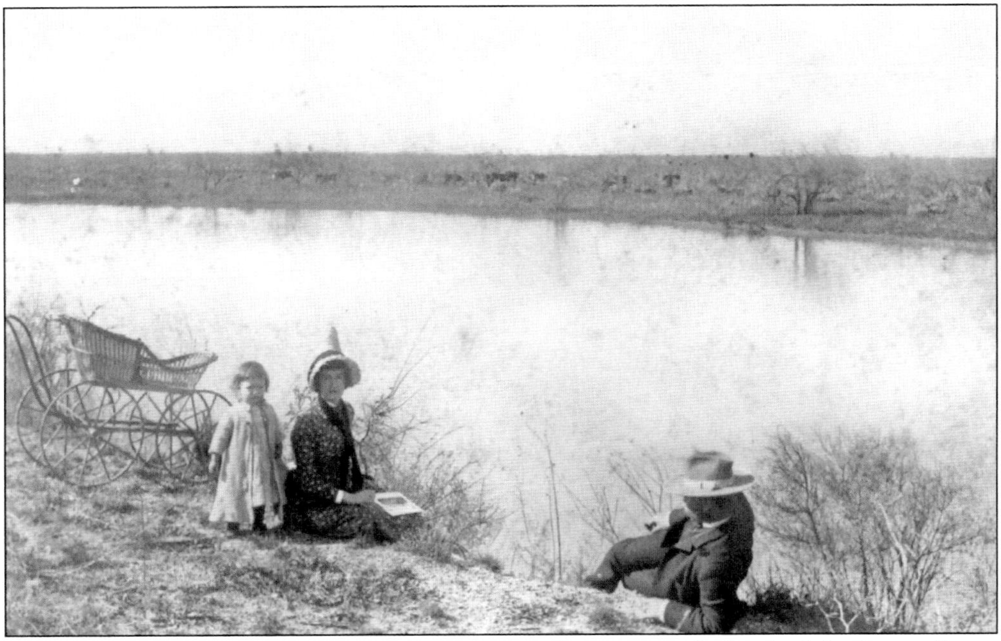

A young family is pictured enjoying a lazy summer afternoon on the bank of the Nueces River. The baby has abandoned her wicker carriage to walk in the sand. A herd of cattle are seen grazing on the opposite side of the river.

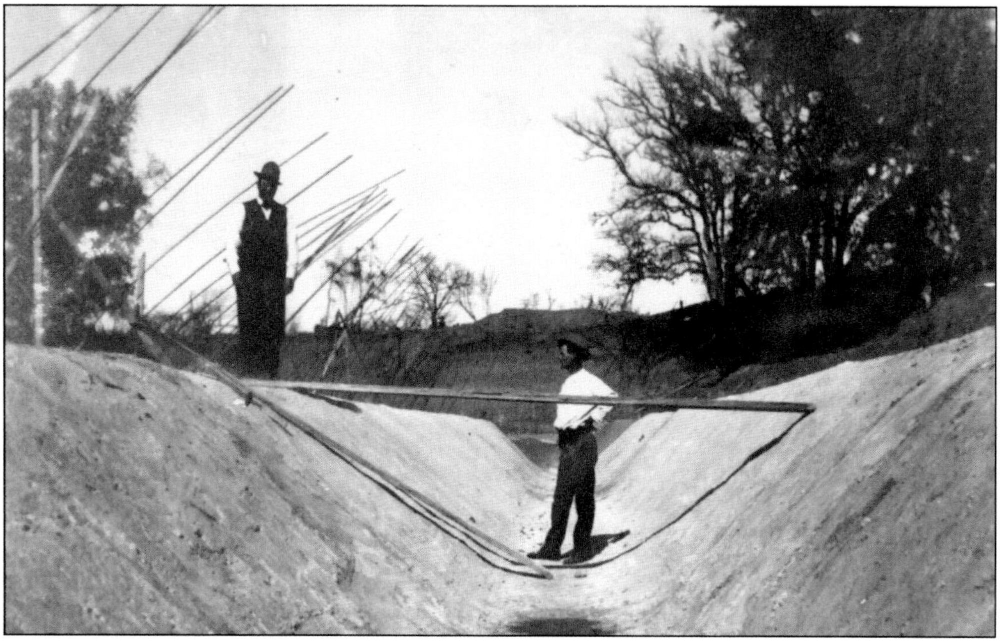

Holland Texas Dam and Irrigation Company was formed in the early 1900s by a group of landowners along the Nueces River. In 1911, a dam was constructed about 10 miles southwest of Cotulla. Pictured are George and Frank Reeder during the early days of construction.

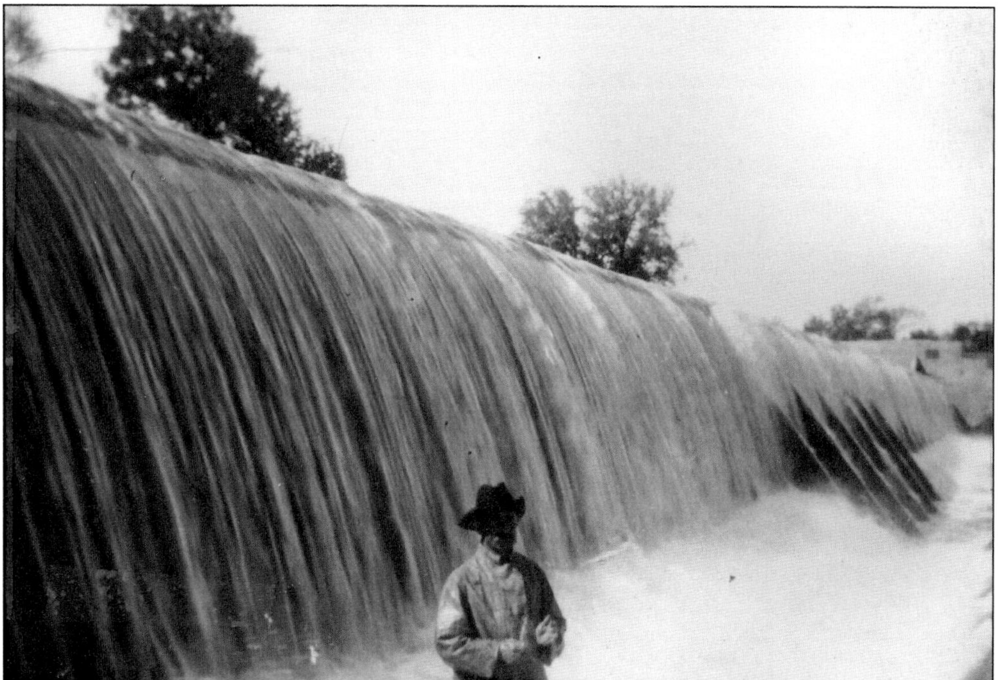

The primary purpose of the Holland Texas Dam was for irrigation, but the dam and lake soon became a favorite fishing, swimming, and picnic spot for the local residents. A scary thing to do was to cross the river on the walkway behind the dam.

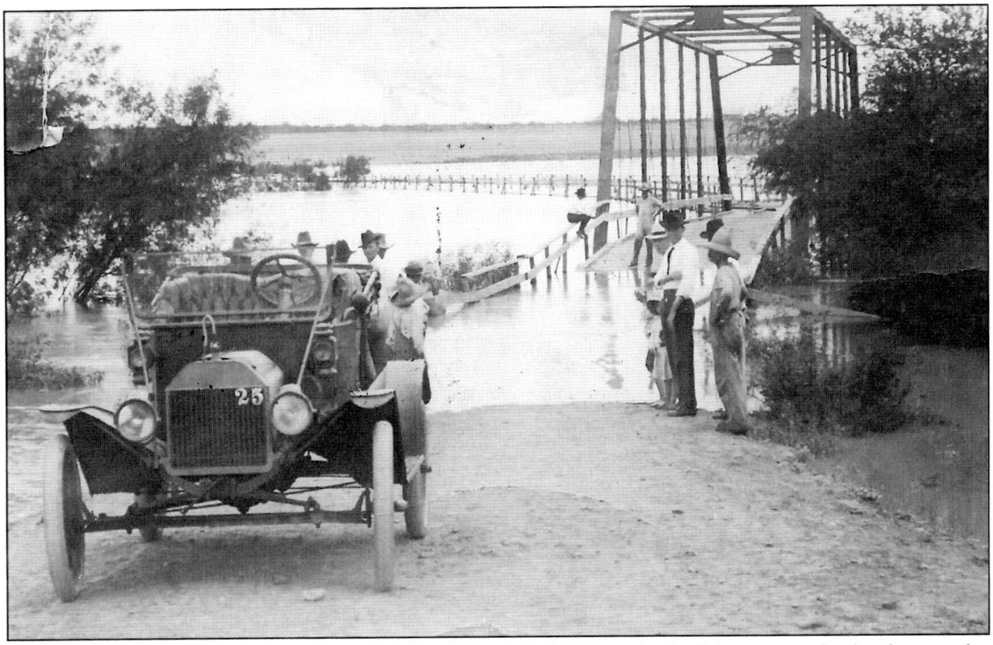

The Nueces River went on a rampage in June 1925. On June 2nd of that year, the bridge on the road from San Antonio to Laredo washed out. The bridge floated into the path of a ferry, which had been brought in to take place of the bridge until the water receded. All traffic from San Antonio to Laredo came to a halt until the ferry could be disentangled from the bridge.

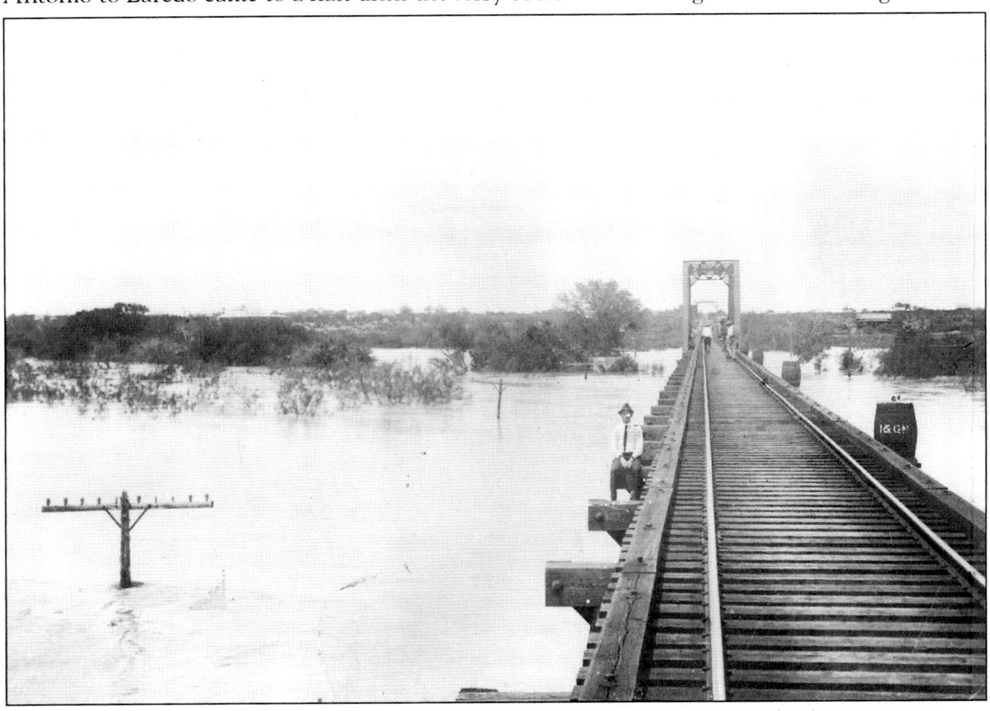

The railroad bridge was unharmed in the great flood of 1925. The mail and other train services were not interrupted. The only way to travel from San Antonio to Laredo was by train, unless travelers and their automobiles crossed the Nueces River by ferry.

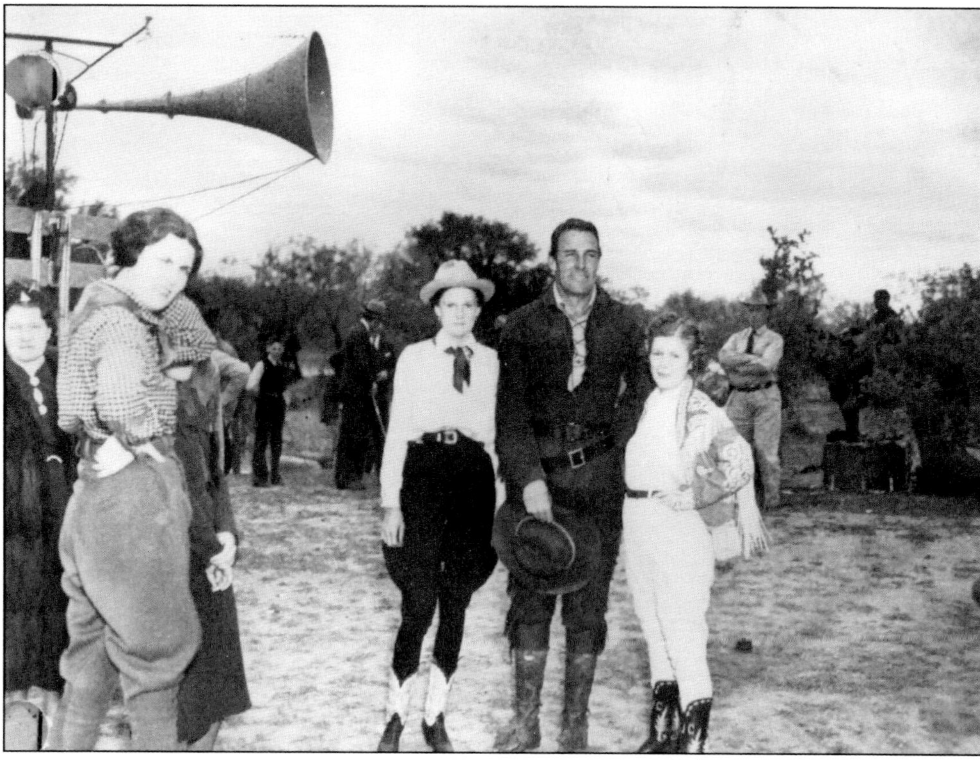

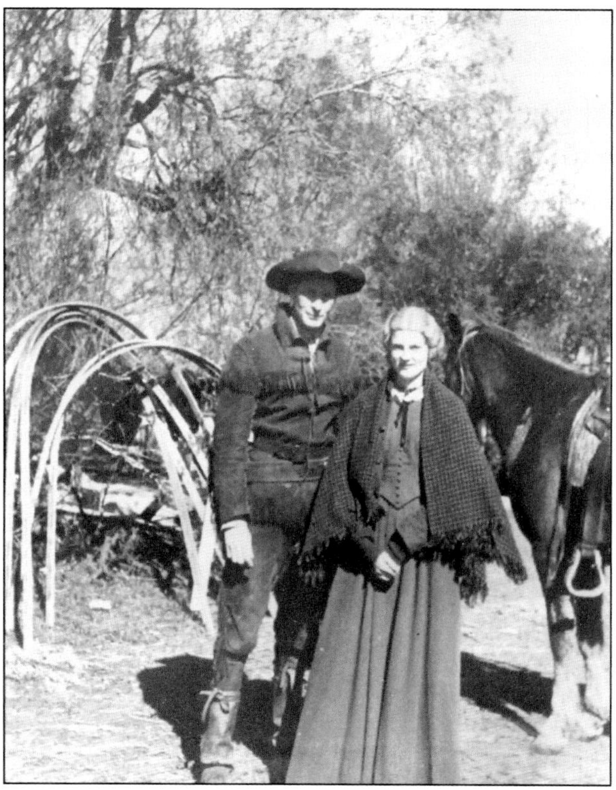

In February 1938, Paramount Pictures filmed *The Texan* on La Mota Ranch about 23 miles southeast of Cotulla. *The Texan* was a romance about Texas after the Civil War, when the carpetbaggers ruled the Southwest. Randolph Scott and Joan Bennett were among the cast members. Many locals were hired to appear in the film, and nearby ranches were contracted to furnish the cattle.

Virginia Bell and Slim Talbott doubled for Joan Bennett and Randolph Scott during the filming of *The Texan*. Before the film was cut and edited it was shown at the Majestic Theater in Cotulla. The theater was filled to capacity as Cotulla residents eagerly awaited the first showing of the film.

Hugh Roy Cullen discovered his first producing oil well in 1921. In 1932, Cullen formed his own company, Quintana Petroleum. He soon made several large discoveries in South Texas, including the Washburn field in La Salle County. Pictured from left to right are Levert V. Chenoweth, Hugh Roy Cullen, Day McNeel, and Hazen L. Rymal.

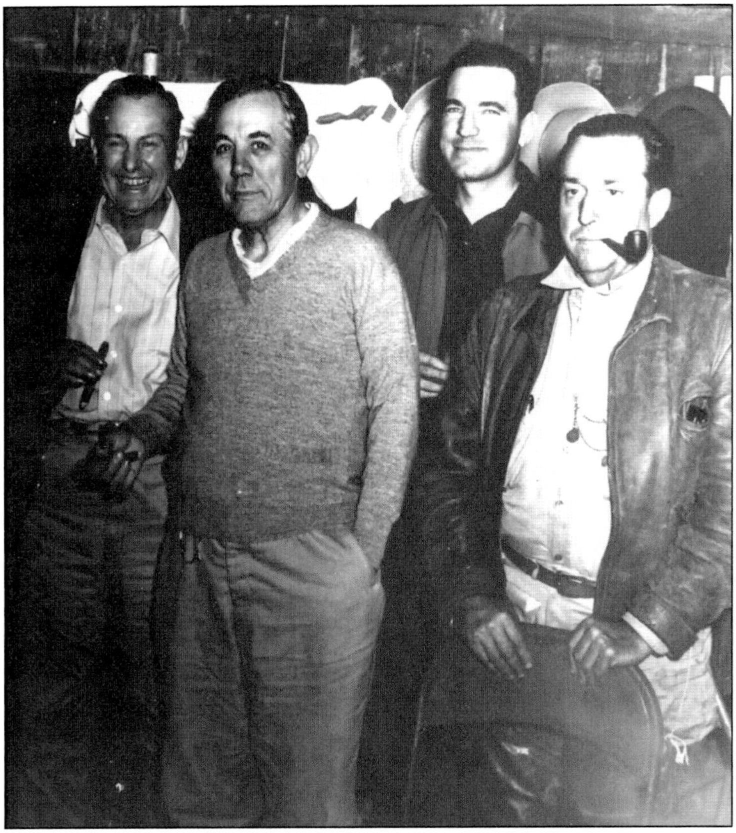

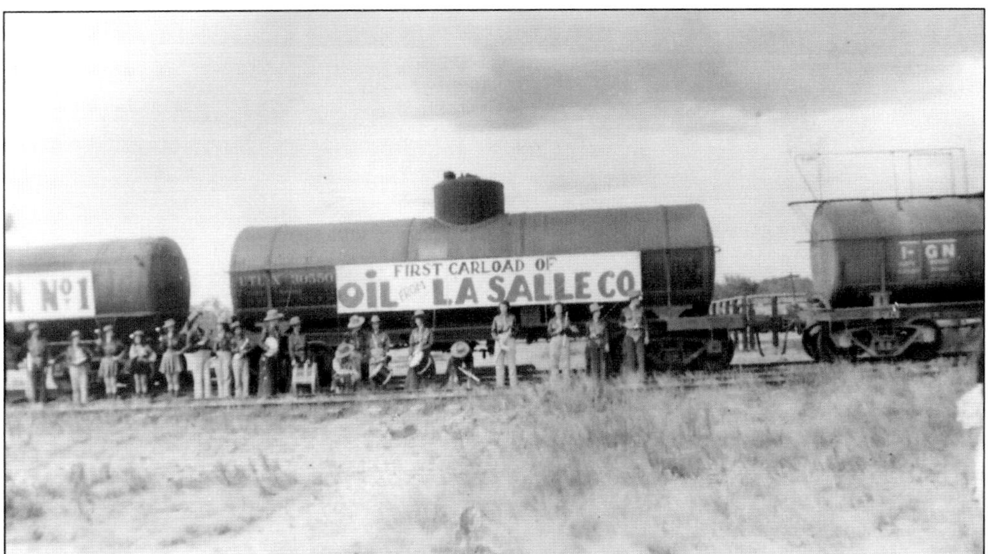

In September 1940, the first carload of oil was shipped from La Salle County. A large crowd attended the celebration and ceremony at Dull switch. The Cotulla Chamber of Commerce arranged a short program, including a barbecue lunch. The guest of honor was Hugh R. Cullen, the oil developer who made the discovery on the Washburn Ranch. The Cotulla Cowboy Band was in attendance and played as the first load of oil left the switch.

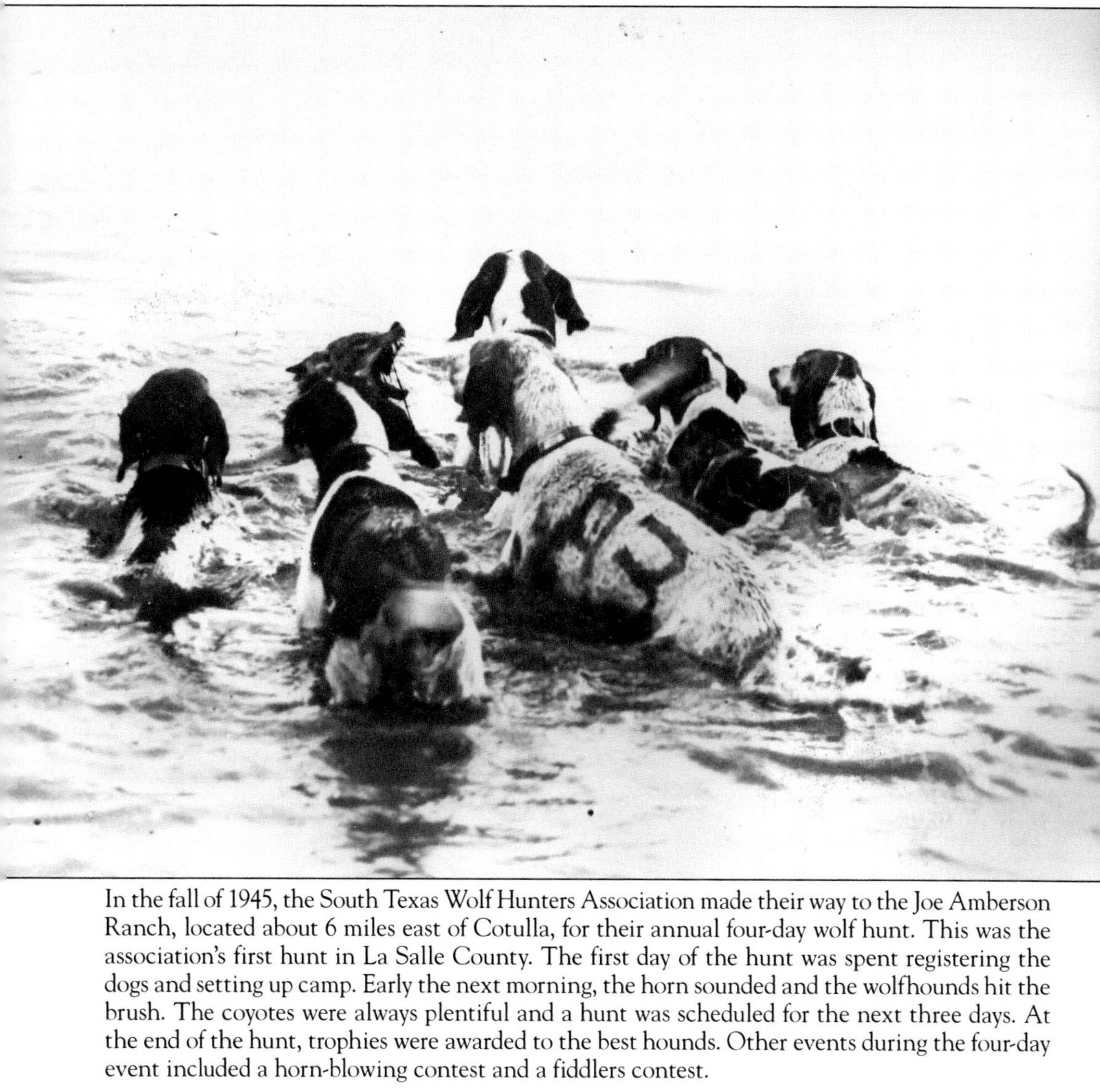

In the fall of 1945, the South Texas Wolf Hunters Association made their way to the Joe Amberson Ranch, located about 6 miles east of Cotulla, for their annual four-day wolf hunt. This was the association's first hunt in La Salle County. The first day of the hunt was spent registering the dogs and setting up camp. Early the next morning, the horn sounded and the wolfhounds hit the brush. The coyotes were always plentiful and a hunt was scheduled for the next three days. At the end of the hunt, trophies were awarded to the best hounds. Other events during the four-day event included a horn-blowing contest and a fiddlers contest.

Five

Farms and Ranches

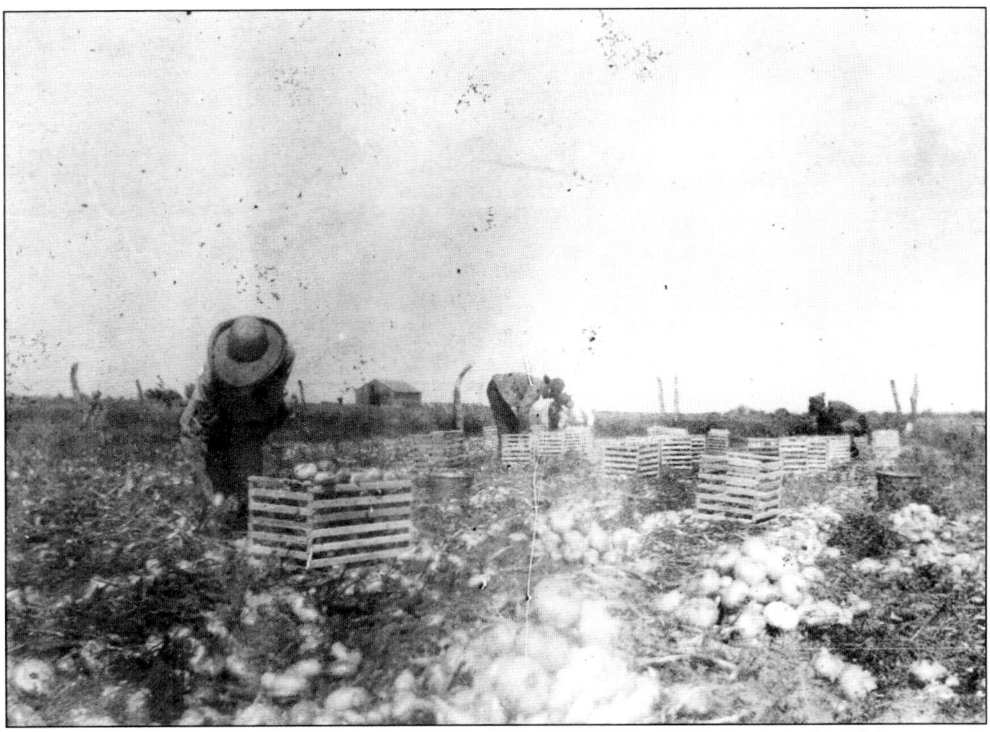

The first Bermuda onions in Texas were planted by George Copp. In 1895, he ordered five pounds of onion seed from the Tenerife Island and later shipped the first load of onions out of the state of Texas. The International and Great Northern Railroad built a spur to his land so the onions could be loaded. From this original start, onions were shipped from La Salle County until the 1950s.

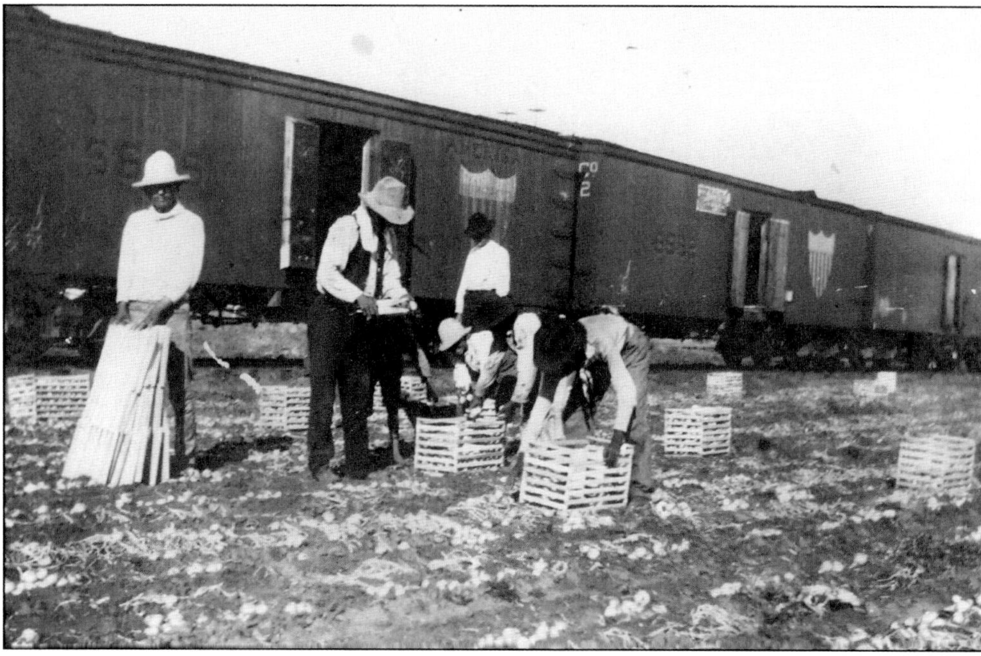

Another early onion farmer was Edgar A. Keck. He operated the Keck farm, located about 8 miles west of Cotulla. Pictured is a group of workers gathering onions out of the field. The onions were put in crates for shipment. A spur was built next to the onion field, so crates could be loaded directly in railroad cars.

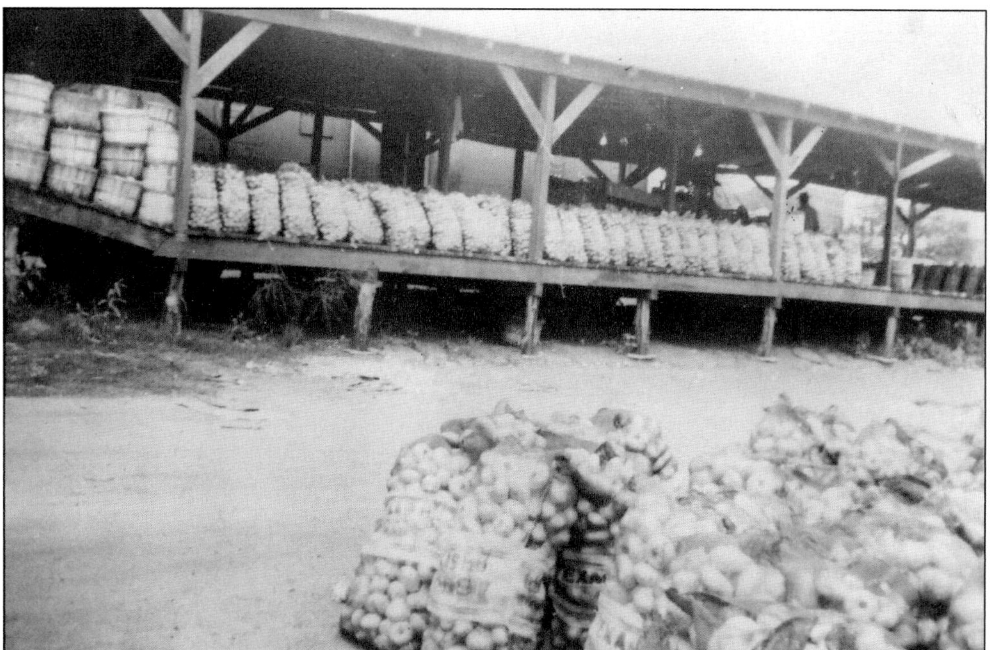

Hundreds of acres of onions were grown on farms all along the Nueces River. Wagonloads of onions were brought into Cotulla daily to be crated and shipped nationwide. Shipping sheds were built along the railroad next to the depot to handle the onions.

QUOTATIONS ON

QUALITY PLANTS

We now have millions of Onion Plants ready and are now shipping daily Crystal Wax and Yellow Bermuda, 500—80c; 1000—$1.25; Postpaid. In large lots by Express collect, 6000 plants per crate

$__________

Sweet Spanish, Prizetakers, 500—$1.00; 1000—$1.50 Postpaid. Crate lots 6000 by Express collect

$__________

TOMATO PLANTS

Ready March 20th and on

Leading Varieties

100—35c; 500—$1.00; 1000—$1.75

Postpaid. Large lots by Express collect $1.00 per thousand. Cabbage Plants same price.

SWEET AND HOT PEPPERS

Ready April 1st.

100—35c; 500—$1.00; 1000—$2.50

Postpaid. By Express collect $2.25 per thousand. Book orders now for Tomato and Pepper Plants. Can supply any amount.

Terms cash with order or we will ship COD

LIND PLANT FARMS

COTULLA, TEXAS

One of the pioneers in the plant business was Louis A. Lind. Lind moved his plant business to La Salle County when he bought property on the Nueces River in 1919. The Lind Plant Farm advertised nationally and did big business raising and shipping plants all over the United States. His slogan was, "When you buy plants, buy them from us and get the very best." Pictured is an example of his advertising.

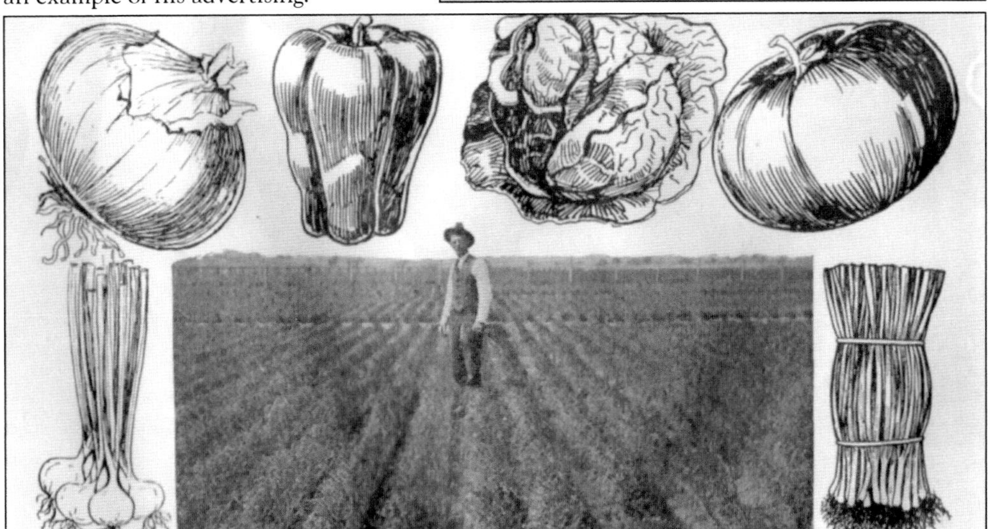

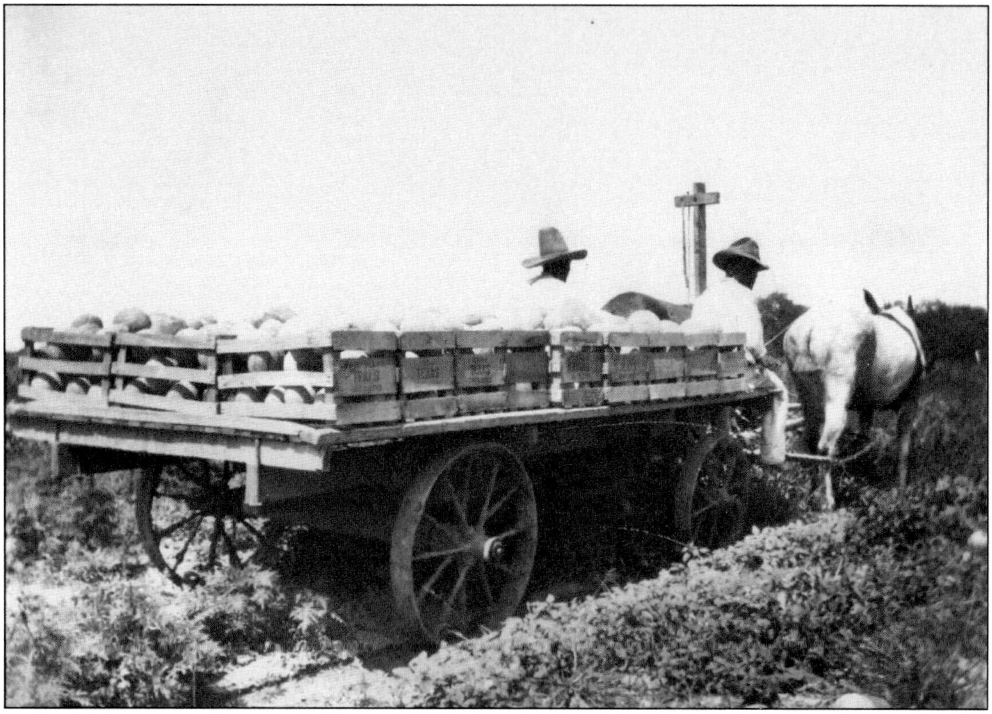

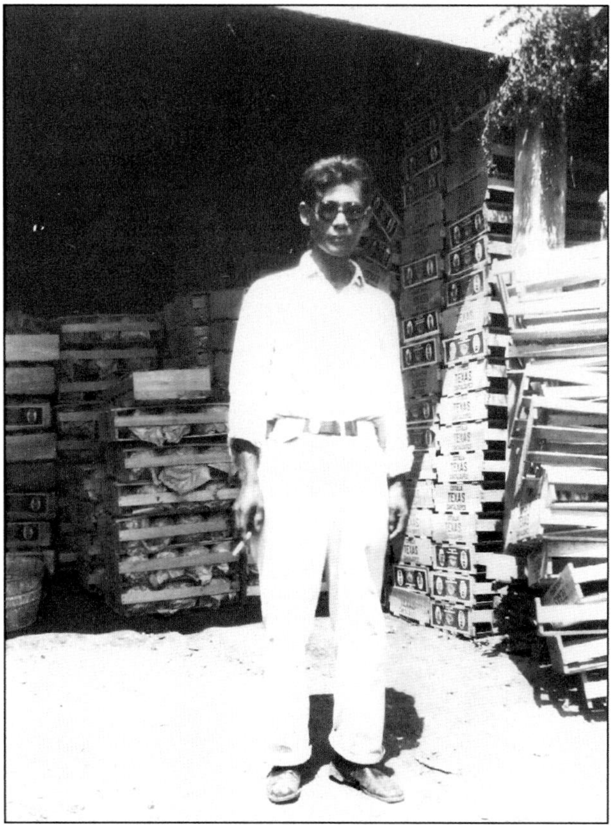

John B. Henderson had an irrigated farm on the Nueces River near the Holland Dam. He hired a Japanese farmer, Robert Y. Naito (shown at left), to work for him. Naito talked Henderson into planting 40 acres of cantaloupes. The 40 acres of cantaloupes produced over 12,500 crates of cantaloupes and cleared $22,000. Pickers were imported to pick and crate the cantaloupes, which were shipped as far as New York.

Naito came to work for John B. Henderson in 1929. He had spent 12 years growing cantaloupes in other areas. Henderson paid Naito $250 per month and 5¢ for every crate of cantaloupes he sold. When it came time to harvest the cantaloupes, Naito imported experienced workers from California to harvest the melons.

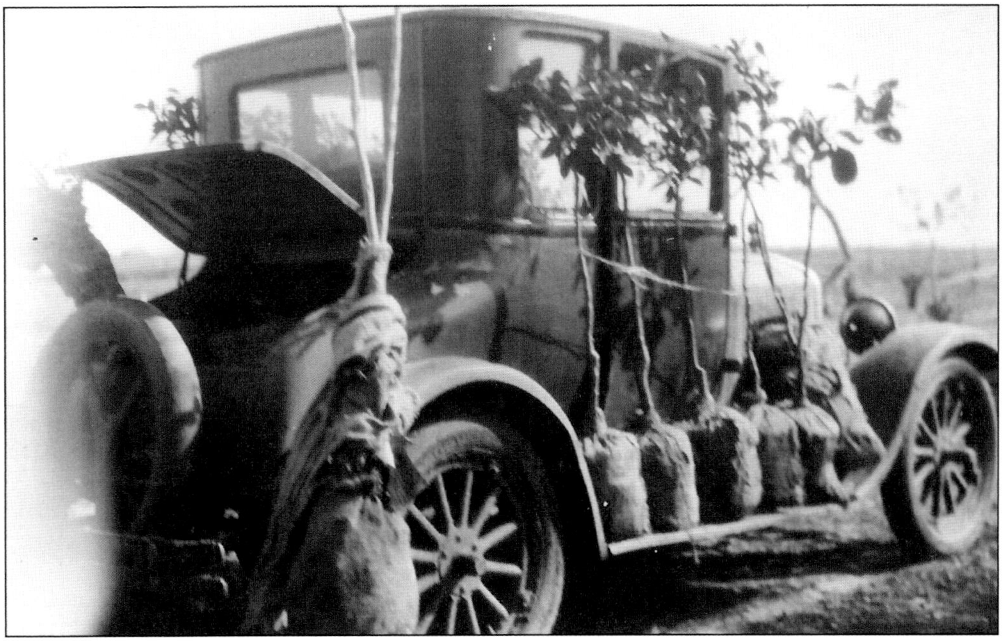

The Riverdale Farm was located on the Nueces River and owned and operated by Frederick W. Streuter. A Model T Ford is well loaded with young citrus trees, balled and ready for shipment. The young citrus trees and other plants were sold by Riverdale Nursery.

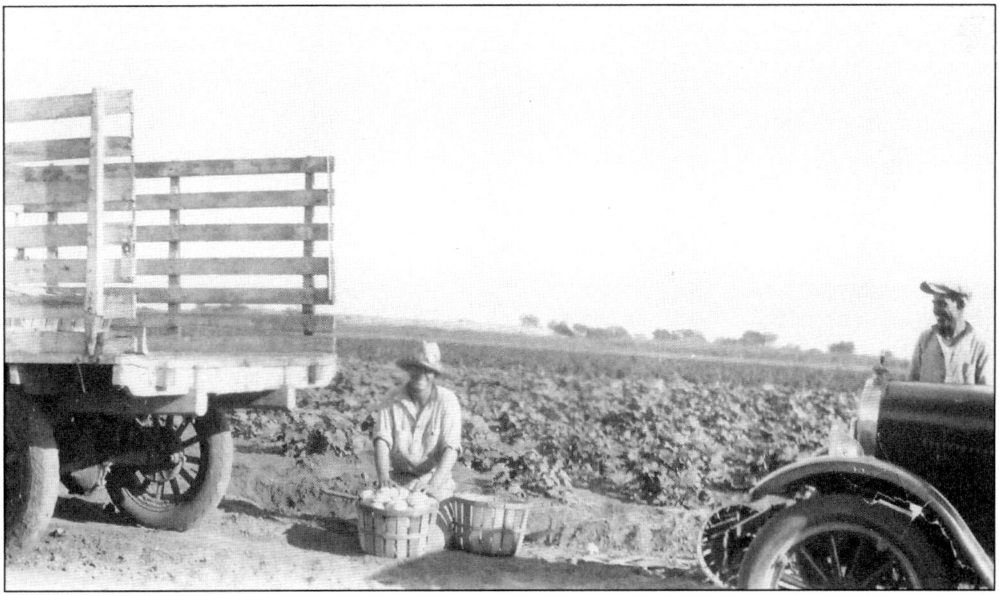

In 1929, Frederick W. Streuter of Riverdale Farm planted an acre of parsley, which he cut and sold for $200. A short time later, the parsley was ready to cut again. Streuter again sold the parsley for $200. After a third cutting, Streuter had made $600 on 1 acre of land. Pictured is Gerald D. Streuter hard at work on the farm.

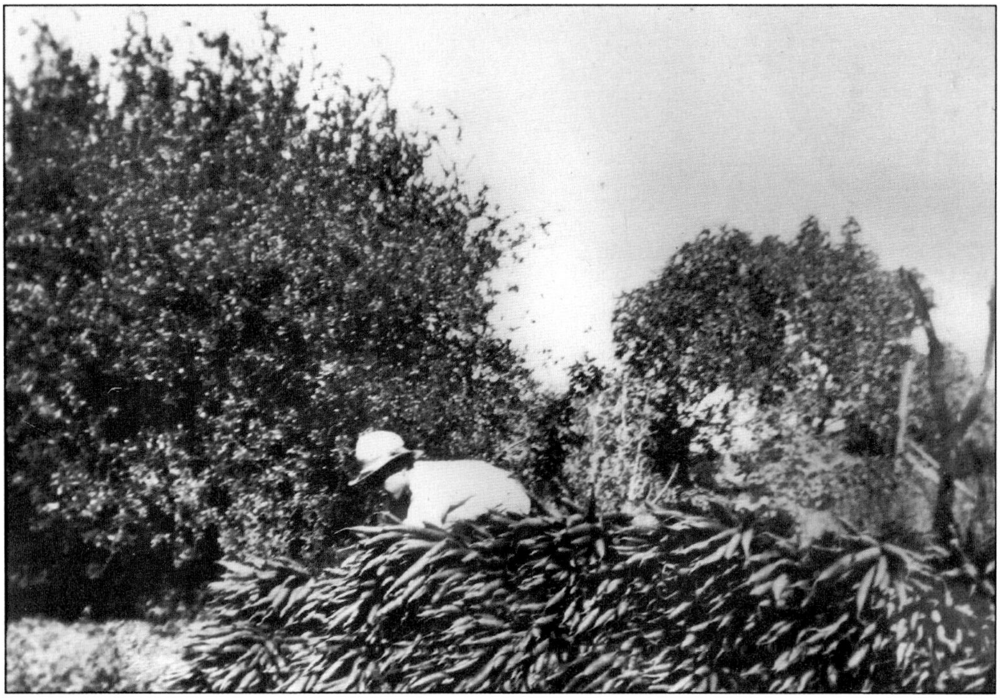

Carrots raised on the Freddie Johnson farm by Lacey Herrin were irrigated from the Nueces River. The carrots were carefully pulled by hand, then washed in the irrigation ditch, after which they were loaded onto a truck for shipment to San Antonio where they would be sold.

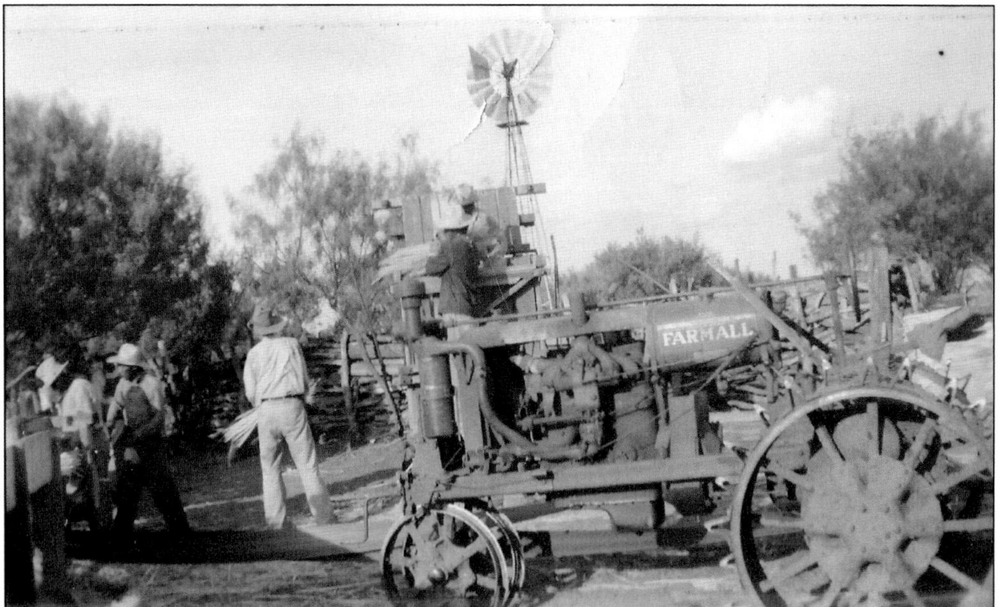

The first Farmall tractors were made in the late 1920s. George D. Crisp's first tractor was a Farmall Iron Wheeler that he bought in 1935. Crisp farmed near Artesia Wells. He is pictured with his sons in 1940 bailing broomcorn along with his first tractor.

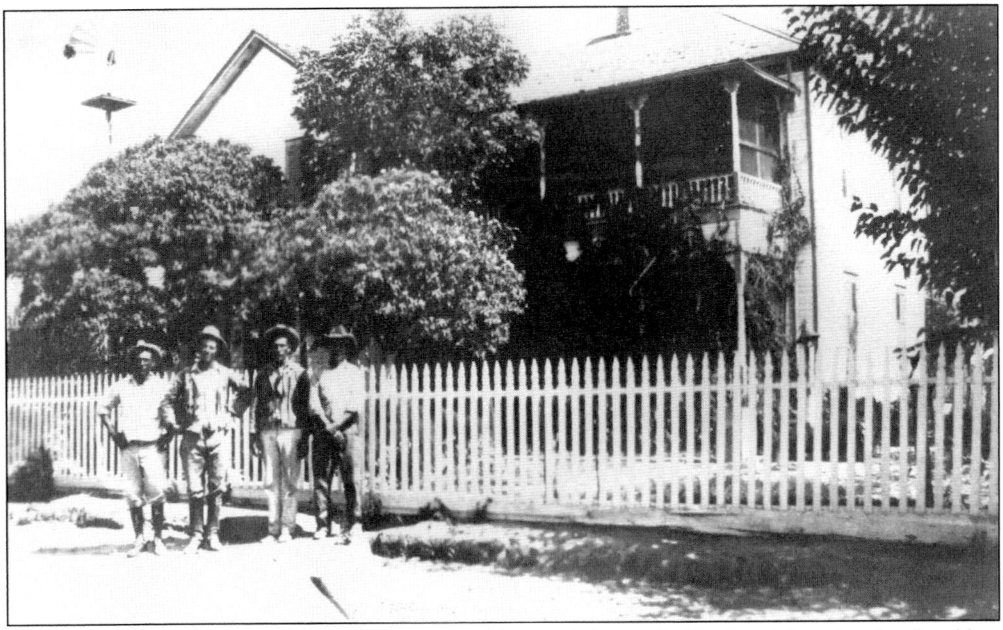

La Mota Ranch was owned by William Franklin and Amanda Burks. After the death of her husband, Amanda continued to operate the ranch and increased its size until it contained 42,000 acres stocked with 3,000 head of cattle. A large two-story house was built on the ranch. Pictured from left to right are Chon Rodriguez, Juan Martinez, Juan Rodriguez, and Andres Lopez.

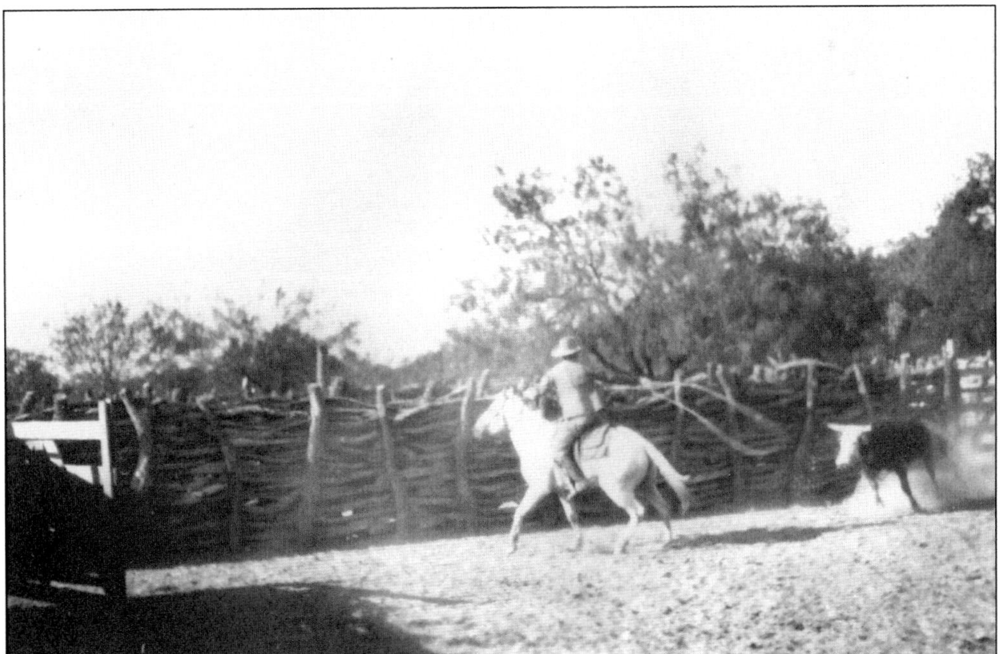

Amanda Burks, left a widow at an early age, owned and operated La Mota Ranch. She depended on the help of her trusted employees to see to the day-to-day operation of the ranch. Jose Lopez, a vaquero on La Mota Ranch, is pictured roping a steer around 1928.

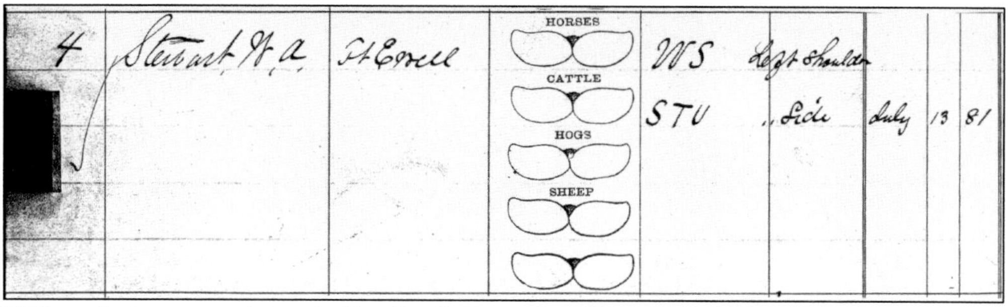

William A. Stewart settled in the Fort Ewell area in the 1850s. He was known as "Peg Leg" because he had lost a leg earlier in life. When the county was organized in 1880, Stewart's Rancho became the county seat. Stewart was one of the first ranchers to register his cattle brand WS on the left shoulder and STU on the left side.

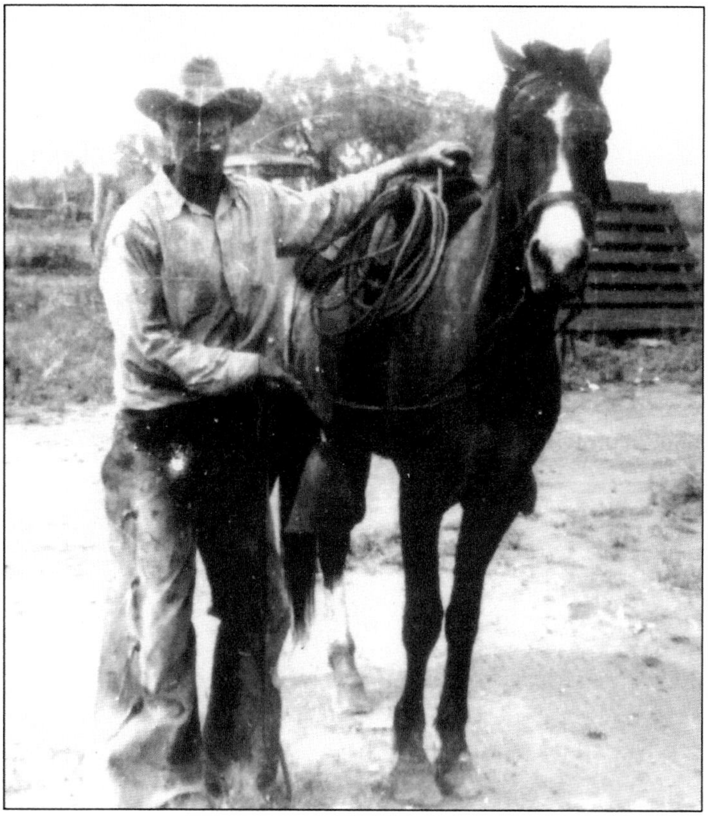

Ezra F. Alderman, oldest son of Emery W. Alderman, is pictured on the Alderman Ranch with his horse. Emery W. came to La Salle County with his family in 1871 at the age of 12. He later purchased the land on which they settled and started the Alderman Ranch. His sons followed in his footsteps to become ranchers.

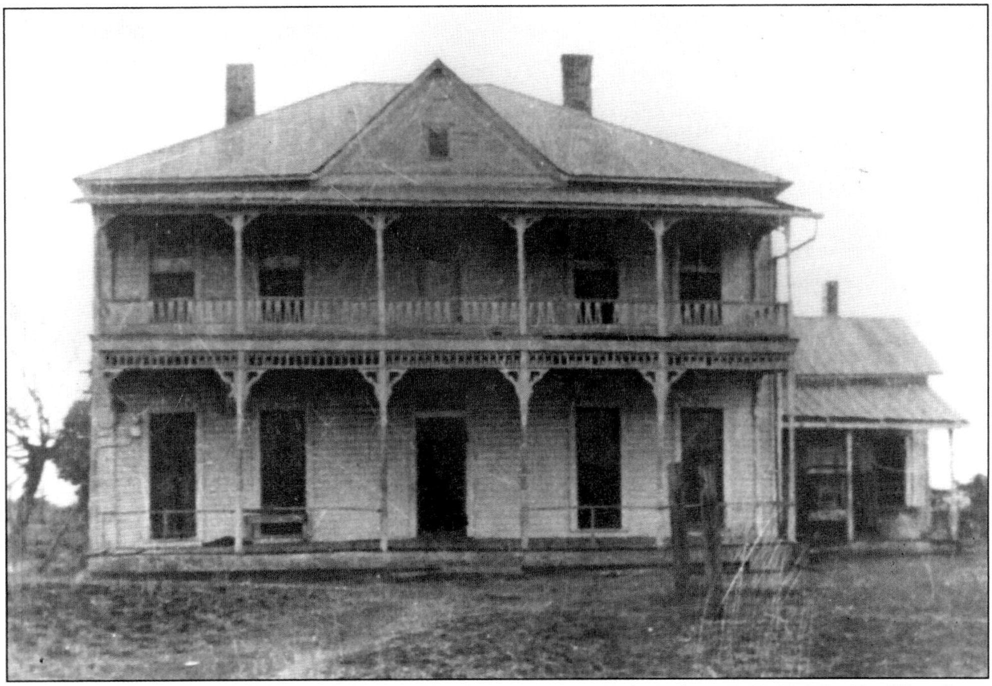

In the 1880s, William A. Waugh sold his ranch to James J. and Andrew J. Dull. The Dull brothers put together a vast ranching enterprise. When William Sydney Porter was a young man he worked as a ranch hand and sheepherder on the Dull Ranch and stayed at the Dull ranch house. Porter, later a famed story writer, went by the pen name O'Henry.

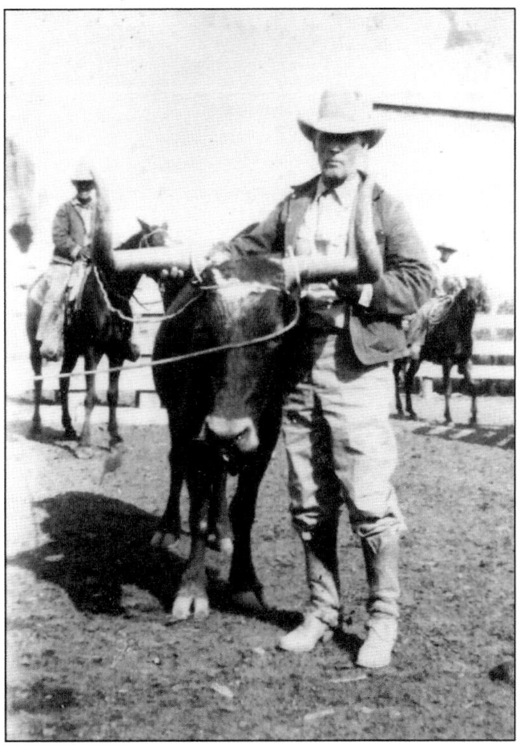

In 1901, the Dull brothers sold their ranch to Brazilla L. Naylor and Augustus H. Jones. Robert Hall "Bob" Lansford, a trusted employee of Naylor and Jones, was foreman on the Dull Ranch for many years. Bob is pictured with the lead steer at the Dull pens around 1932.

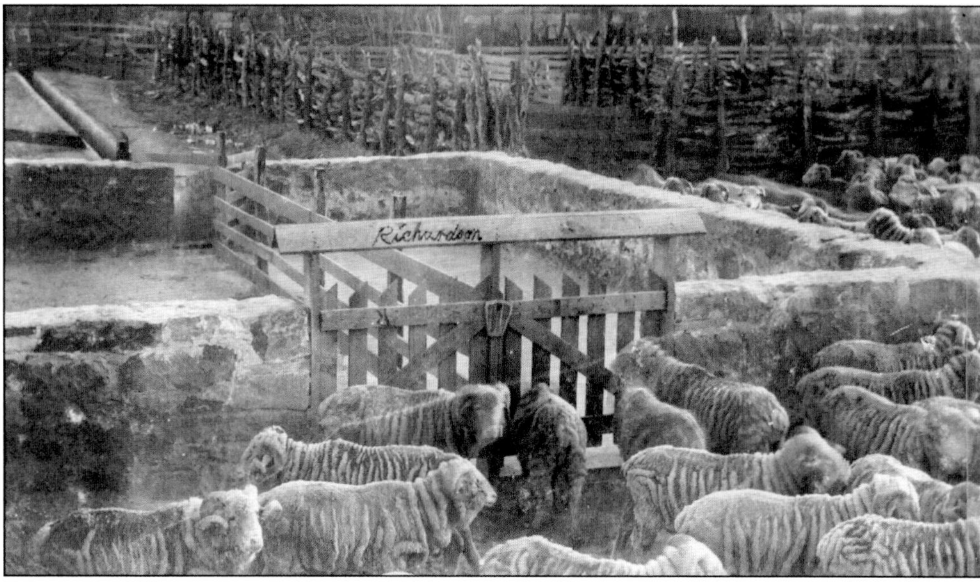

Before 1900, sheep outnumbered cattle in La Salle County. On the 1882 tax rolls there were over 152,000 head of sheep and only 16,000 head of cattle. As the prairie grass decreased and the brush took over, the terrain was no longer suitable for raising sheep.

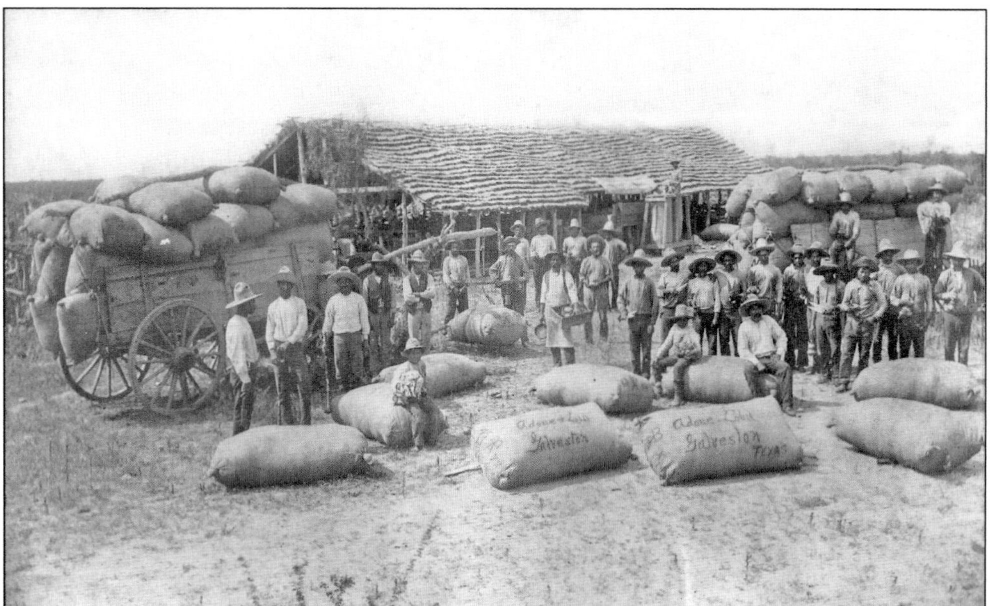

In April 1889, out-of-county buyers at Encinal were sold 100,000 pounds of wool. The wool was unusually fine and some of the larger clips sold at 19¢ and 20¢ per pound. After the wool was clipped, it was bagged and loaded for shipping.

In 1868, Joseph Cotulla started ranching along the Nueces River in La Salle County. He continued to add to his ranch land until he owned 30,000 acres in La Salle, Dimmit, and Webb Counties. Pictured at right are his son Simon Cotulla and his saddle horse riding the range.

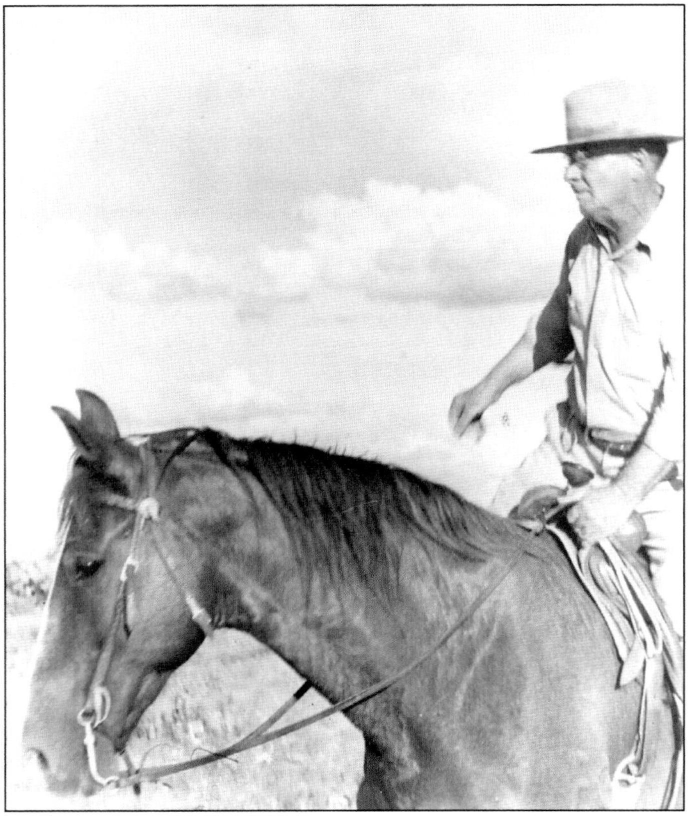

James M. Dobie owned Los Olmos Ranch, located about 33 miles southeast of Cotulla. At one time, Dobie owned 56,000 acres of land and leased 200,000 more. Onie J. Sherran, pictured below, was manager of Los Olmos for many years.

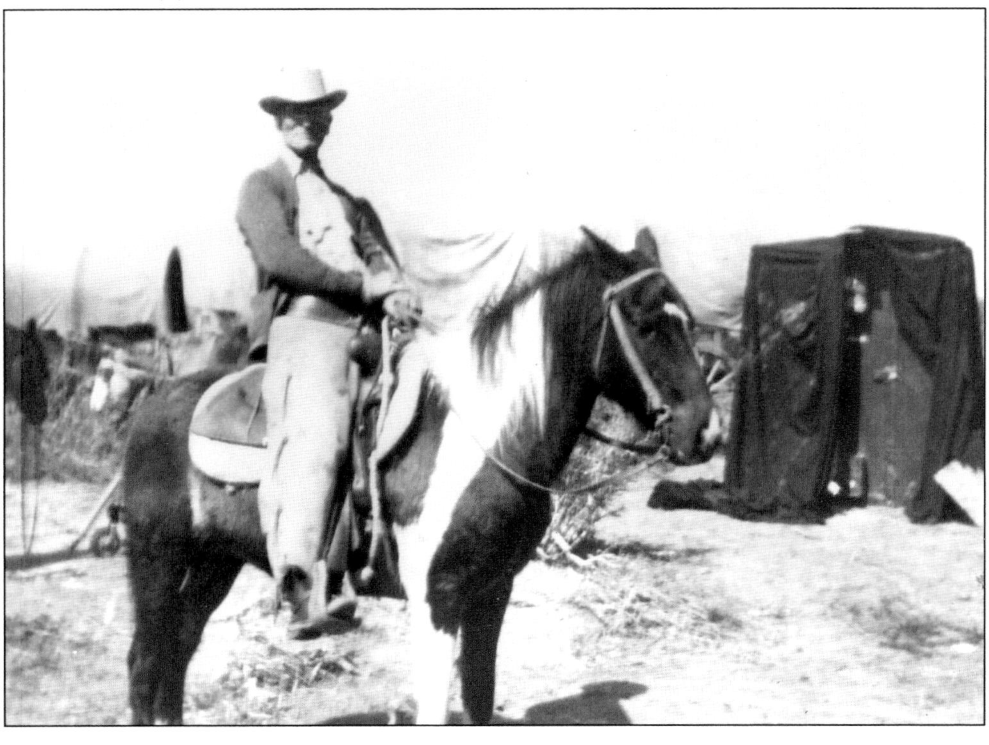

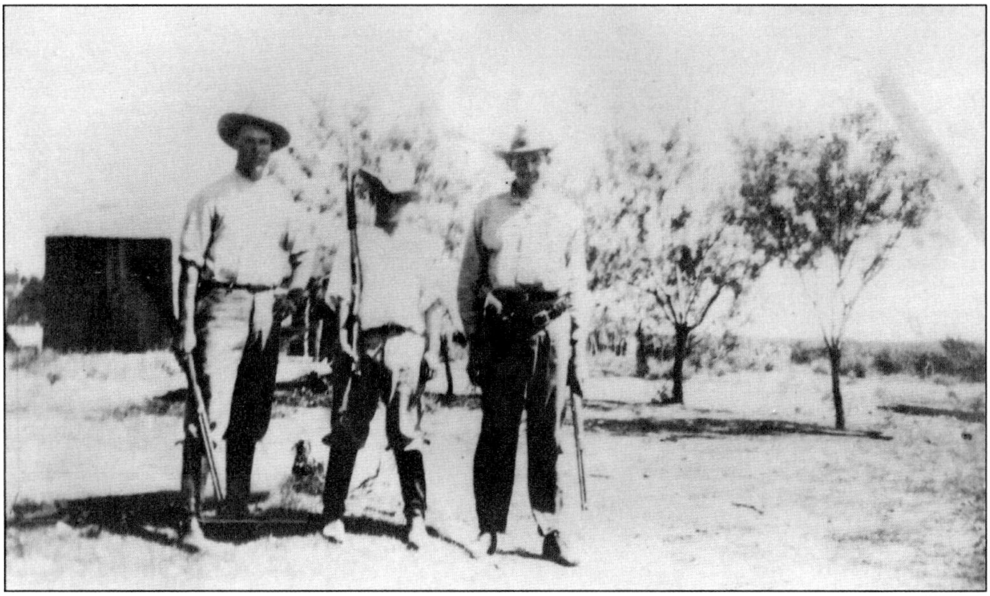

Willie Copp, Buck West, and Charles W. Burwell, pictured from left to right, have their guns ready to hunt a big buck on the H. Dudley Storey Ranch, east of Cotulla. Storey started ranching in La Salle County in 1906 and acquired vast acreage. He was a prominent rancher and rodeo promoter.

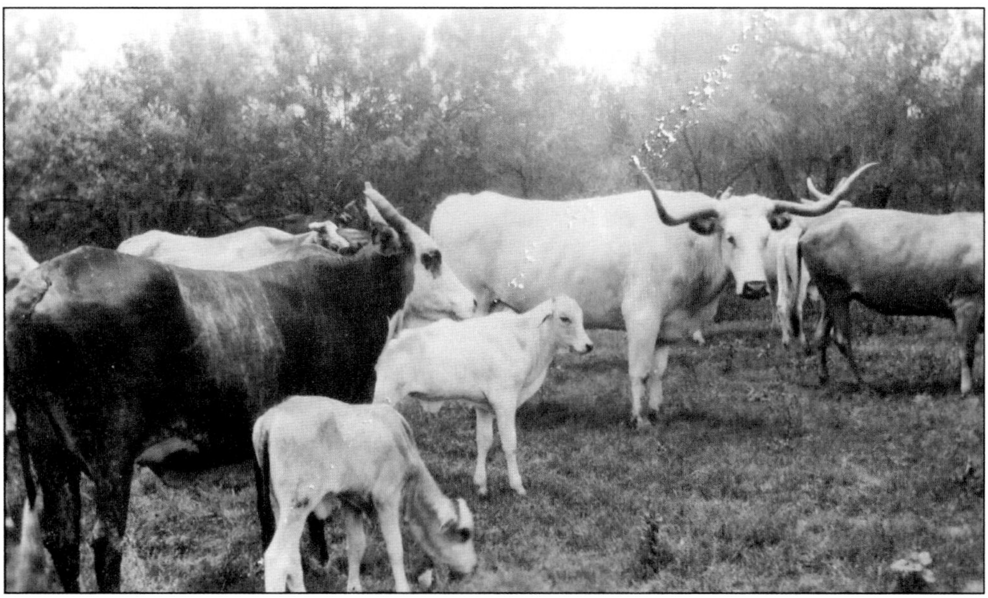

Handlebar Hank was a longhorn born on the Martin Ranch in eastern La Salle County about 1920. The steer was later sold to Charles Schreiner. In 1936, Schreiner took Hank to the Texas Centennial at the state fair in Dallas. Hank spent the last years of his life in Breckenridge Park in San Antonio. At his death, his horns were hung in the Old Trail Driver's Museum in San Antonio.

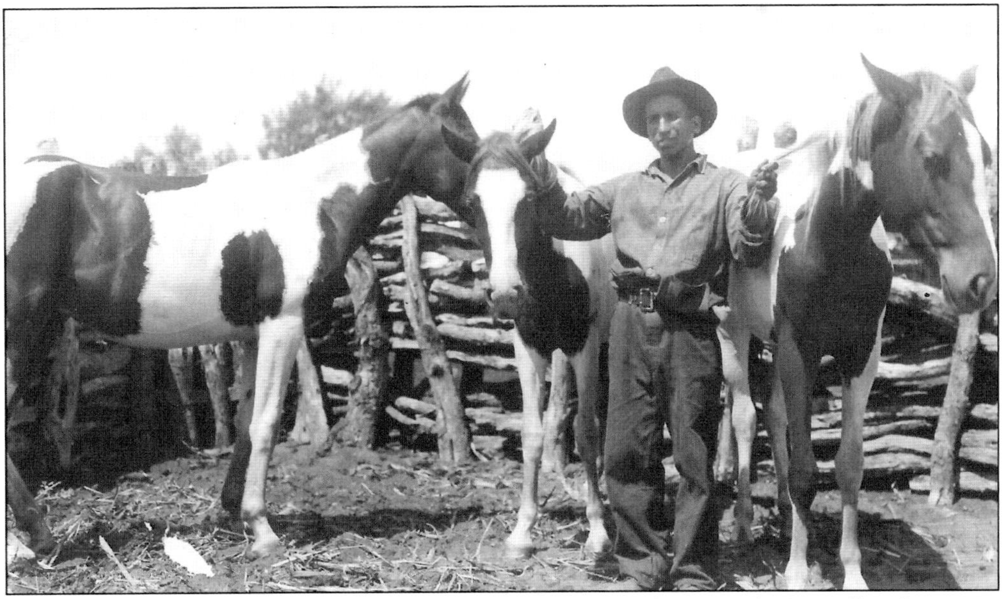

Encarnacion (Chon) Aguilar was employed on the John E. Bishop Ranch. One of his duties was to train the young horses raised on the ranch. He is standing in front of a pole fence with three two-year-old paint horses he is training for Bishop.

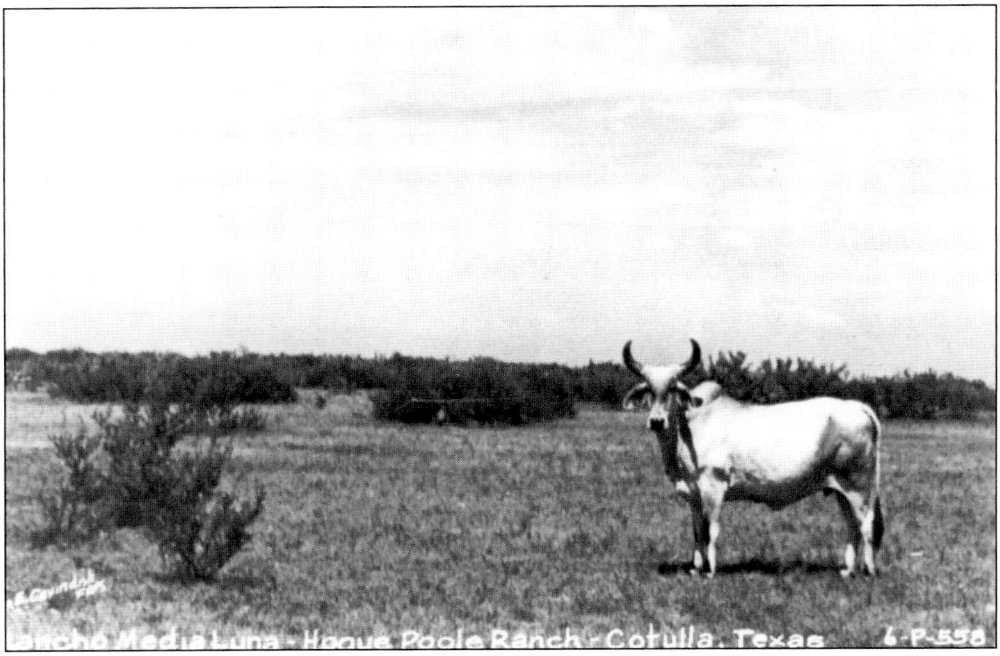

Rancho Media Luna was founded around 1900 by Travis Hogue Poole. Poole took over operation of the ranch after his father's death and raised registered Zebu cattle. The ranch contained 35,000 acres of land and ran 1,500 head of cattle. The ranch brand was the *media luna*, or half-moon.

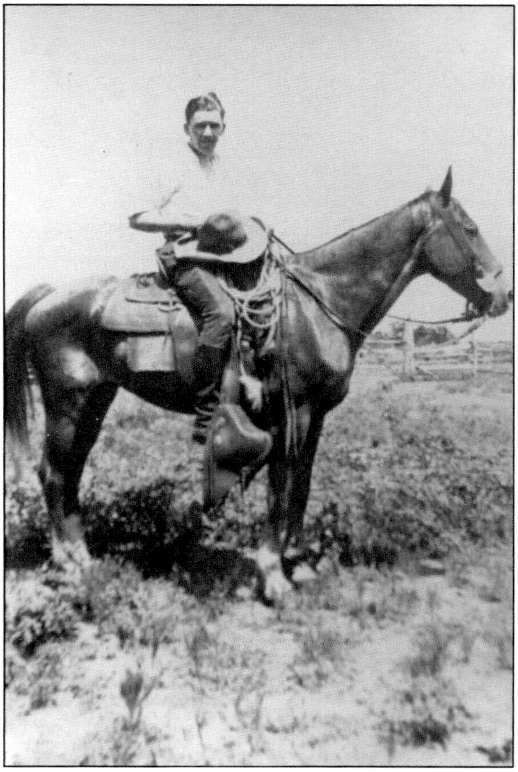

Troy Howard came to La Salle County in 1935. Not only was he a rancher, but he was also a renowned saddle maker. His saddles were known throughout the Southwest. His was probably the only manufacturing business in La Salle County. His first saddle is on display in the Brush Country Museum in Cotulla.

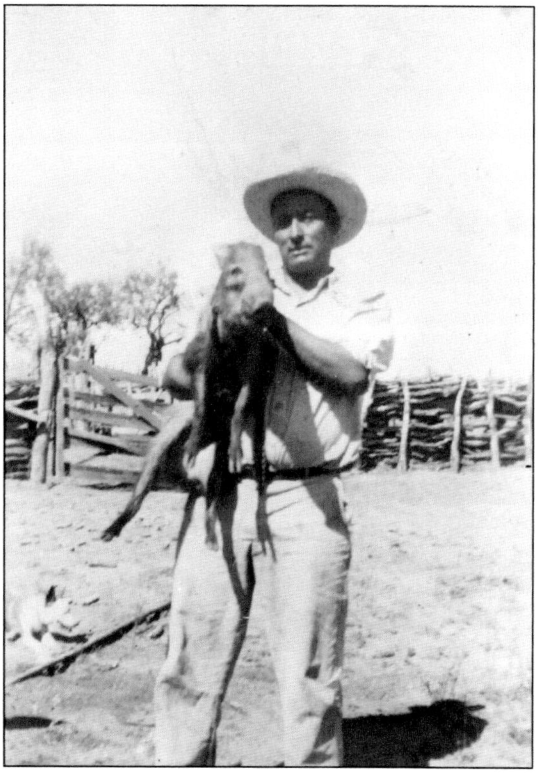

Teodoro "Lolo" Gonzalez was a renowned fence builder in La Salle County and the surrounding area. He built fences on many of the area ranches. Pictured at right is Gonzalez with a baby javelina he caught while working on the Pena Ranch, located northwest of Cotulla.

Six

Learning the ABCs

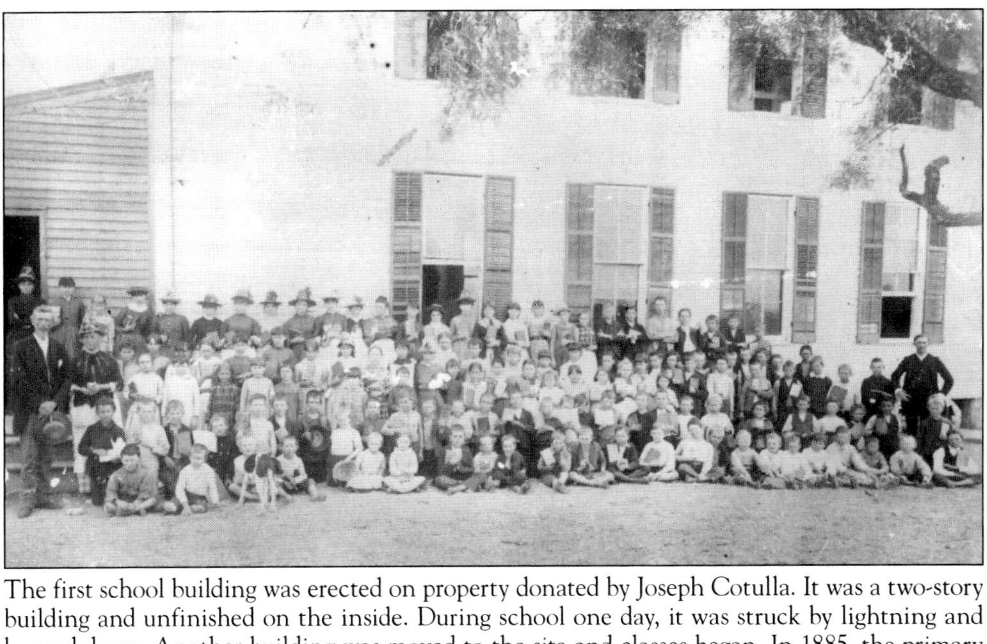

The first school building was erected on property donated by Joseph Cotulla. It was a two-story building and unfinished on the inside. During school one day, it was struck by lightning and burned down. Another building was moved to the site and classes began. In 1885, the primary students were charged $2 to attend school, intermediates were charged $2.50, and advanced students $3.50.

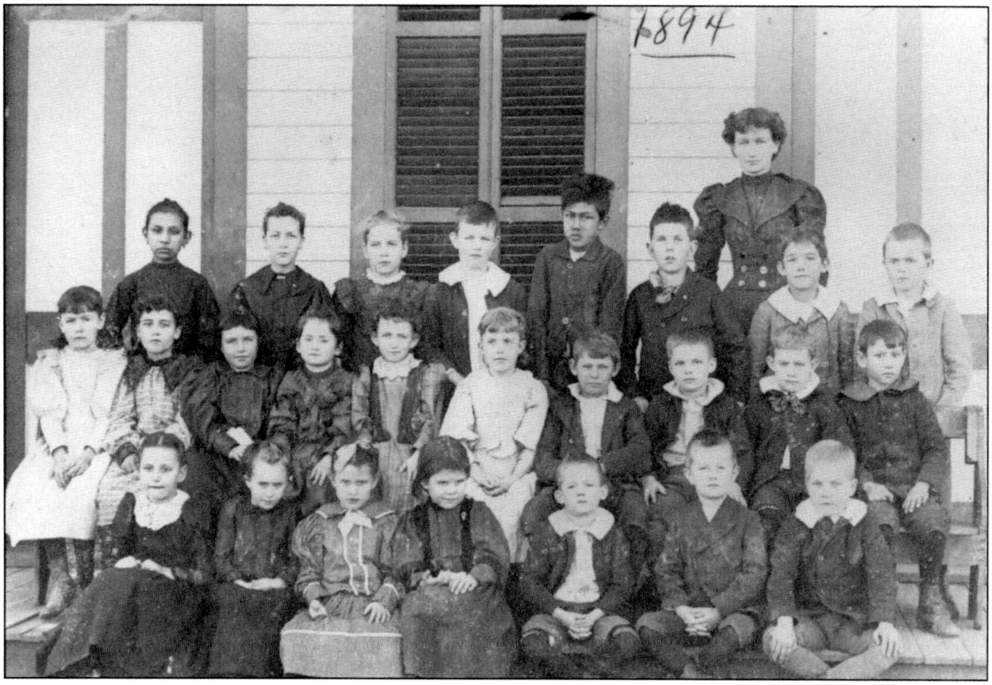

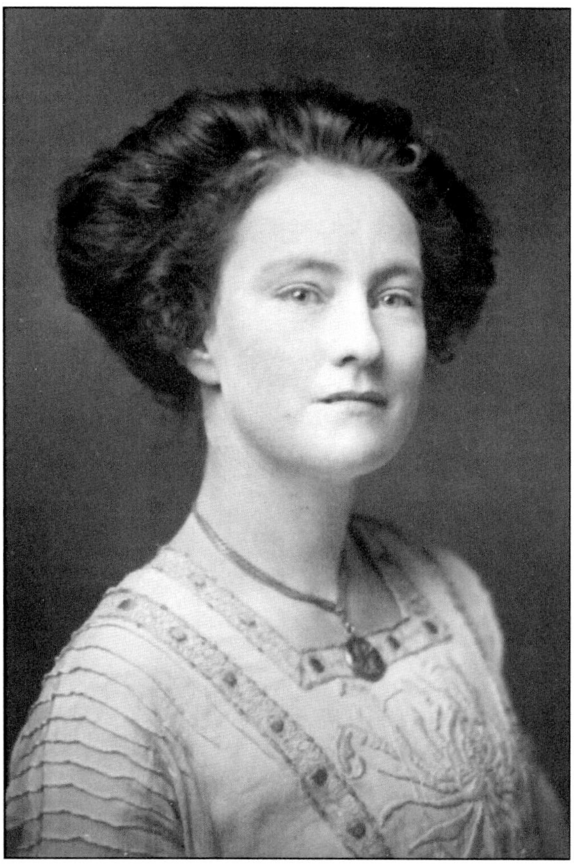

The early school in Cotulla was located on the corner of Stewart and Carrizo Streets. The 1894 students and their teacher take time out from their studies to have their picture taken alongside their school. By 1895, the enrollment had increased to 132.

Christy Steele was the daughter of William H. and Jean Steele. She was one of the first teachers in the Cotulla School. Steele taught first grade in the early 1900s and was much loved by her students.

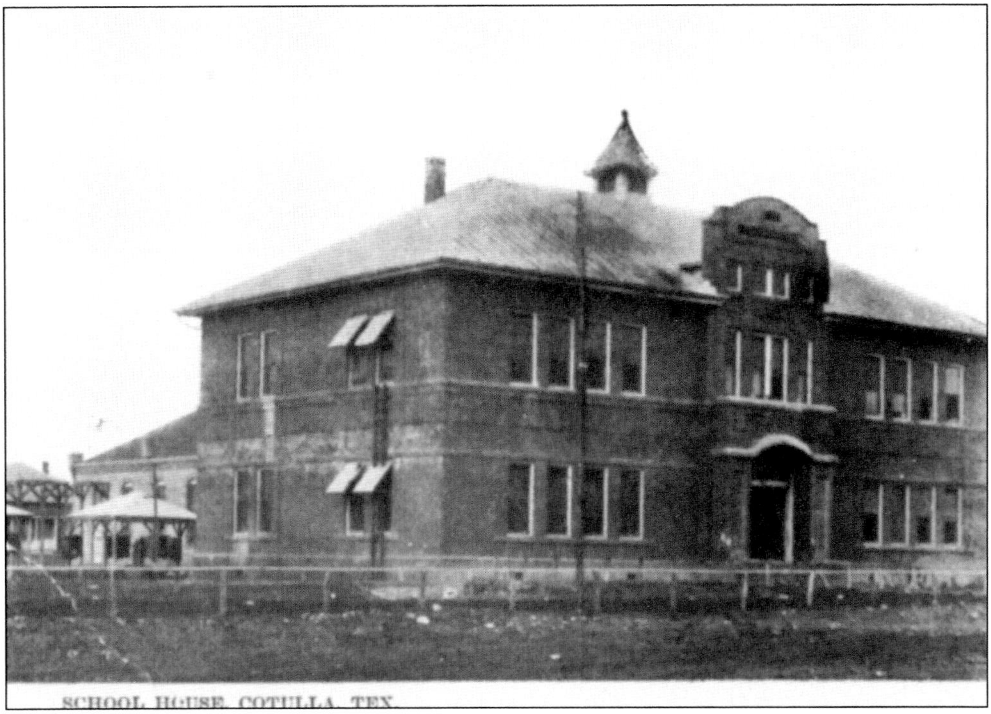

In 1909, a two-story, brick school building was constructed in Cotulla. It housed all 10 grades. That same year, a long building was constructed to the north of the original one. This was referred to as the opera house or auditorium. In June 1911, the Southwest Texas Summer Normal opened in the auditorium. Judge Frank B. Earnest gave the opening address. Music was furnished by the Cotulla Concert Band. When a high school was built, the 1909 structure became an elementary school and was named the Amanda Burks School.

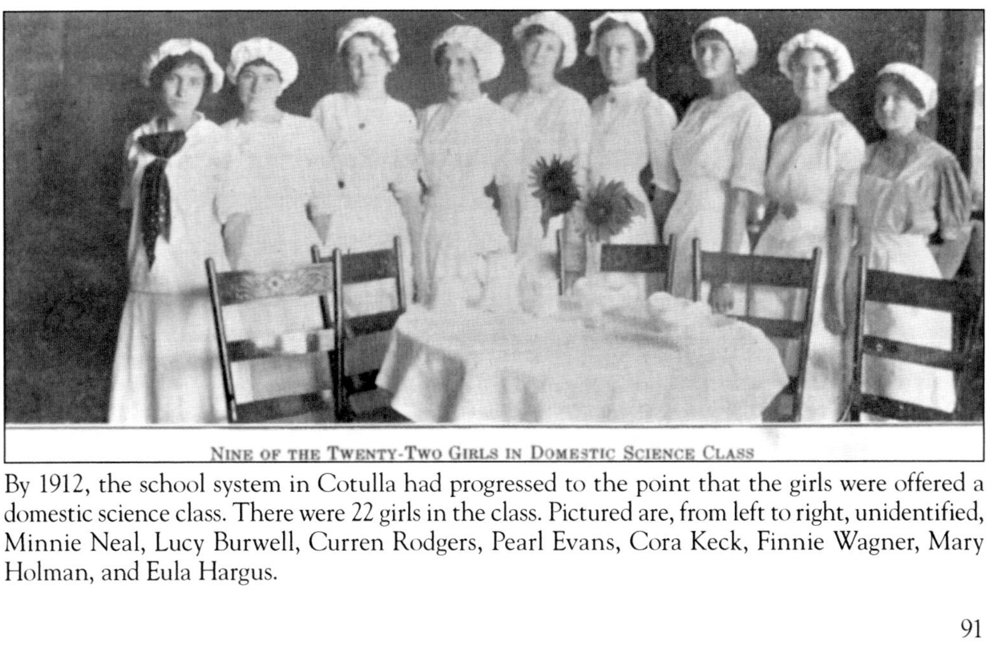

NINE OF THE TWENTY-TWO GIRLS IN DOMESTIC SCIENCE CLASS

By 1912, the school system in Cotulla had progressed to the point that the girls were offered a domestic science class. There were 22 girls in the class. Pictured are, from left to right, unidentified, Minnie Neal, Lucy Burwell, Curren Rodgers, Pearl Evans, Cora Keck, Finnie Wagner, Mary Holman, and Eula Hargus.

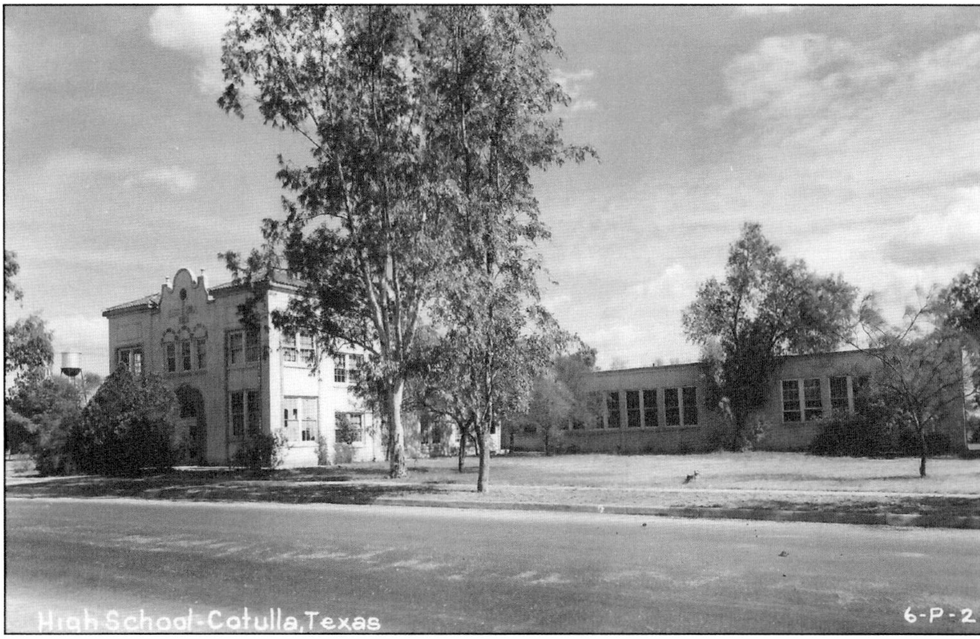

The first Cotulla High School was erected in 1927 on the block adjoining the existing school. The class of 1928–1929 was the first to graduate from the new building. There were 14 graduating seniors that year. The school was used until 1978 when a new high school was constructed.

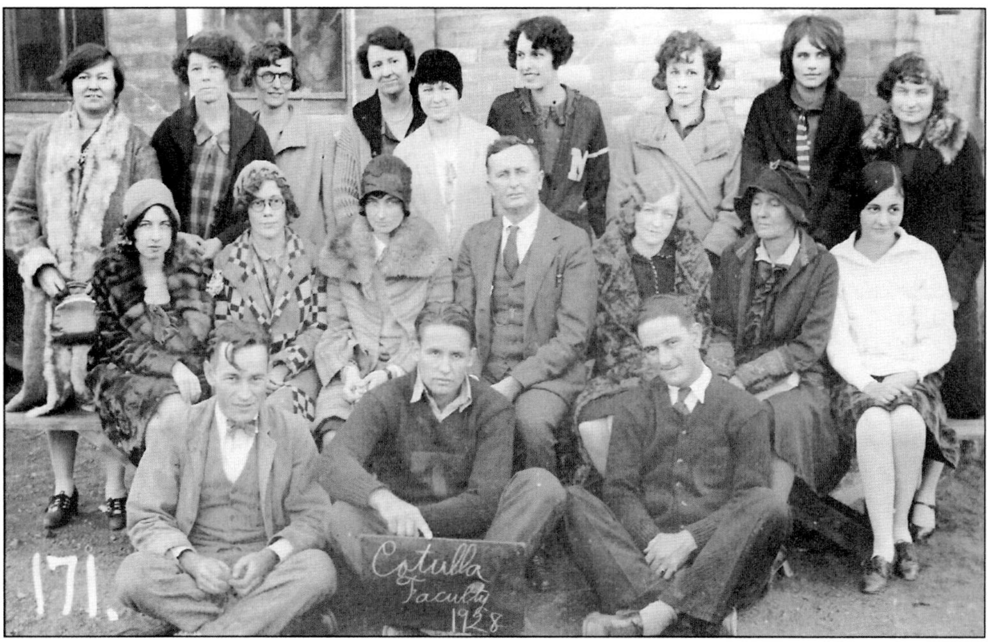

The 1928–1929 faculty of the Cotulla school system did not know they had a future U.S. president in their midst when they all gathered to have their picture taken. Lyndon Baines Johnson, a teacher in Welhausen School, is seated at the right on the first row.

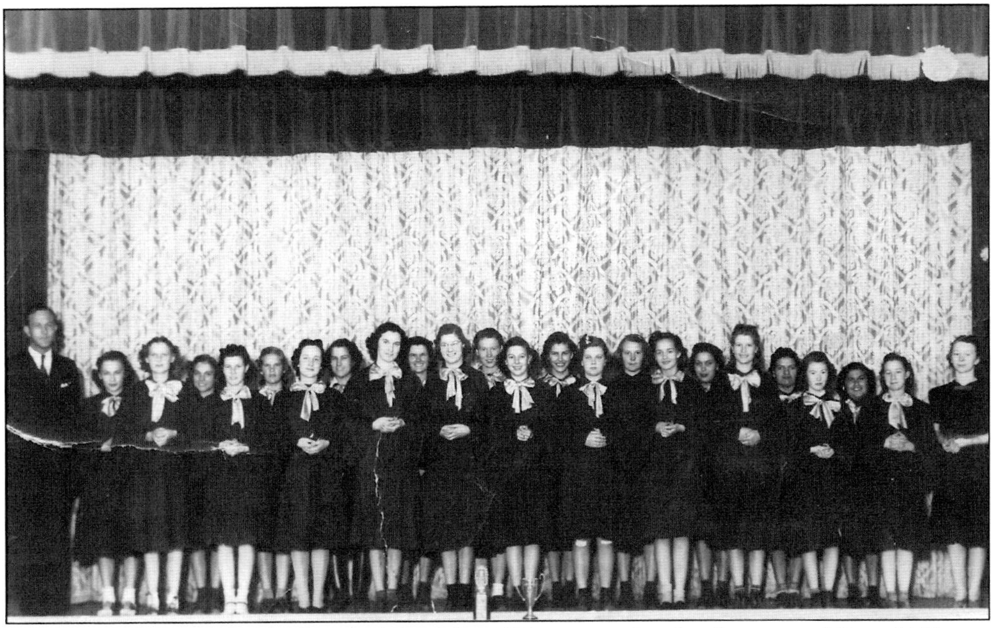

The Cotulla High School Choral Club of the 1930s was under the direction of Donald Peters. Under his leadership, the choral club grew in number and became a much better organization. Each year, the choral club presented an annual recital in the high school auditorium.

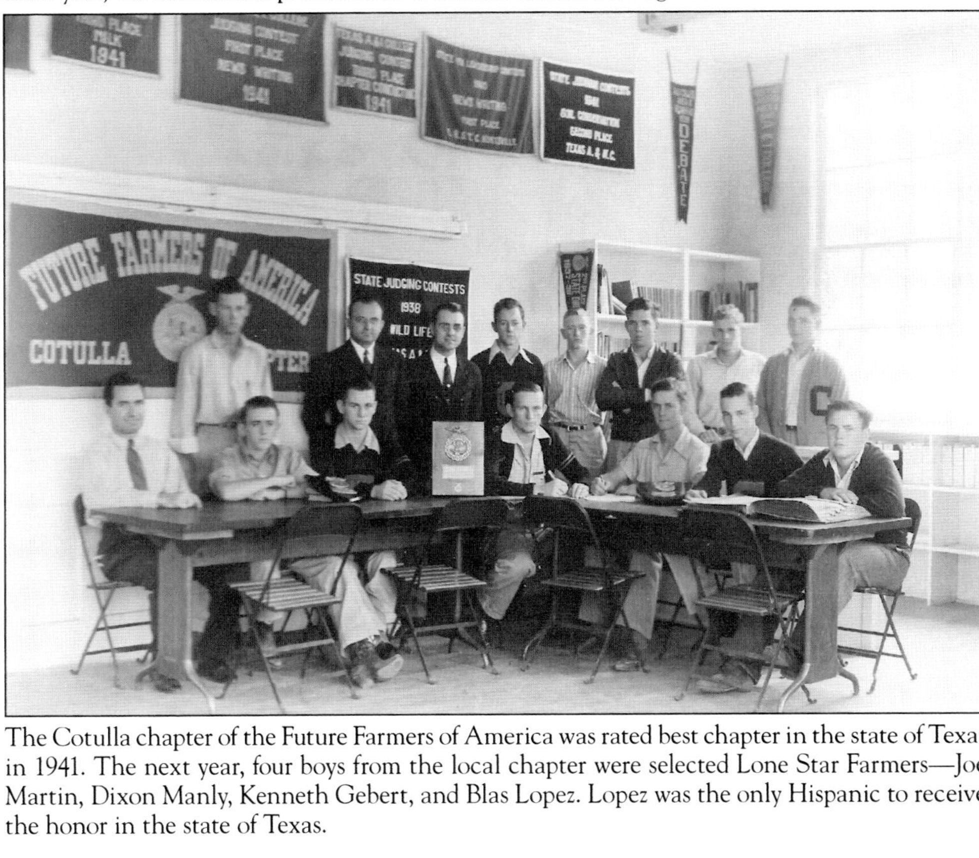

The Cotulla chapter of the Future Farmers of America was rated best chapter in the state of Texas in 1941. The next year, four boys from the local chapter were selected Lone Star Farmers—Joe Martin, Dixon Manly, Kenneth Gebert, and Blas Lopez. Lopez was the only Hispanic to receive the honor in the state of Texas.

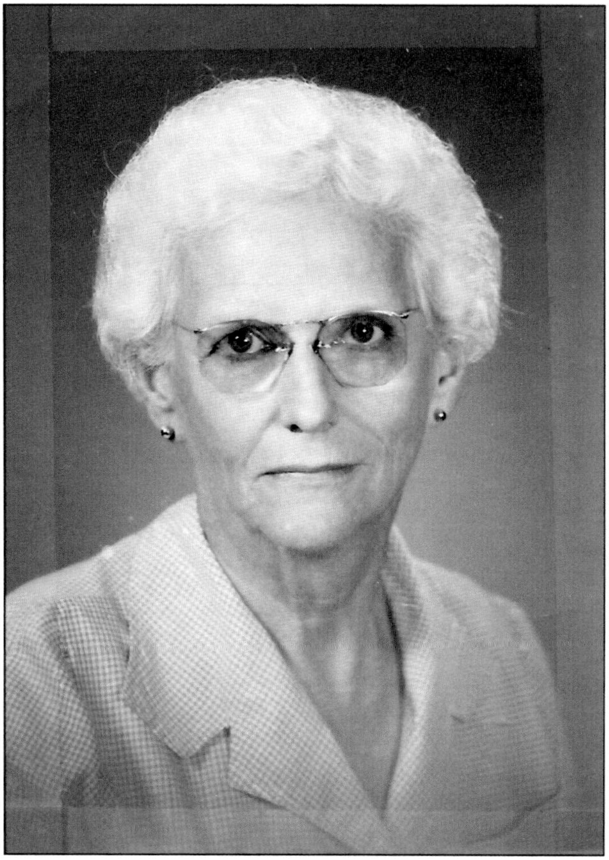

Lois Pearce Wildenthal was one of those teachers who no student ever forgot. She was very strict, and she expected her students to do their very best. Wildenthal will always be remembered for her famous 100 or zero tests. One question was given and if the question was not correct, a grade of zero was given. At the end of the six weeks, if only one zero was received, it was not averaged into the final grade.

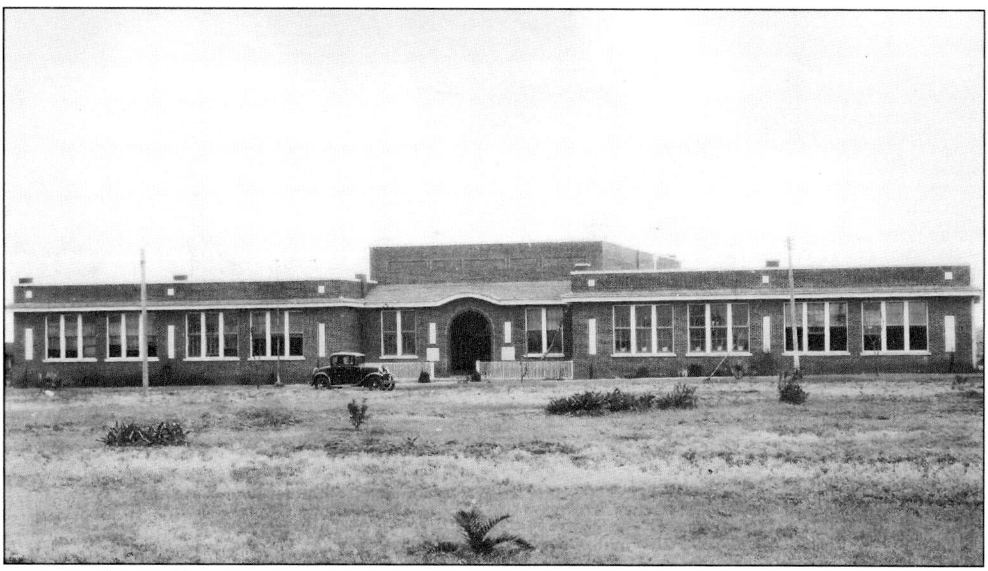

In 1926, the Welhausen School was built for the Mexican American children. It was built on the east side of Cotulla. After the students completed all seven grades at Welhausen, they would then attend Cotulla High School to complete their education. Sadly many students dropped out after the seventh grade.

Elizabeth Woolls, Twila Kerr, future U.S. president Lyndon Baines Johnson, and Mamie Wildenthal, pictured from left to right, were all teachers at Welhausen School in 1928–1929. Lyndon B. Johnson was only 20 years old. He needed money to complete his education, so he left college to teach and make some money.

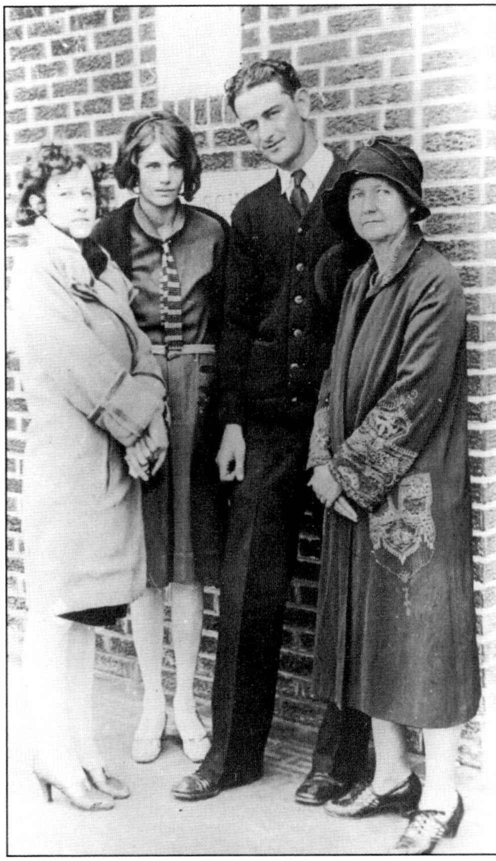

Lyndon B. Johnson taught at Welhausen School starting in December 1928. He was appalled at the poverty and immediately endeavored to improve the students' way of life. In November 1966, President Johnson returned to Welhausen School and addressed his former students and the present students of Welhausen School. A large crowd of townspeople converged on Welhausen School to hear the president. Pictured below are President Johnson and his class.

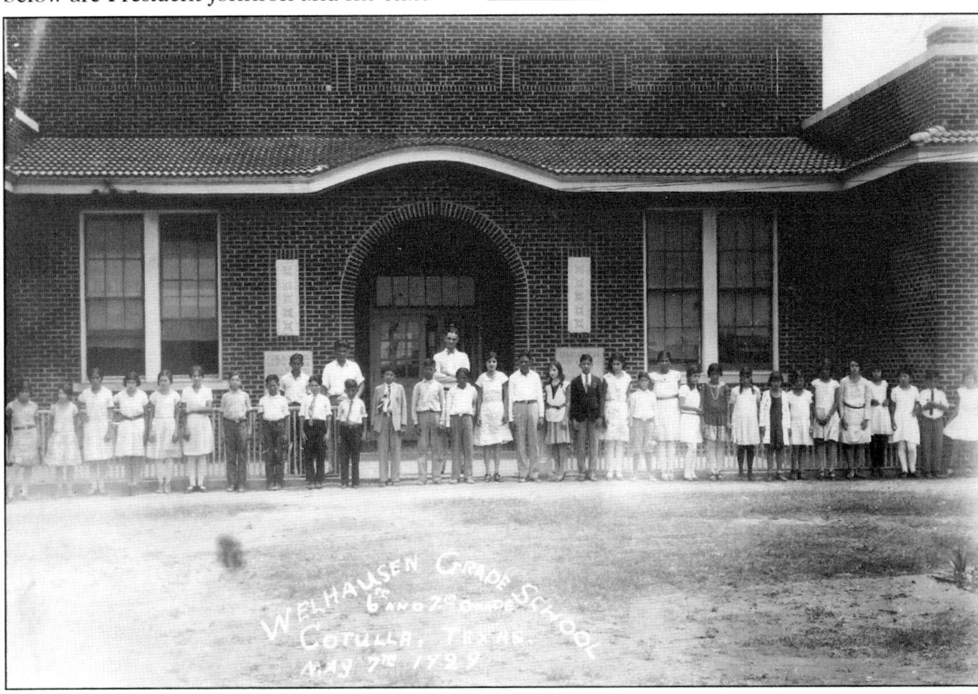

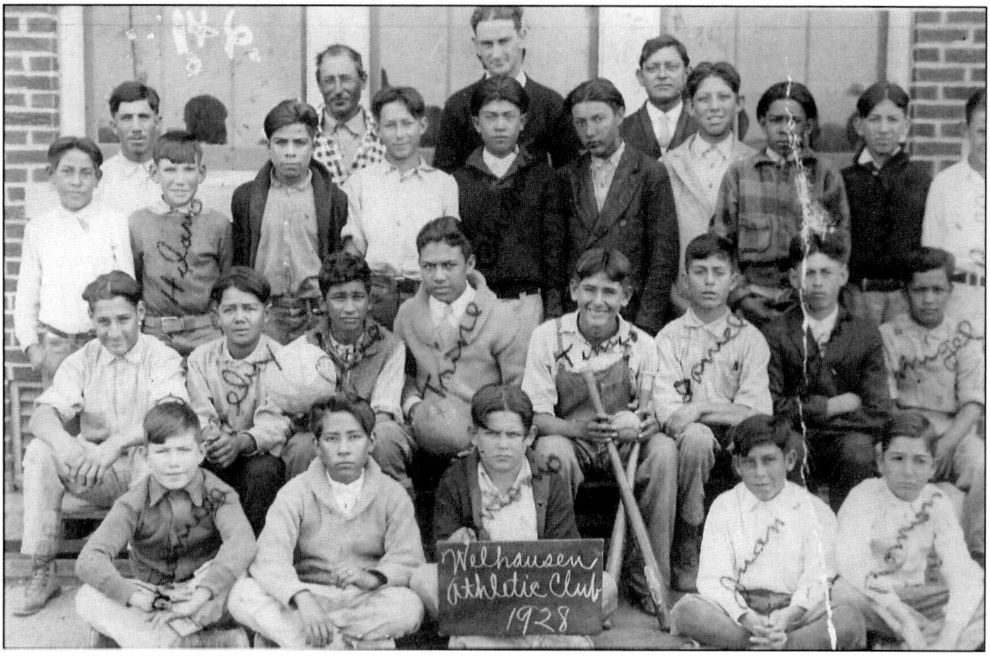

Lyndon B. Johnson and the 1928 Welhausen Athletic Club have their picture taken in front of the Welhausen School. He was much loved by his students, and years later they all remembered him with much love and devotion as a teacher that really cared.

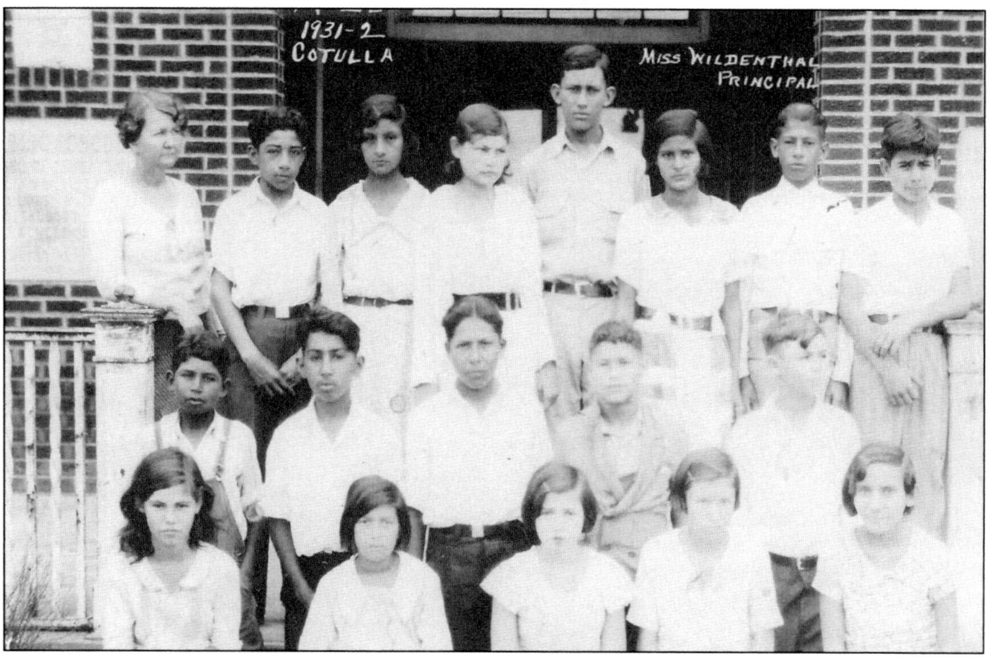

The 1931–1932 fifth-grade class of Welhausen School is pictured with their teacher Mamie Wildenthal. Pictured from left to right are (first row) Julia Garcia, Hortensia Rodriguez, Paulita Sanchez, Susie Linares, and Ignacia Coronado; (second row) Crecencio Marlez, Jose Sanchez, unidentified, Arturo Velez, and Tristan Ramirez; (third row) Mamie Wildenthal, Jose Munoz, Cuca Santoya, Ofelia Ramirez, Luis Aguero, Lupe Garza, Pedro Muriel, and Frank Gonzalez.

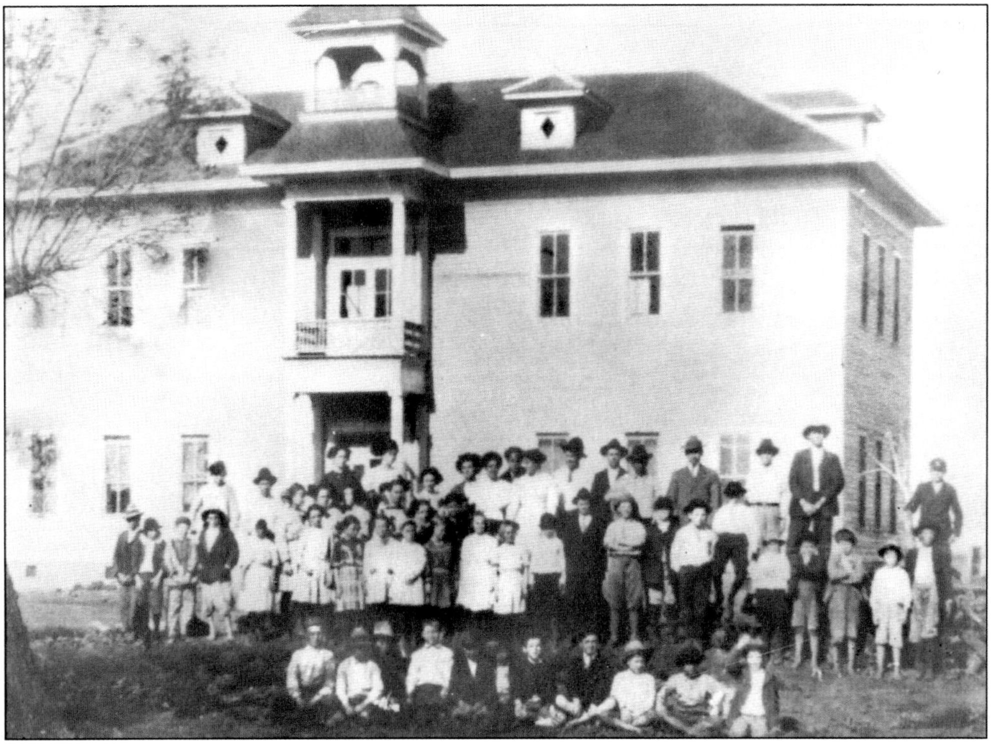

The first school in Millett was a small frame building erected in the late 1890s. As the area continued to grow, a new two-story building with a bell tower was constructed that was the pride of the community. In 1923, a contract was let for a new brick building. When finished, it was described as one of the most modern school buildings in La Salle County.

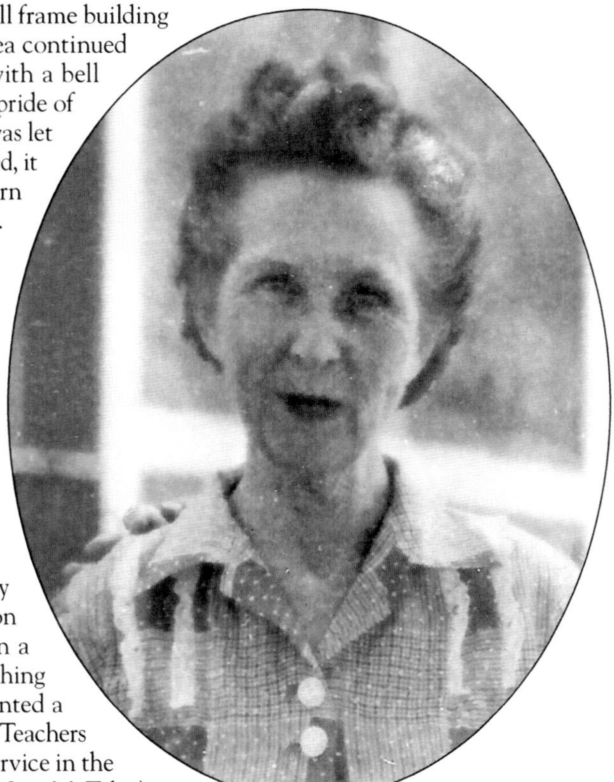

Clara Ellison was a much-loved primary teacher at the Millett School. Ellison started teaching at the age of 18 on a ranch near Twohig and continued teaching for the next 61 years. She was presented a Golden Certificate by the Texas State Teachers Association recognizing 50 years of service in the public schools of Texas. (Courtesy of Nora M. Tyler.)

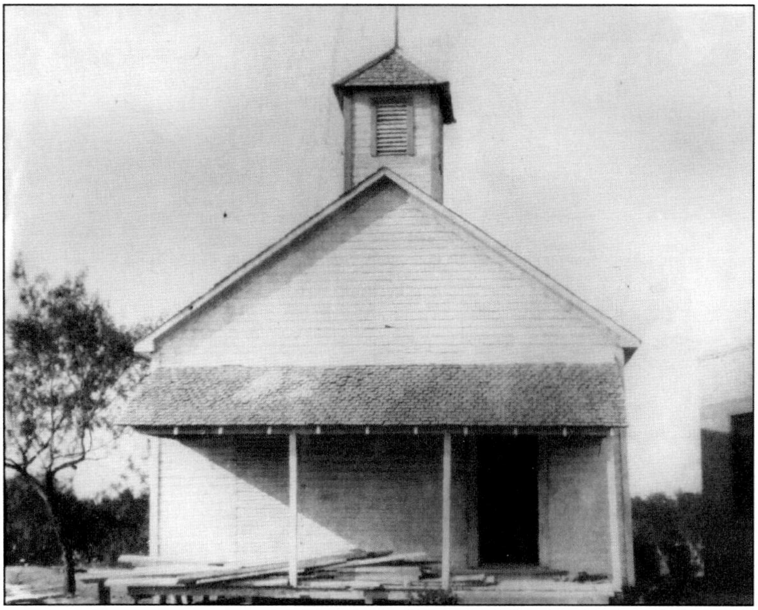

Gardendale's first school was erected in 1907. It was a small wooden frame building and was one of the first buildings erected in the new town of Gardendale. Pearl Hammond, a young college student, was one of the early teachers in the Gardendale School.

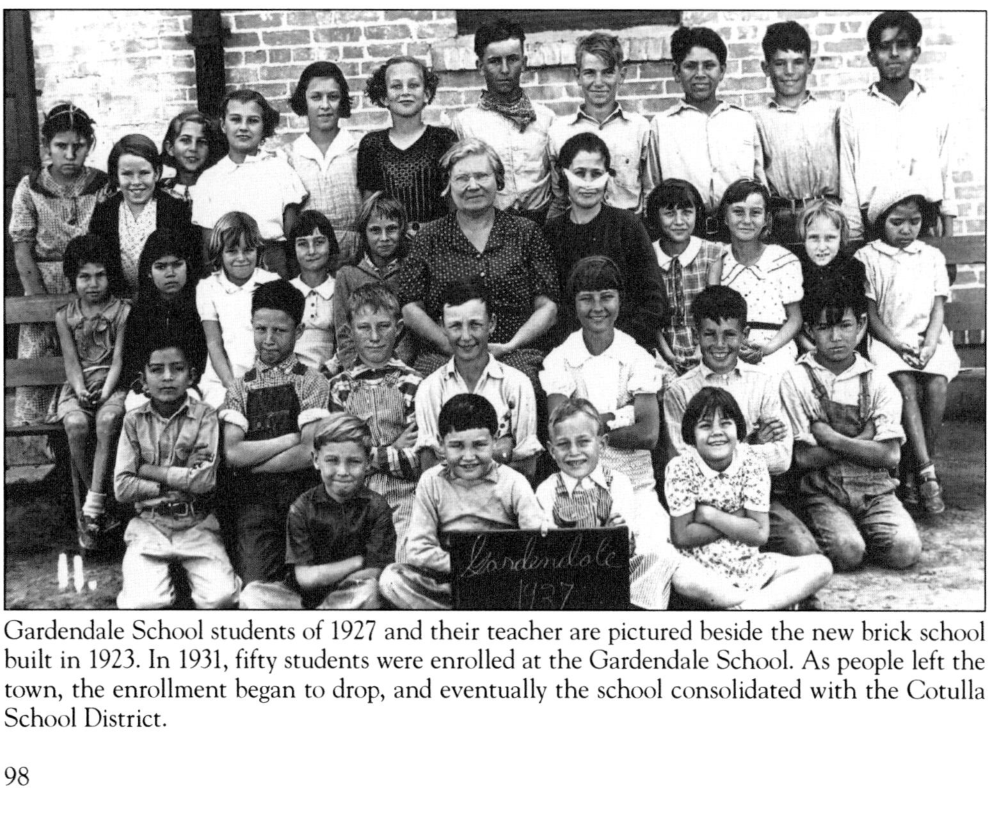

Gardendale School students of 1927 and their teacher are pictured beside the new brick school built in 1923. In 1931, fifty students were enrolled at the Gardendale School. As people left the town, the enrollment began to drop, and eventually the school consolidated with the Cotulla School District.

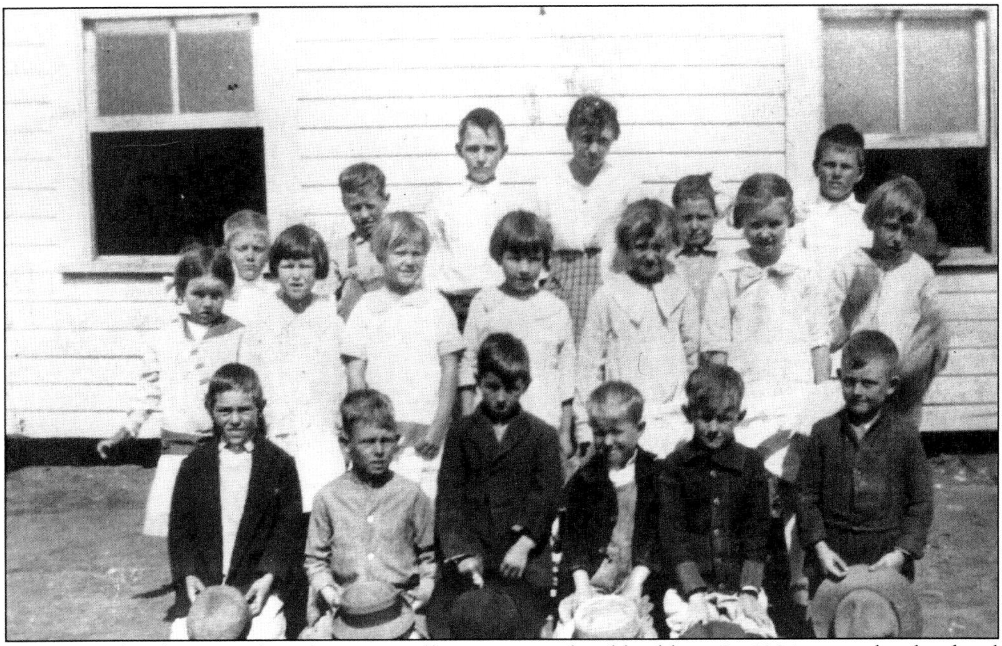

The first school in Woodward was a small one-room school building. In 1924, a new brick school was erected and was considered the bright spot in the Woodward community. The 1917–1918 students are, from left to right, (first row) Edgar Sample, two unidentified, Ray Arnold, Jack Barnes, and Victor Sample; (second row) unidentified, Ruth Arnold, unidentified, Lola Coovert, Nellie Mae Ferguson, unidentified, and Tressie Arnold; (third row) unidentified, Burrell Lann, Dessie Covert, unidentified teacher, two more unidentified.

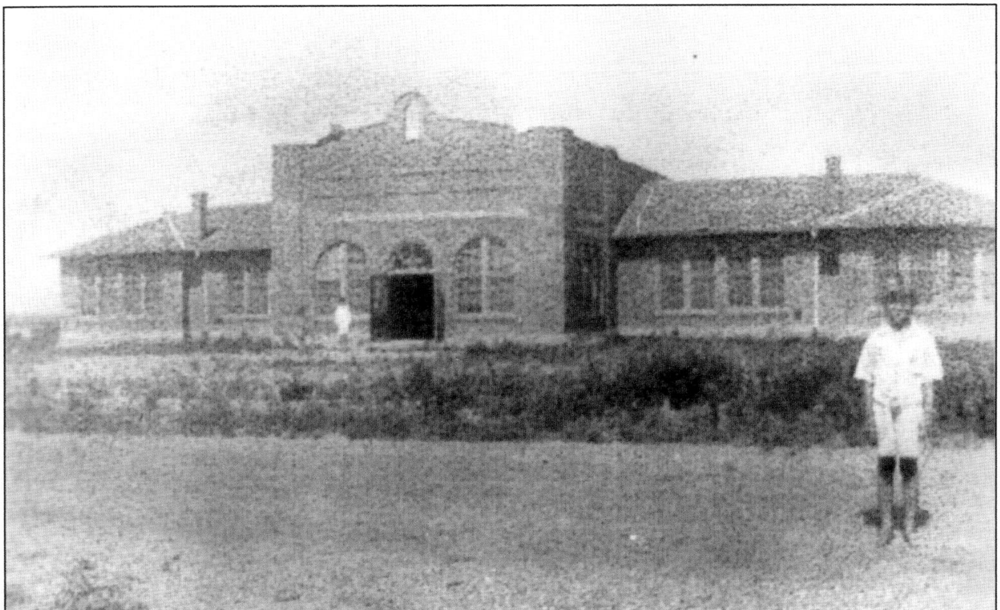

The children of Los Angeles first attended school in a three-room frame building. In 1926, a new brick school was constructed. High school students as well as elementary students attended school in Los Angeles. In 1935, the high school students traveled to Cotulla to finish their education.

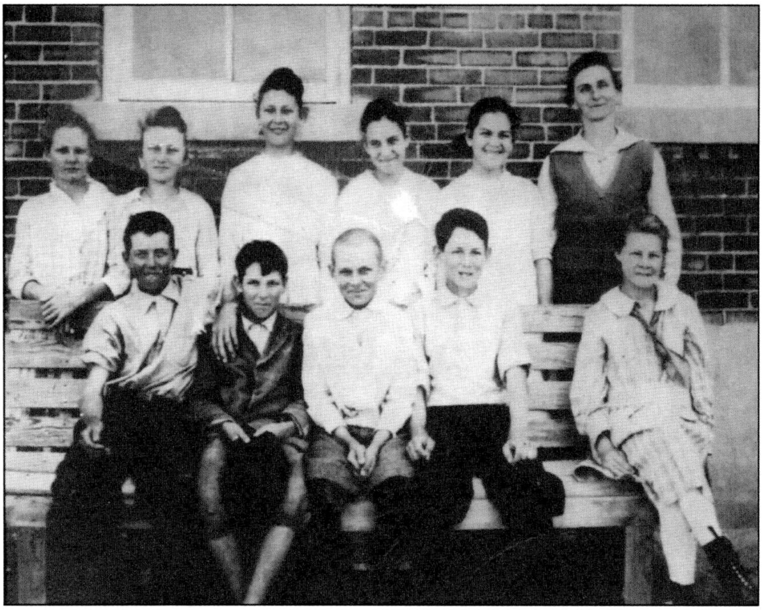

When school opened in 1913, the Fowlerton children started in a new brick building. The new building had a laboratory and library. That year, 227 students were enrolled. A 1913 class is pictured, from left to right, (first row) Oden Walker, Tom Lansford, Stanley A. Smith, Francis Sponseller, and Mattie Lee Booth; (second row) all unidentified.

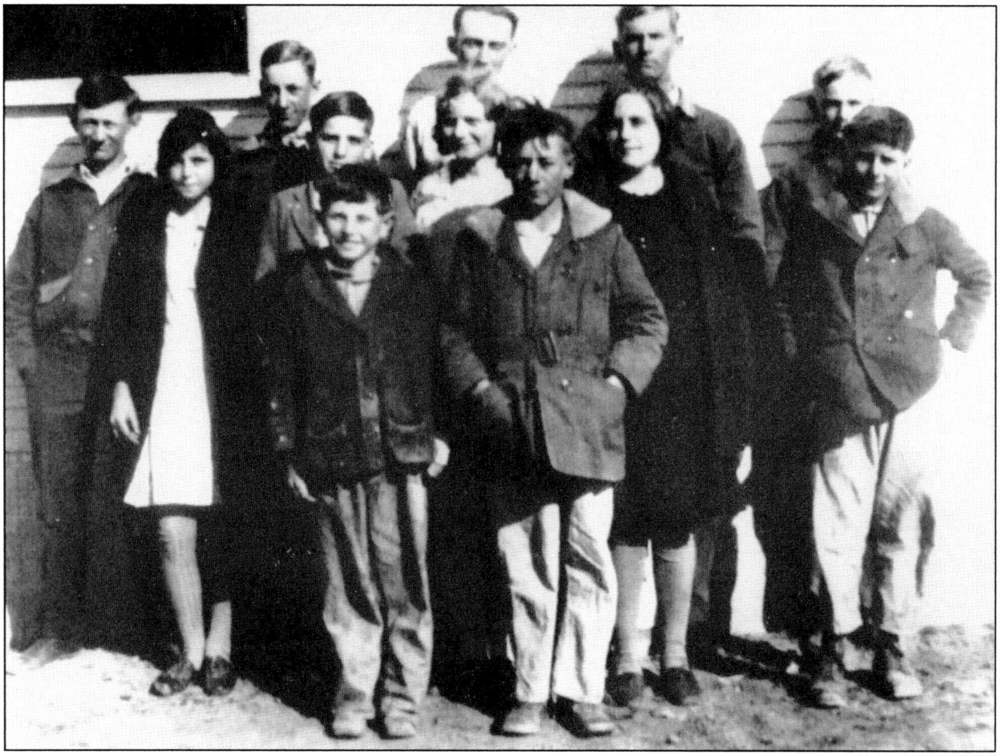

The first school at Buckholt was a small one-room building. When the first teacher arrived, she disembarked from the train at Los Angeles and was met by a Buckholt resident. When she saw the remoteness of the area, she began to cry; she left the next morning. The Buckholt students pictured here are, from left to right, (first row) Herbert Fiedler and Malvin Plocek; (second row) Tillie Fiedler, Medford Keath, Pauline Smith, Lexadine Keath, and Frank Maldsky; (third row) Roy Plocek, Leo Vic, unidentified, Theo Smith, and David Smith.

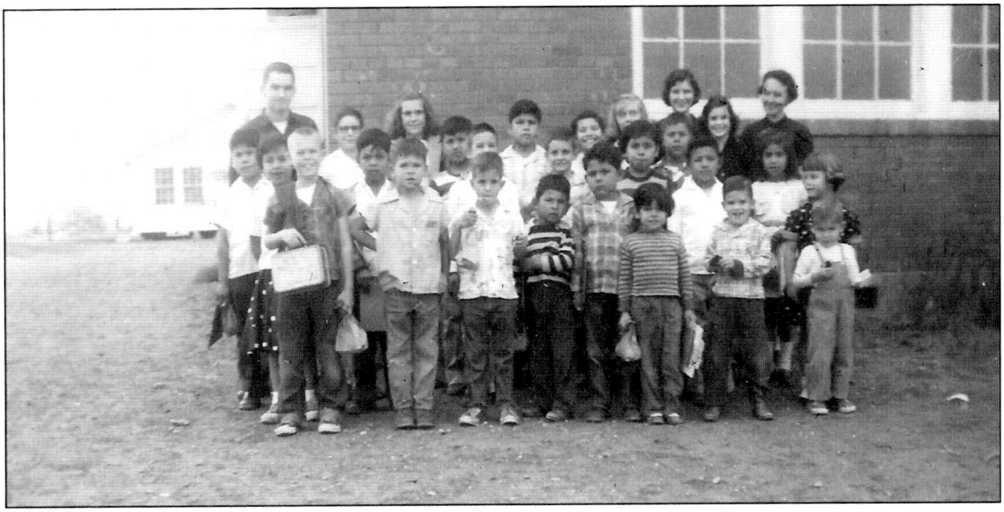

A new brick school was erected in Artesia Wells in 1925. John Marion Ramsey donated the land for the school and the new building became known as the J. M. Ramsey Memorial School. The school was also used for church services and other community events.

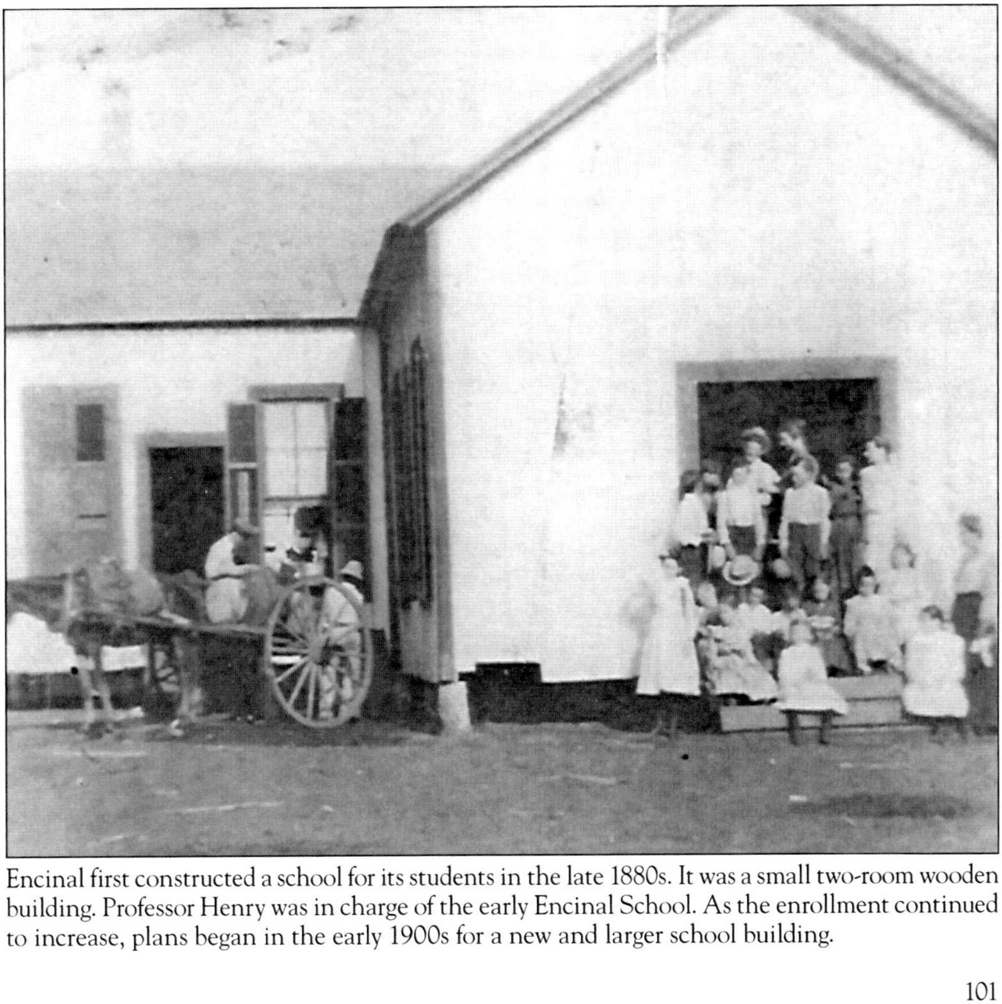

Encinal first constructed a school for its students in the late 1880s. It was a small two-room wooden building. Professor Henry was in charge of the early Encinal School. As the enrollment continued to increase, plans began in the early 1900s for a new and larger school building.

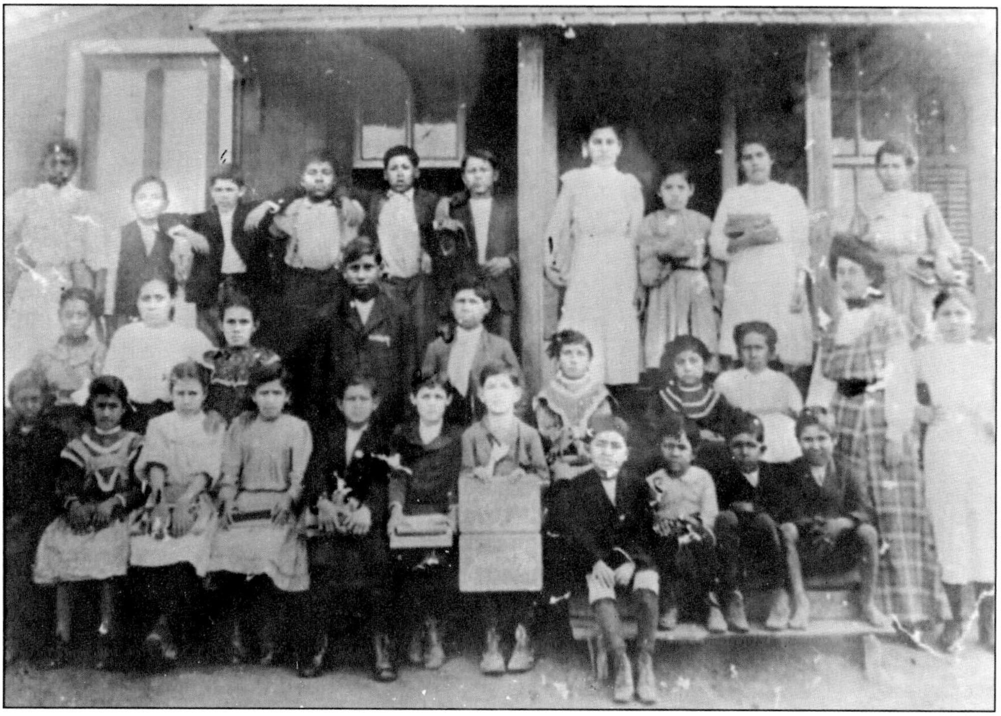

In 1908, Mexican American students attended a separate school. The Mexican American school was known as Encinal School No. 2. The 1908 students of Encinal School No. 2 are pictured in front of their school along with their instructors. Feerner Grober and Margaret Culler were among the school's early teachers.

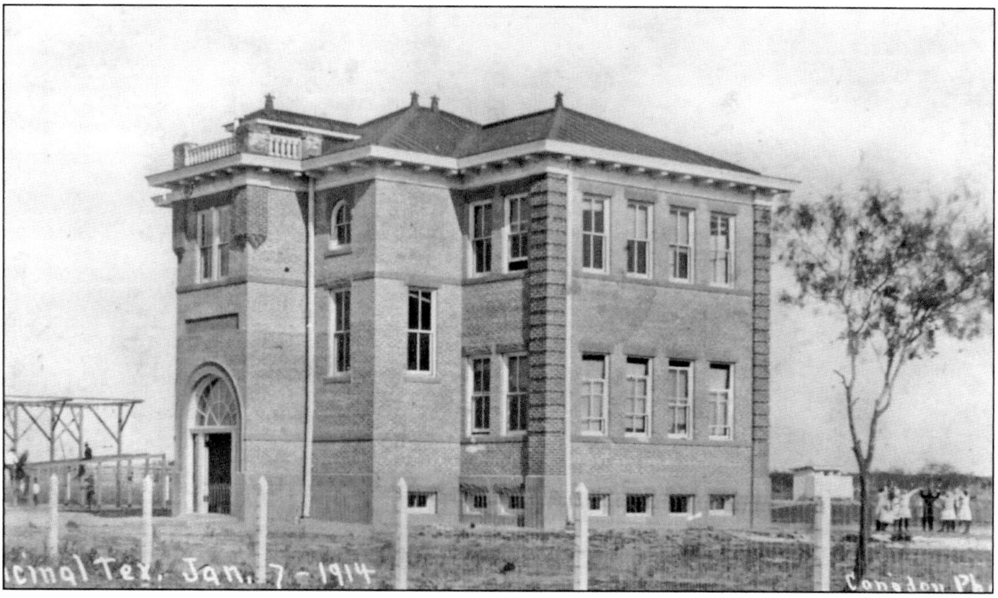

In 1913, a new brick building was erected in Encinal. By the 1920s, the school had over 200 students enrolled. The Encinal school system consisted of a high school and an elementary school. The top enrollment for the Encinal school system was in 1931 when the school had 363 students enrolled. In 1941, the high school students were transported to Cotulla.

Seven

COWBOYS, COWGIRLS, MATADORS, AND CUBS

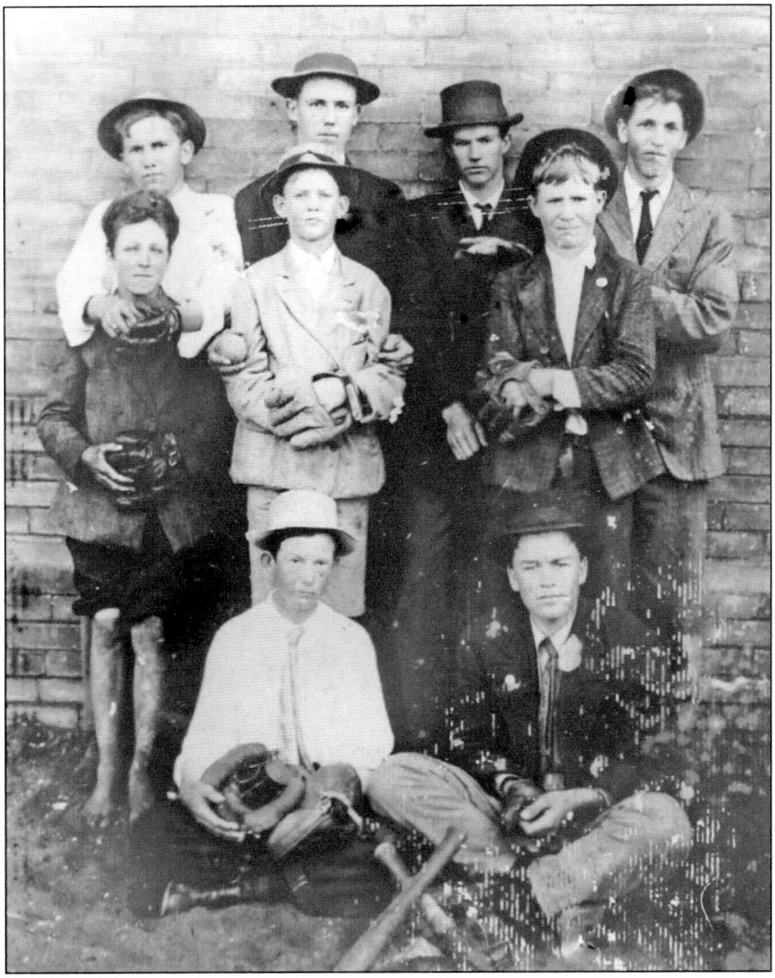

As early as 1899, Cotulla had their first baseball team. Games were played on Saturdays with a nearby town. The team members were, from left to right, (first row) Alonzo Neal and Ray Keck; (second row) two unidentified players and Hap Russell; (third row) Albert U. "Dutch" Knaggs, Willie Copp, Everett Coleman, and Clinton Haney.

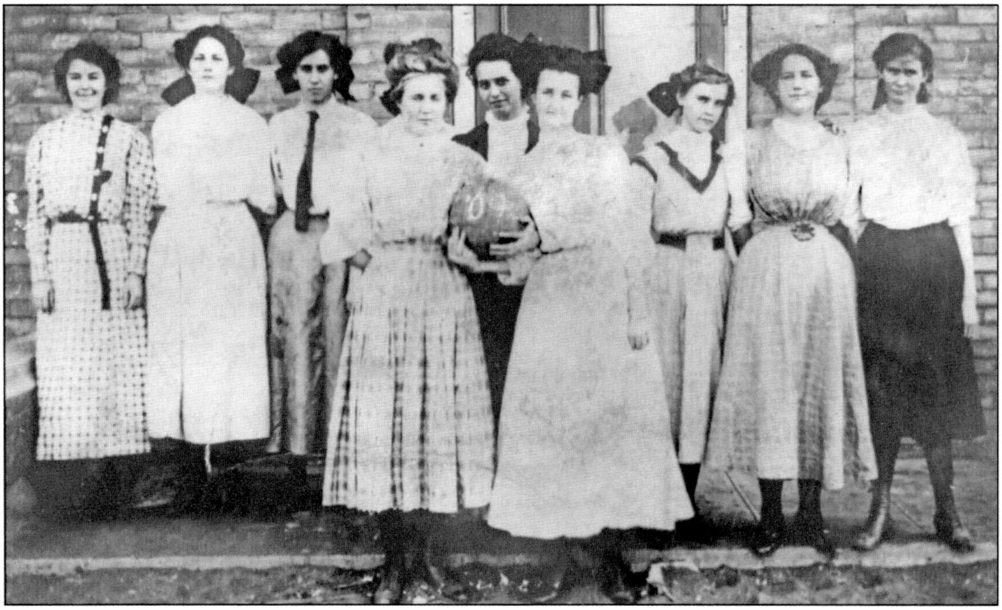

One of the early sports offered to girls in the Cotulla schools was basketball. Matched games were arranged with Encinal or some close by town. The Cotulla girls basketball team of 1909 is pictured in front of the new school. The team members were, from left to right, Lucy Burwell, unidentified, Pearl Landrum, Mamie McHenry, unidentified, Alma Coleman, Nannie Peters, Loretta Binkley, and Rose Earnest.

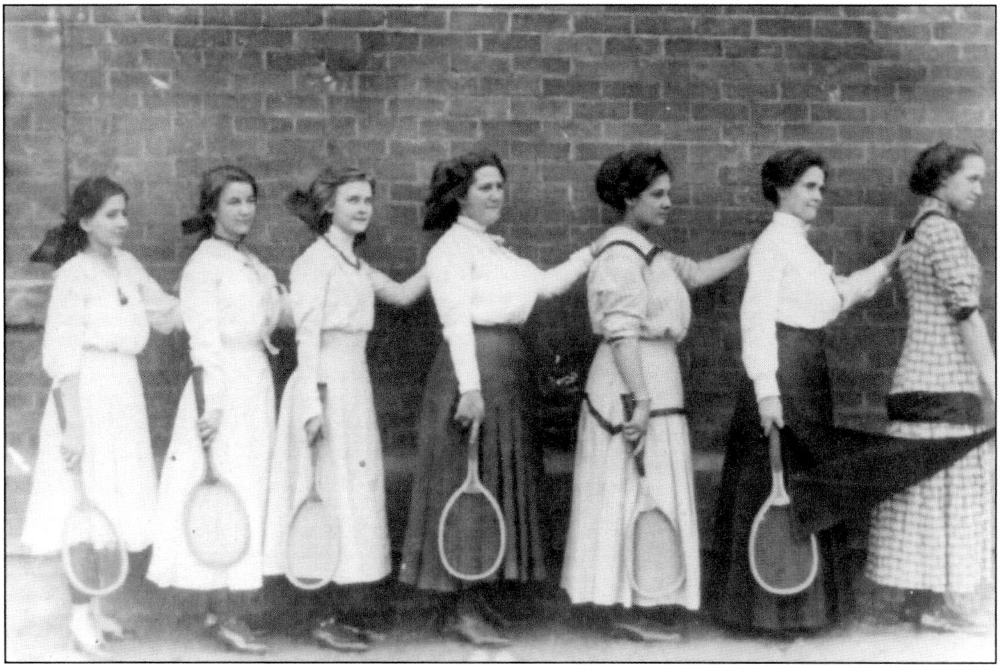

Ozella Loggin was coach of the 1910 girls tennis team. The tennis team members were, from left to right, Elizabeth Kerr, Ethel Gardner, Loretta Binkley, Ida Earnest, Rose Earnest, Ozella Loggin, and Julia Porter. Notice the heavy wooden tennis rackets held by the girls.

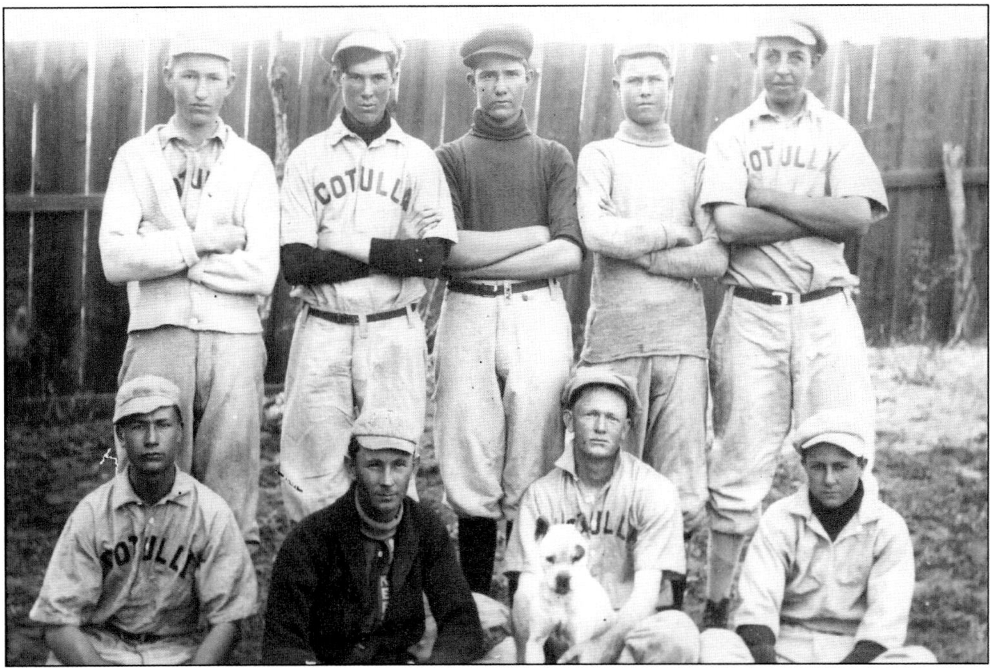

Early sporting events were always arranged with neighboring towns. If the game was in Dilley, the team traveled by wagon. The team traveled by train if the games were with Pearsall or Devine. The 1912 baseball team members were, from left to right, (first row) Joe Peters, Professor Bledsoe, Walter Manly, and Hobson Wildenthal; (second row) Merton Haynie, Charles Tarver, Arthur Knaggs, Otto Jay, and Fred Dunning. Professor Bledsoe coached the team.

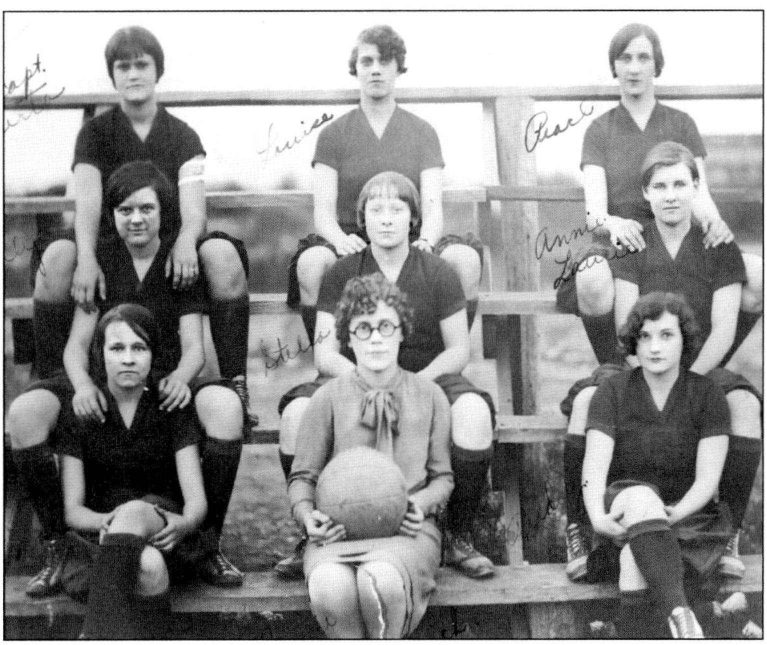

Fannie Herring coached the 1926 Cotulla Cowgirls basketball team. Berta Duncan was elected captain of the team. Team members were, from left to right, (first row) Eva Mae Smith, coach Fannie Herring, and Audrey ?; (second row) Polly ?, Stella Smith, and Annie Laurie Holman; (third row) Berta Duncan, Louise Burris and Pearl Mayes.

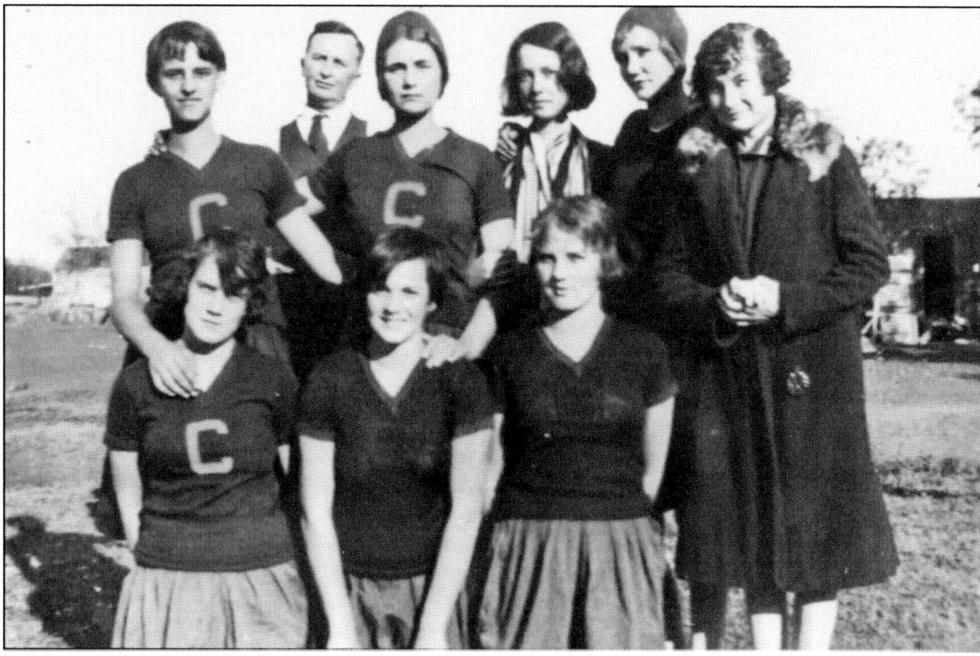

High school football is big in Texas, and no Texas high school football game would be complete without the fans and cheering section. The 1926 Cotulla Cowboy cheerleaders were always on hand to cheer the football team on to victory. "Two bits, four bits, six bits, a dollar! All for Cotulla, stand up and holler!"

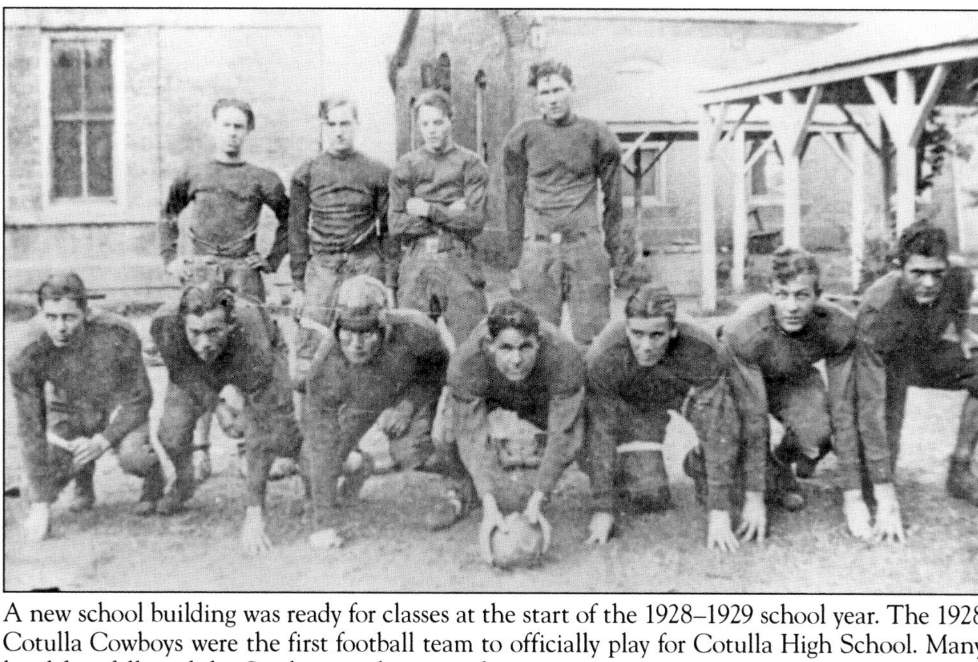

A new school building was ready for classes at the start of the 1928–1929 school year. The 1928 Cotulla Cowboys were the first football team to officially play for Cotulla High School. Many local fans followed the Cowboys to their out-of-town games.

Girls' doubles Martha Swisher and Ethel Woolls won the district tennis title and competed in the 1934 regional tennis meet in Kingsville. Others on the 1934 tennis team were Boncil McNabb, girls' singles; and William A. Tarver and L. Lopez, boys' doubles. The boys' doubles also won the district tennis title and competed in Kingsville at the regional meet.

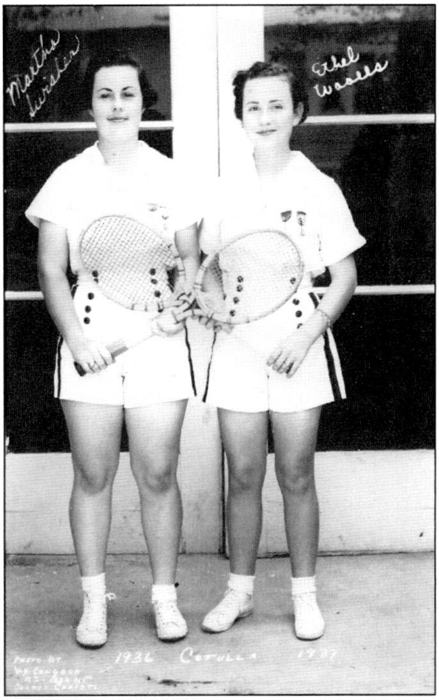

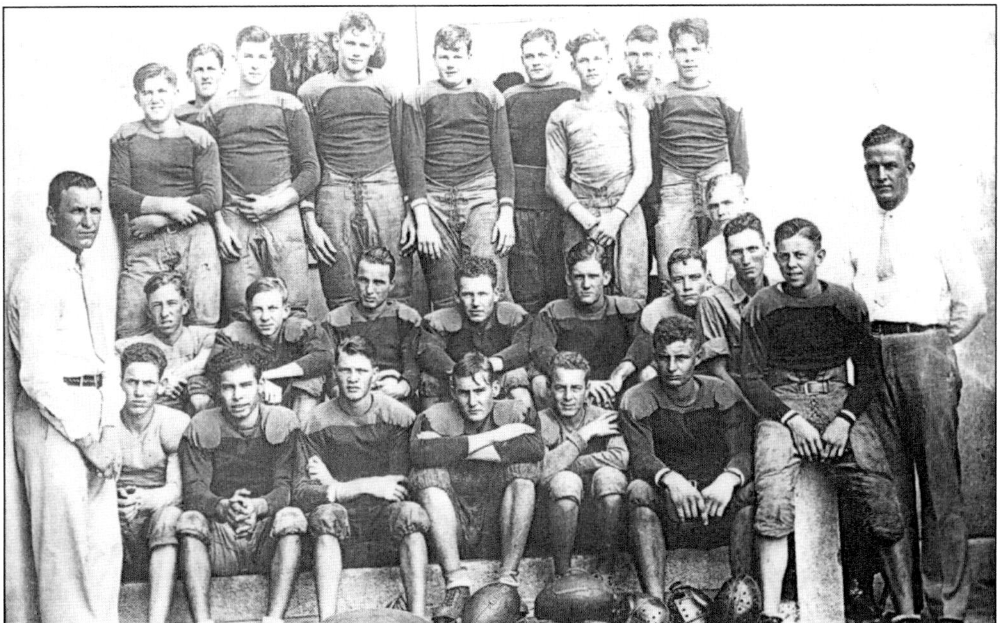

Coach Murry Stephenson, with the aid of assistant coaches Morgan and Spence, put the Cotulla Cowboys through their paces in preparation for the 1934 football season. The Cowboys defeated Uvalde for the first time in 10 years. In the final game of the season, the Pearsall Mavericks were headed for the district championship when defeated by the Cowboys by a score of 13 to 7. Henry Tutor and the backfield played all season with the precision of a well-oiled machine. Raymond Marsh and Walter Earnest cocaptained the team.

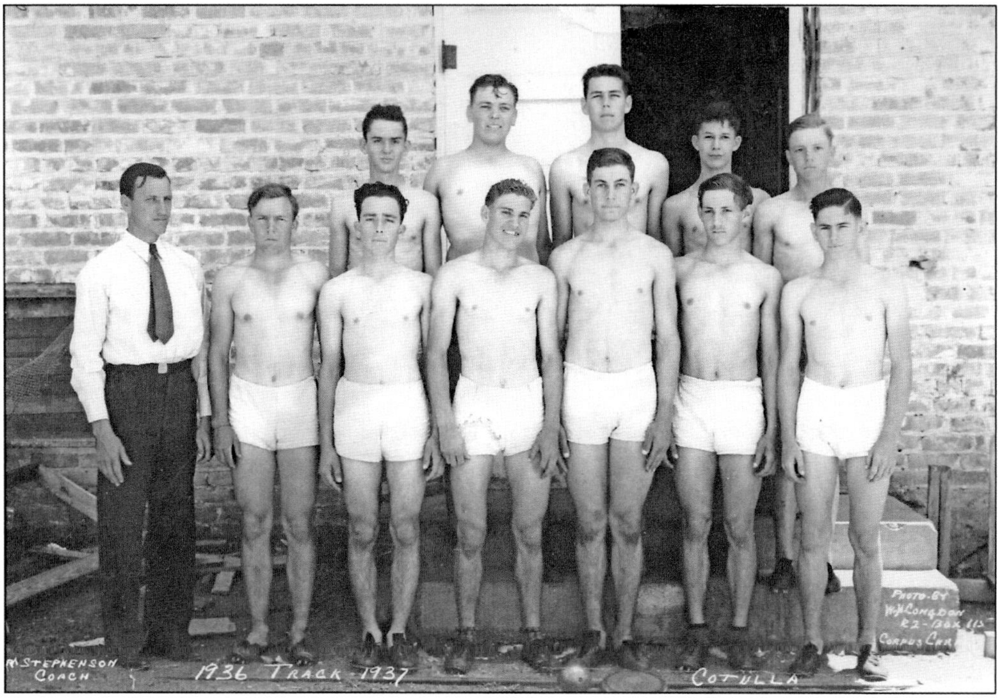

The Cowboy track team of 1936–1937 had 11 members and was coached by Murry Stephenson. According to a newspaper report, the team had several good runners and was expected to do well at the district meet. The Region VII, District 27 track and tennis meet was held in Laredo.

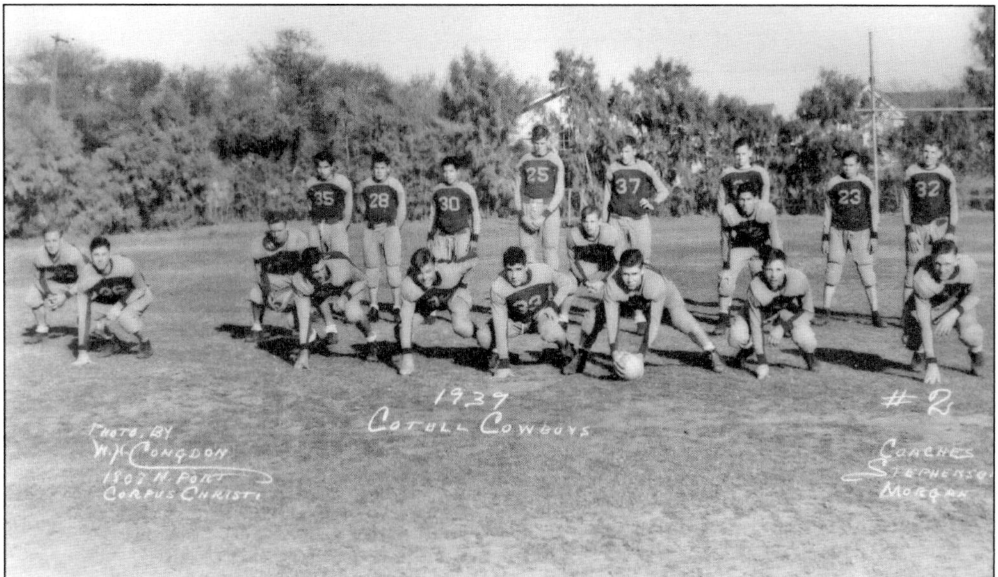

Coach Murry Stephenson started the 1937 football season with 10 returning Cowboy lettermen and hoped for a district championship. Ray Darnell and Warren Pickens were cocaptains of the team. The Cowboys' hopes for a district championship were dashed when the team was defeated by the Hondo Owls.

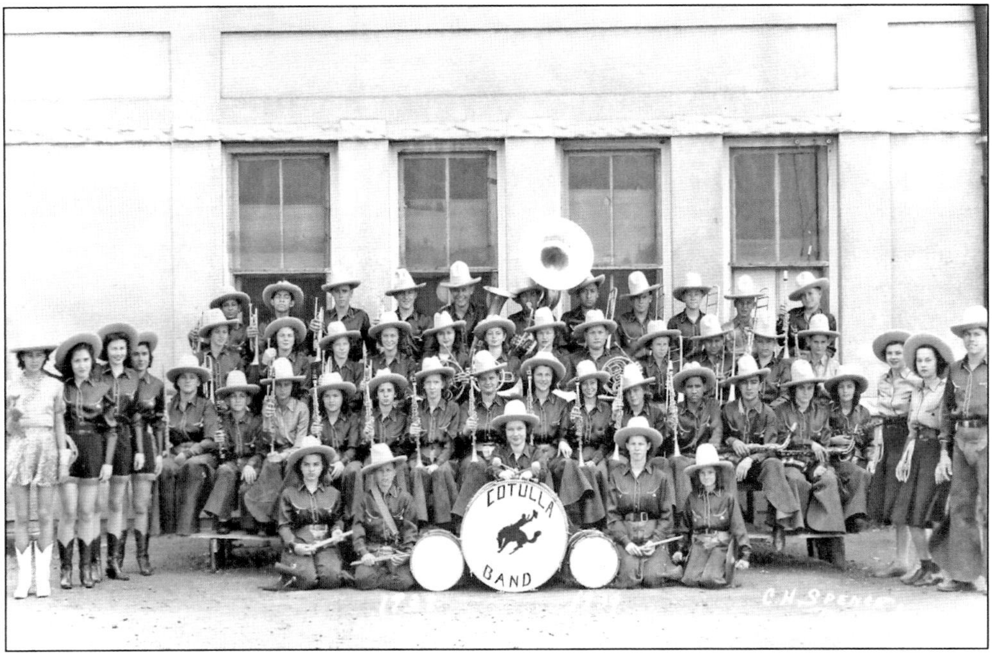

The Cotulla Cowboy Band was always on hand to cheer on the Cowboys. The band carried out the cowboy theme by dressing in the traditional cowboy garb of leather chaps and vest. Maroon or gold shirts with maroon trousers and a Stetson hat finished the uniform.

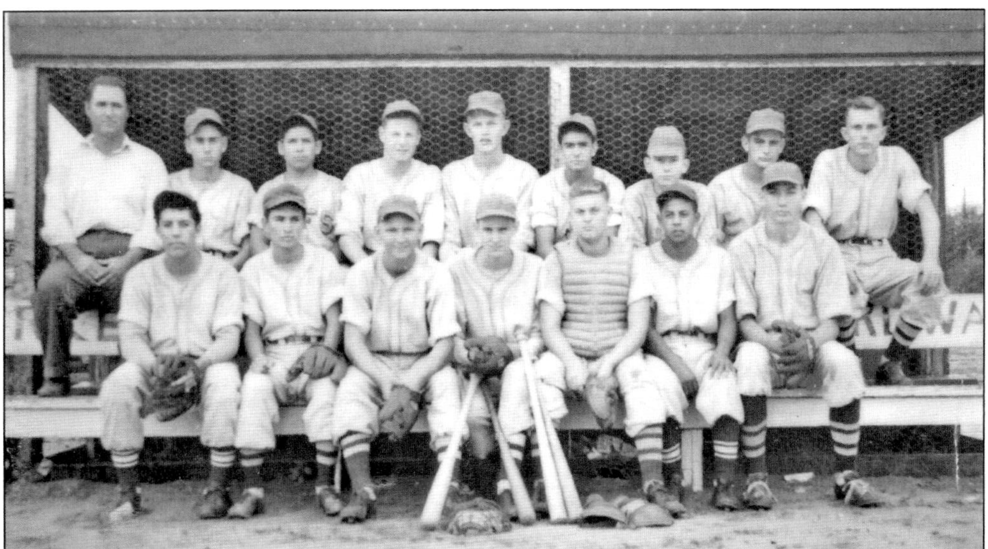

When the 1948 baseball season opened, coach Clyde Morgan had hopes of a good team, with a number of experienced players from the previous year. That year coach Morgan led the Cowboys to a district championship. The Cowboys defeated San Felipe of Del Rio for the 46B district title.

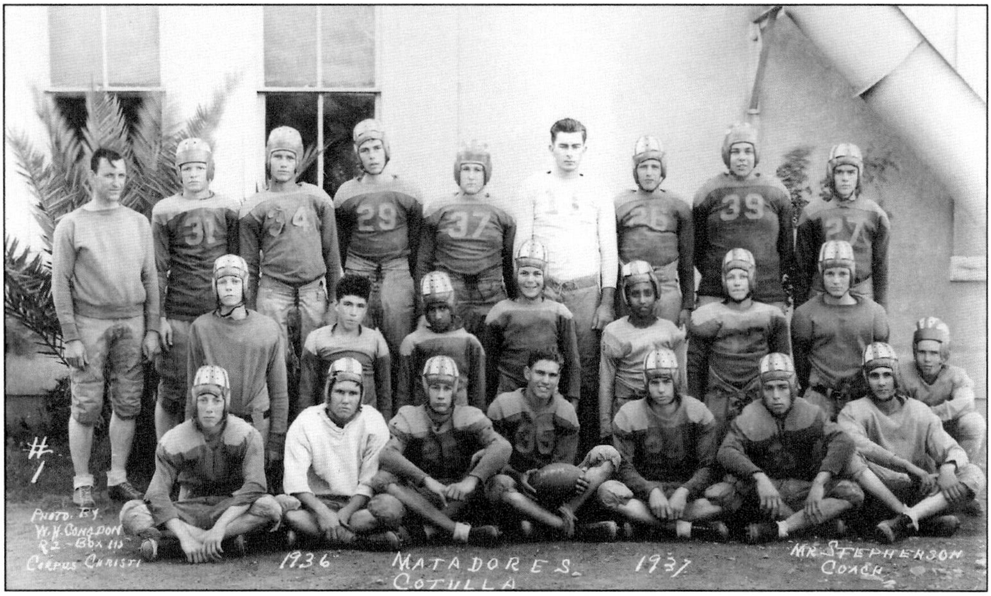

In the 1930s, ex-high school and college players formed an amateur sports team, known as the Cotulla Matadors. The Matadors were primarily a basketball club, but they did play other sports, too. Games were arranged with area towns. Russell Reeder and Albert U. "Dutch" Knaggs managed the team. Members of the team included Preston Reeder, John Cotulla, Murry Stephenson, Joe Young, Bill Williams, Clyde Morgan, Hubert Jemeyson, and Eddie Healey. Pictured above is the 1936 Cotulla Matadors football team.

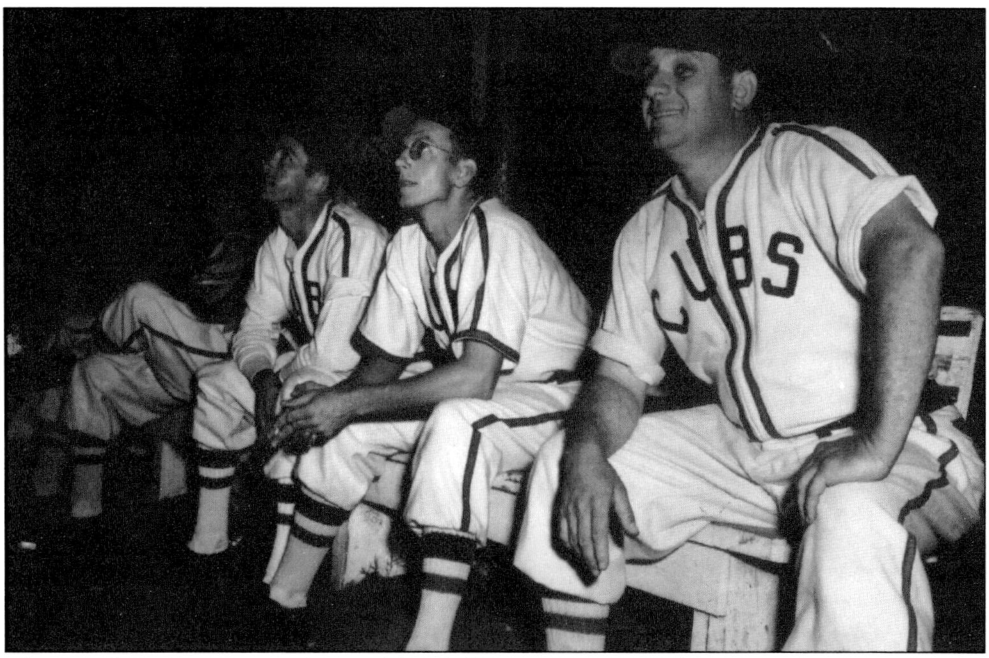

The Cotulla Cubs, a semiprofessional baseball team, was managed by Marvin Brown (far right). In 1948, the team won the Tournament of Champions. The Cubs played in a modern lighted field with a seating capacity of 2,000. In 1949, the Cotulla Chamber of Commerce presented the Cubs manager, Marvin Brown, with a gold watch in appreciation for his outstanding team.

Eight

Preaching the Gospel

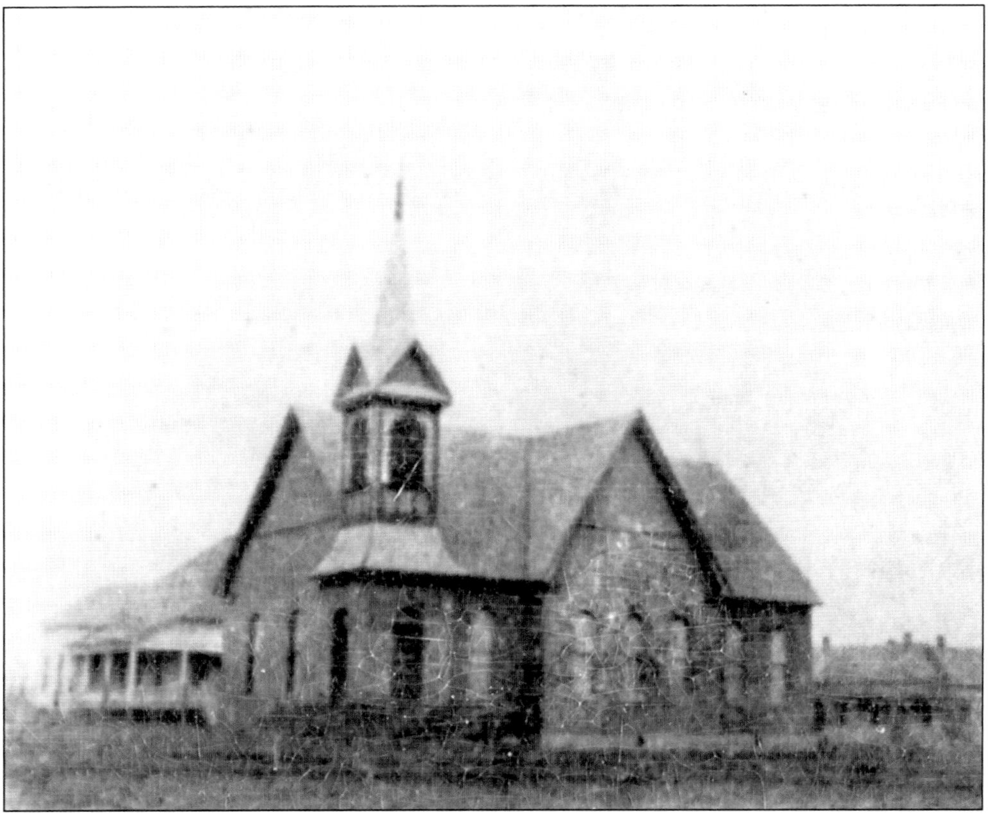

The First United Methodist Church of Cotulla was built in the early 1880s. The Methodist church was the first one to be built in Cotulla and had 26 members. Rev. William H. Keck preached the first sermon. The first church was a wooden structure. Later the church purchased a new location and in 1906 erected a new brick building. A parsonage was erected on the site of the original church. In the early days, the Methodists shared their building with the Baptists and Presbyterians, each conducting services on alternating Sundays.

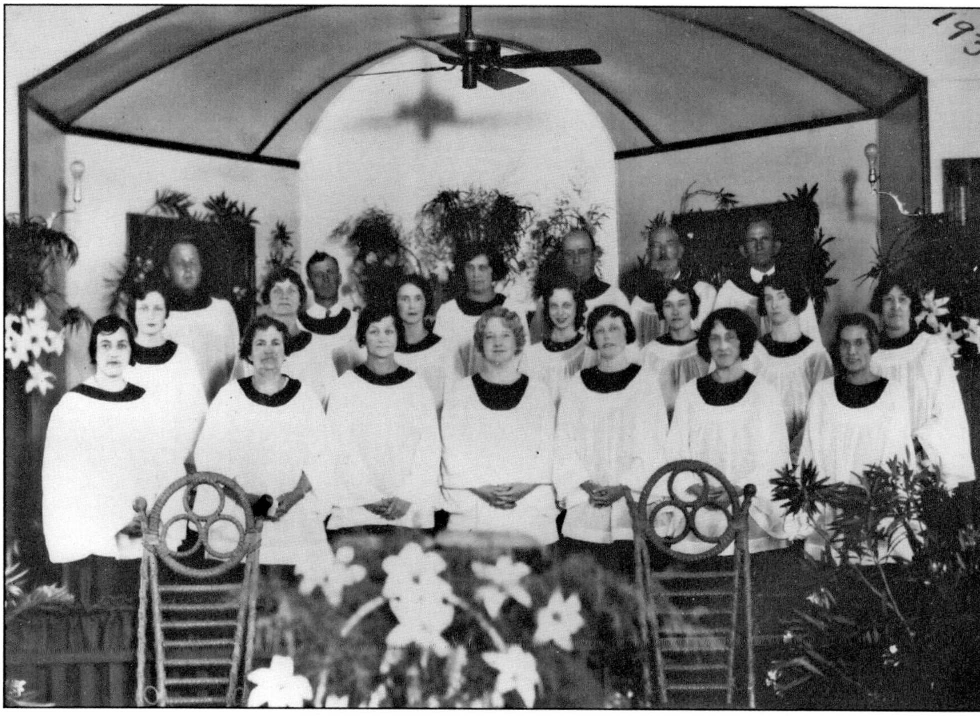

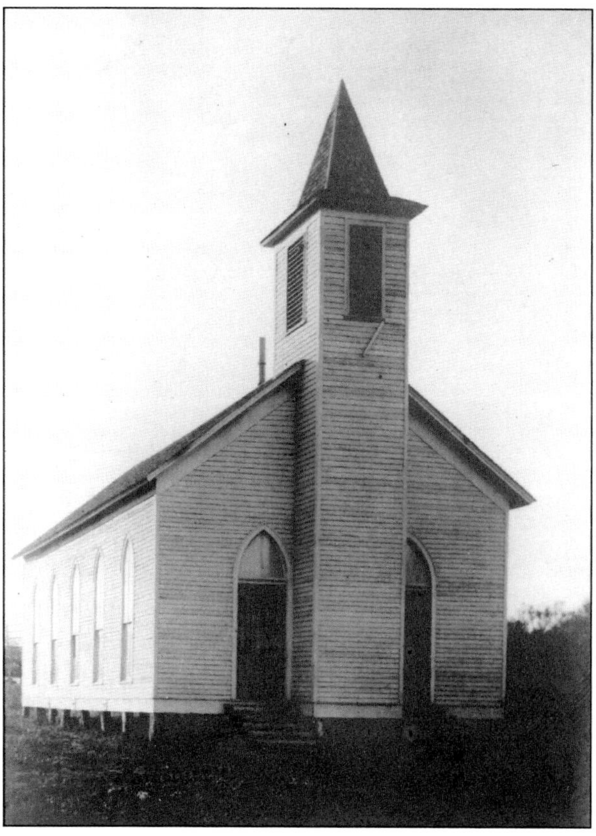

The First United Methodist Church choir is pictured in front of the choir loft. In 1946, Marion Neeley installed a new choir loft, altar, and communion rail at the church in memory of his parents, David L. and Delia Fullerton Neeley. David and Delia were early members of the church.

The First Baptist Church in Cotulla was erected in the late 1880s. The 30 members had been meeting in the Methodist church. The church was constructed of wood and had tall, arched windows. Rev. John Van Epps Covey preached the first sermon, and Loula Bowen was the first pianist.

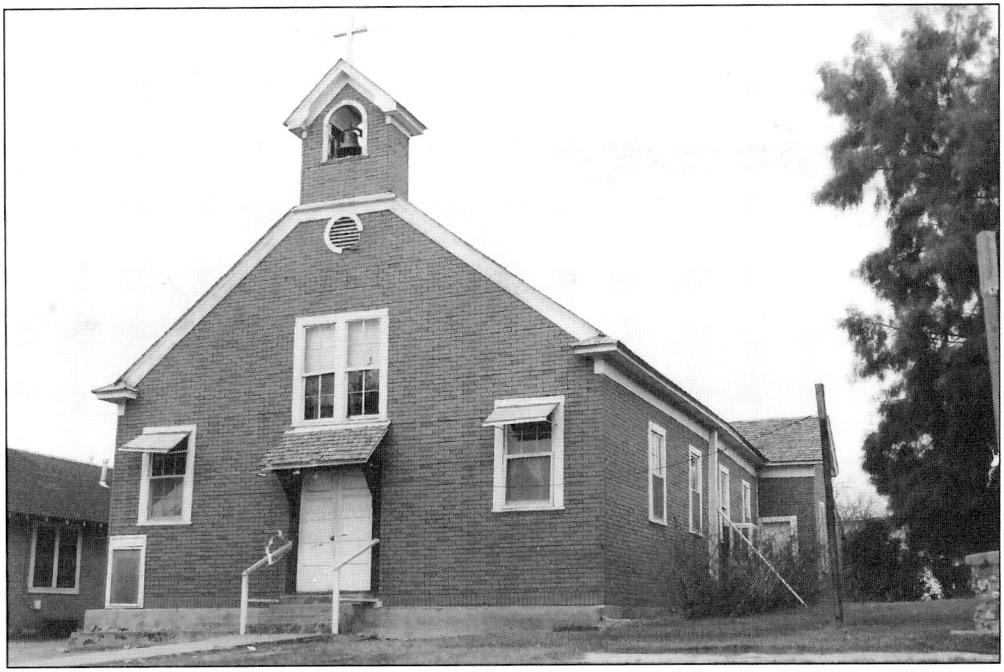

The Catholic Church in Cotulla purchased property on Main Street in 1883 for the purpose of building a church. The first church was destroyed by fire in 1910. The Sacred Heart Catholic Church or *La Iglesia del Sagrado Corazon* was built in 1912 and continued to serve its parishioners until a new church opened in 1958. During that period of time, 10,000 masses were offered, and there were 6,600 baptisms, 3,255 confirmations, and 876 marriages.

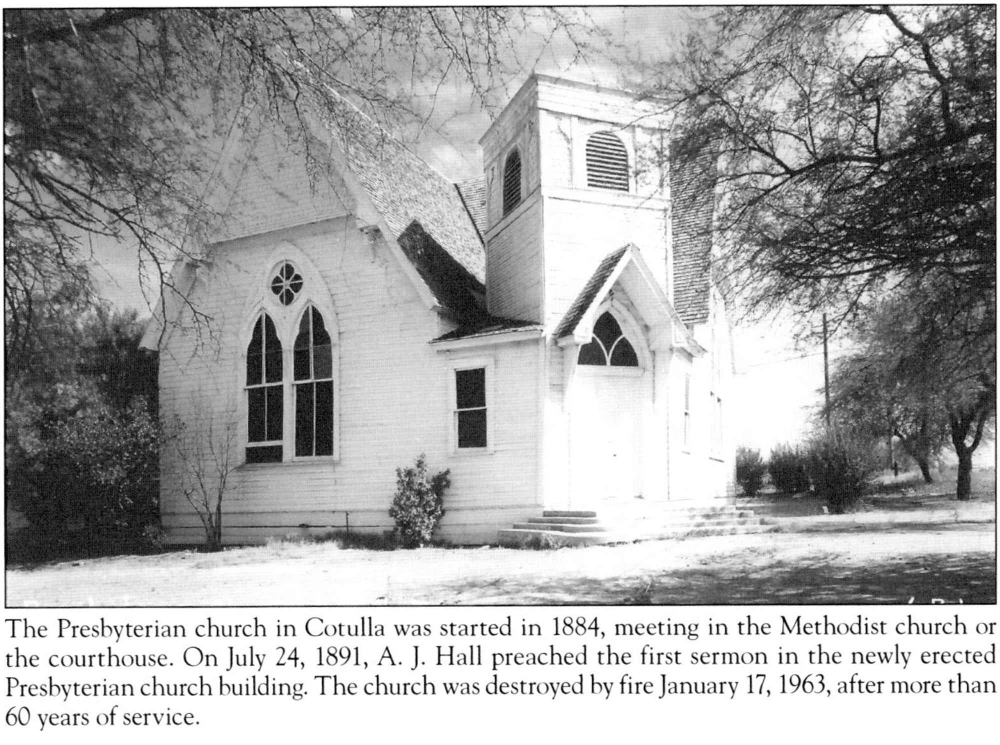

The Presbyterian church in Cotulla was started in 1884, meeting in the Methodist church or the courthouse. On July 24, 1891, A. J. Hall preached the first sermon in the newly erected Presbyterian church building. The church was destroyed by fire January 17, 1963, after more than 60 years of service.

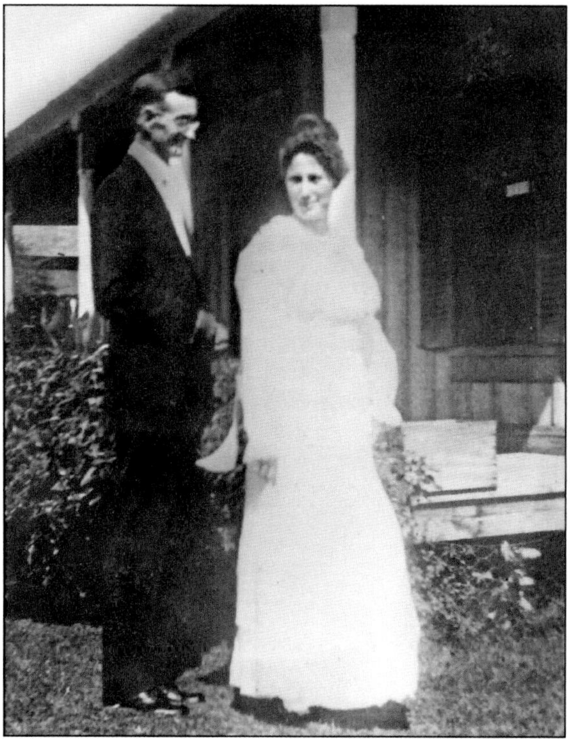

In 1909, a young preacher named Harry W. Hamilton was installed as pastor of the Presbyterian Church. Rev. Hamilton soon married a local girl, Jessie Ann Copp. He was so loved by the church members and the local citizens that he remained pastor of the church for 31 years.

The Church of Christ first met in the home of Travis and Pearl Huddleston. In 1948, C. C. and Maggie Mae Taylor bought two lots and gave them to the church for a building. The members purchased a house and converted it into a church building. The first services in the building were held in May 1948 when Br. Edgar Furr held a revival meeting. (Photograph courtesy Darlene Taylor Meyer.)

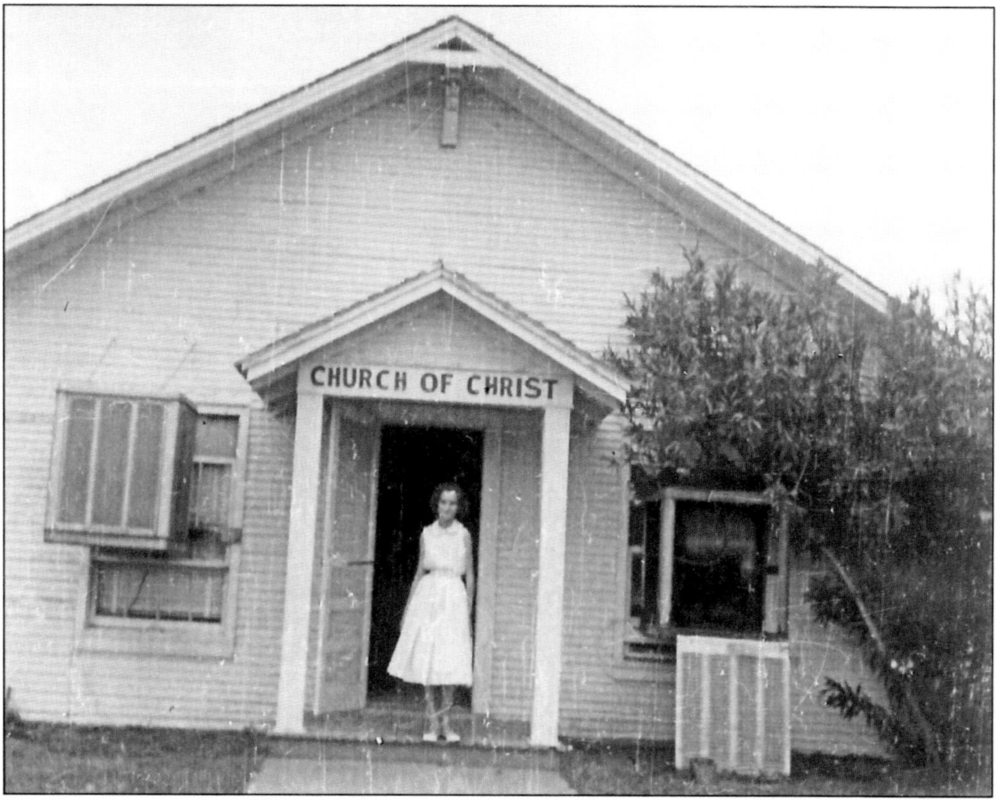

The first church in Millett was built in 1905. Originally it was a community church and was shared by the Methodists and Baptists. When the Baptists erected their own building in 1923, it became the Methodist church. The building was torn down in the early 1940s.

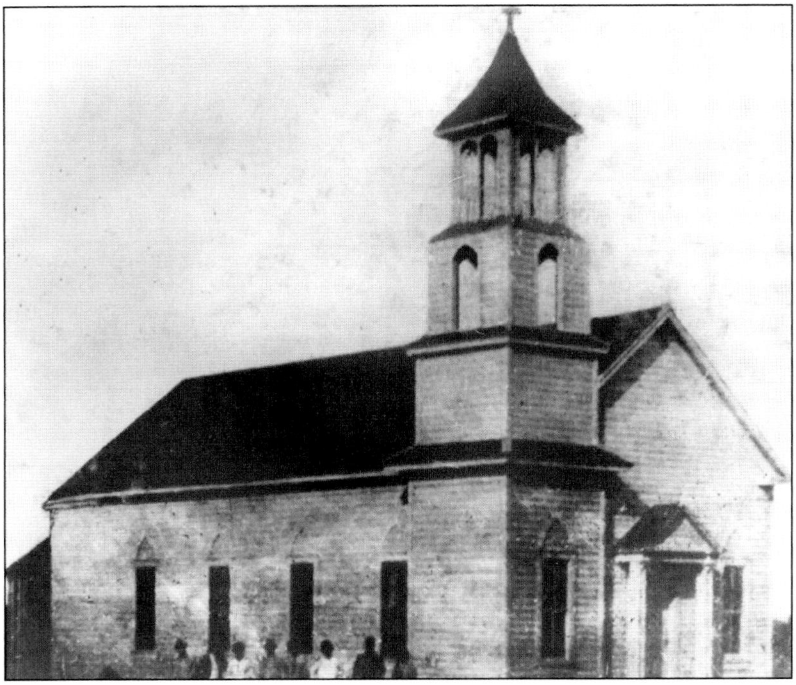

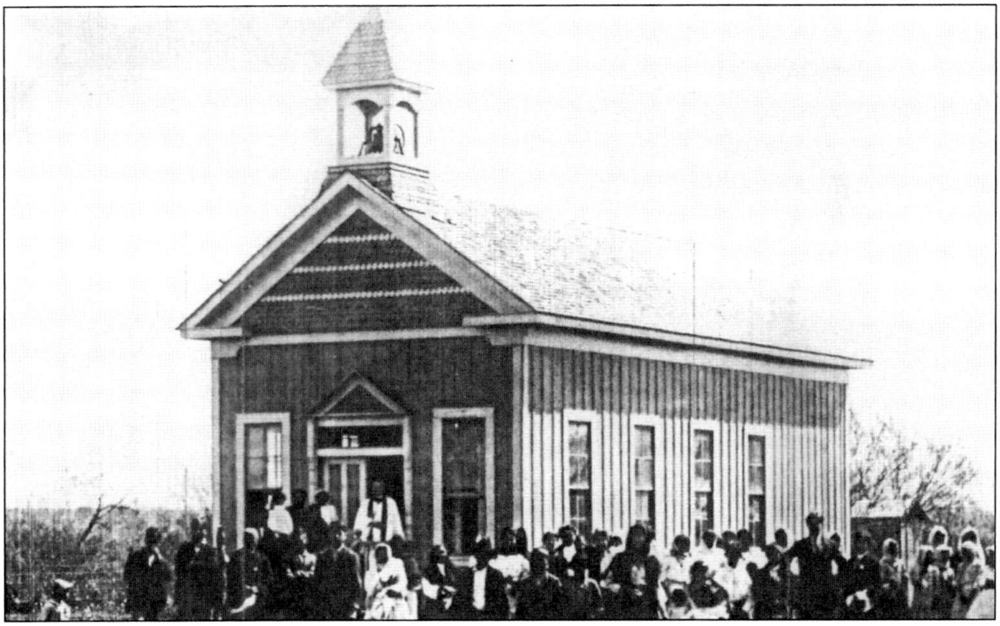

People of the Catholic faith first met in private homes in Millett. In 1911, a small church was built, but was destroyed by fire in 1920. Later Our Lady of Guadalupe Mission Catholic Church was built on Front Street in Millett. The church was the scene of many baptisms and weddings. The structure was torn down in the early 2000s.

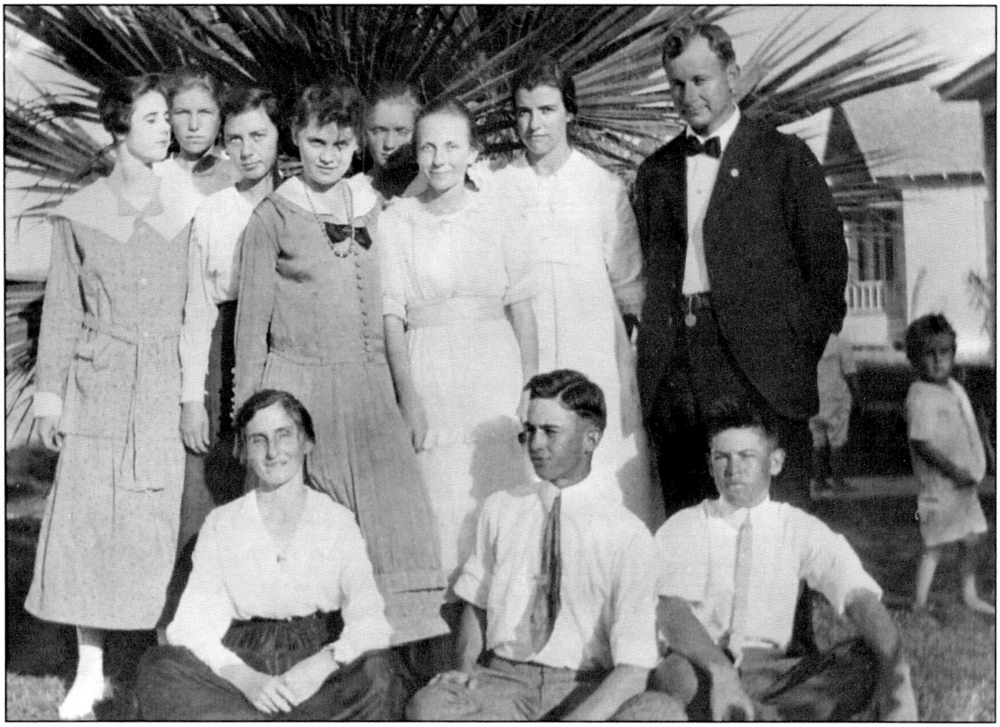

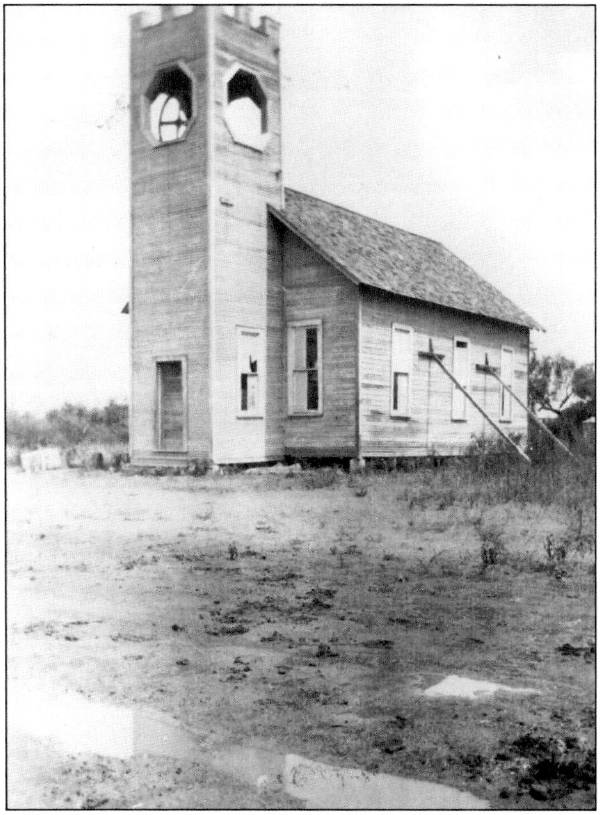

A group of Fowlerton Methodist Church parishioners have their picture taken in 1913. From left to right are (first row) Catherine Cook, John Mossis, and Joe Morris; (second row) Nadine Whitledge, Helen Barnettski, two unidentified, Lucille Loundes, Mary Cook, Ruth Sponseller, and Reverend McKay.

The Baptists were among the first to erect a church building in Fowlerton. In 1922, the church hired a young preacher, Oran W. Nolen, to be their pastor. Reverend Nolen was ordained on December 3, 1922, and the next day made his way to Fowlerton. He so endeared himself to the church members that he remained there until 1927.

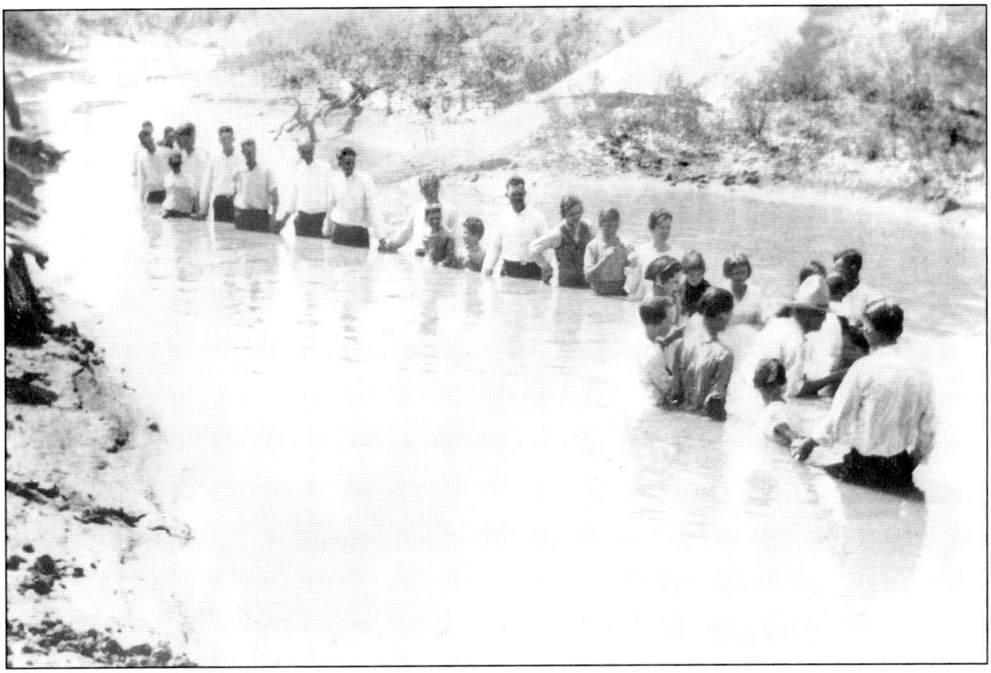

One warm summer day, 29 souls were baptized in the waters of the Frio River near Fowlerton. Rev. Oran W. Nolen, pastor of the Fowlerton Baptist Church, performed the baptisms. Reverend Nolen's new wife, Eula, was the first in line to be baptized.

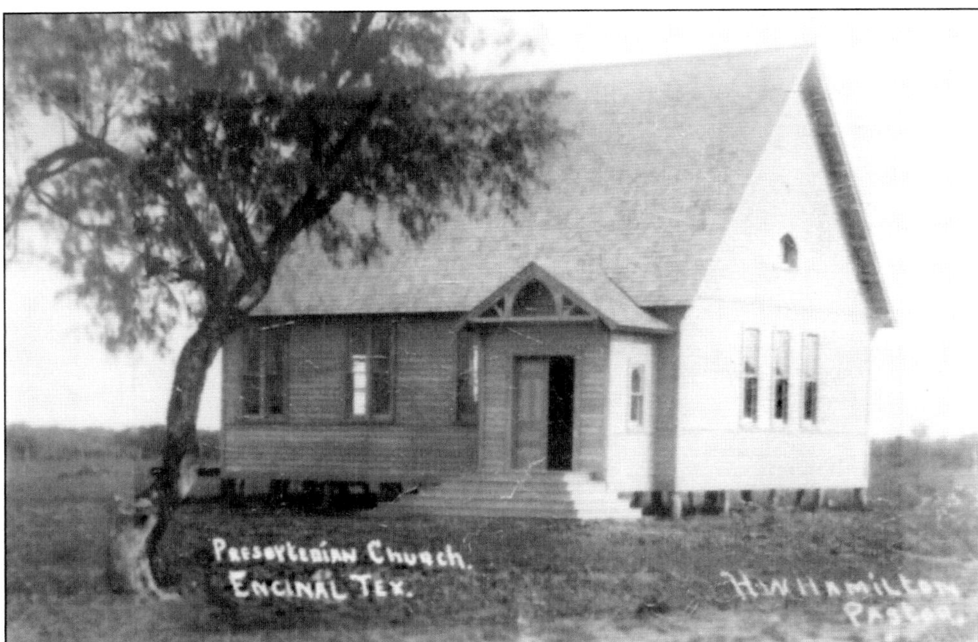

Dr. M. W. Doggett, a Presbyterian evangelist, made a religious census of Encinal in the early 1900s. In 1908, he organized the Presbyterian Church in Encinal. The congregation raised funds and erected a church building in 1910. It was a small, one-room structure, but as the church continued to grow, additional rooms were added.

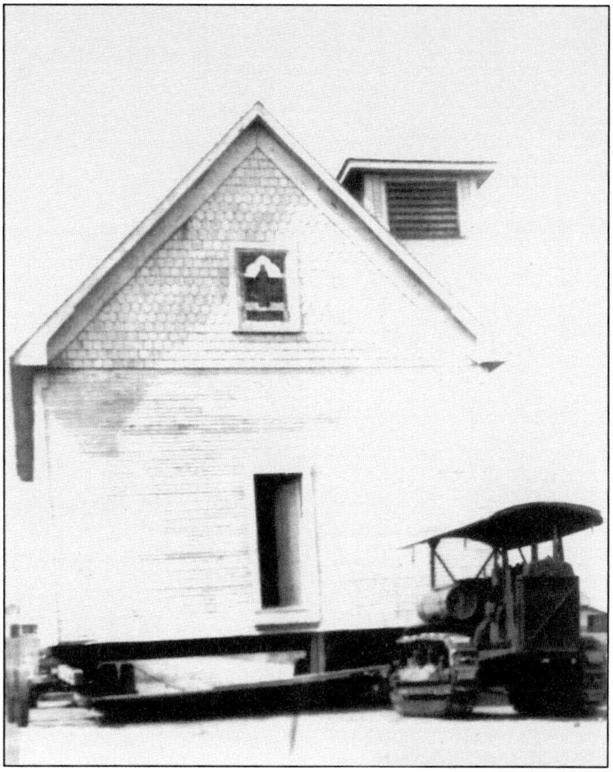

In the early 1920s, a convent for the Benedictine Sisters was built at Harriss Valley. A small chapel was built for their services. The nuns operated a dairy, but due to the arid conditions of the area they were soon forced to leave. Pictured at left is the small chapel being moved to Los Angeles.

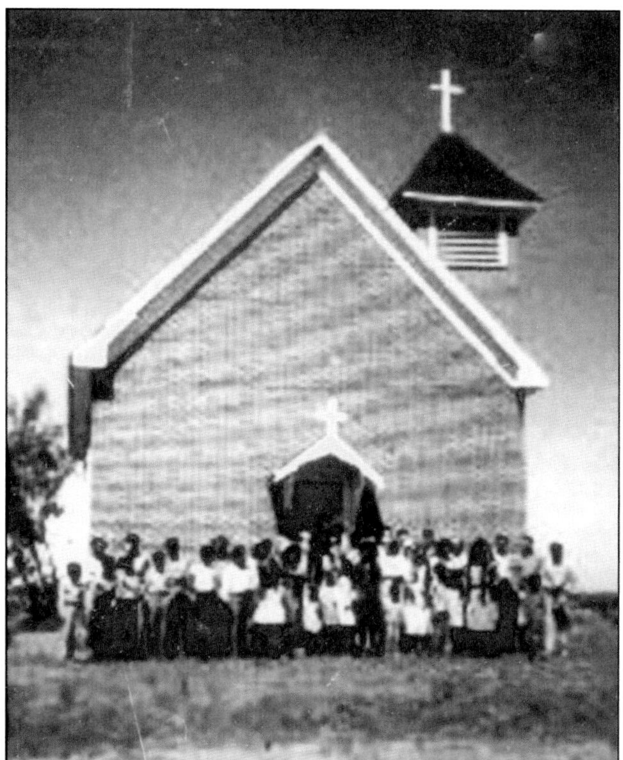

After the Benedictine Sisters abandoned their dairy and left Harriss Valley there was no need for the small church on the ranch. The little chapel was then moved into the town of Los Angeles where it found a new home. The church became known as the Los Angeles Catholic Church.

Nine

Rodeos, Parades, and Fiestas

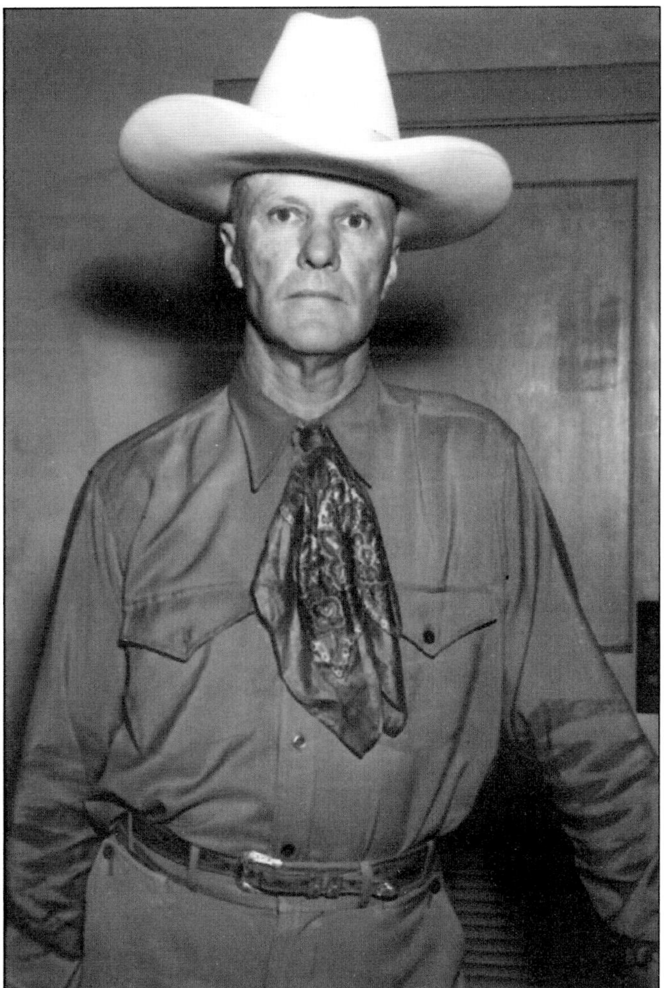

The Frontier Days Celebration and Rodeo, held on the Fourth of July, was promoted and managed by H. Dudley Storey. The first celebration was in 1922 and continued to grow in numbers each year. During the 1930s and early 1940s, the celebration was a huge success. As the crowds continued to grow, more seats were added to the arena to accommodate the large crowds attending. In 1938, a local citizen credited Storey with putting Cotulla on the map. With the onset of World War II the rodeo and celebration were cancelled. After World War II, the rodeo was sponsored by the American Legion.

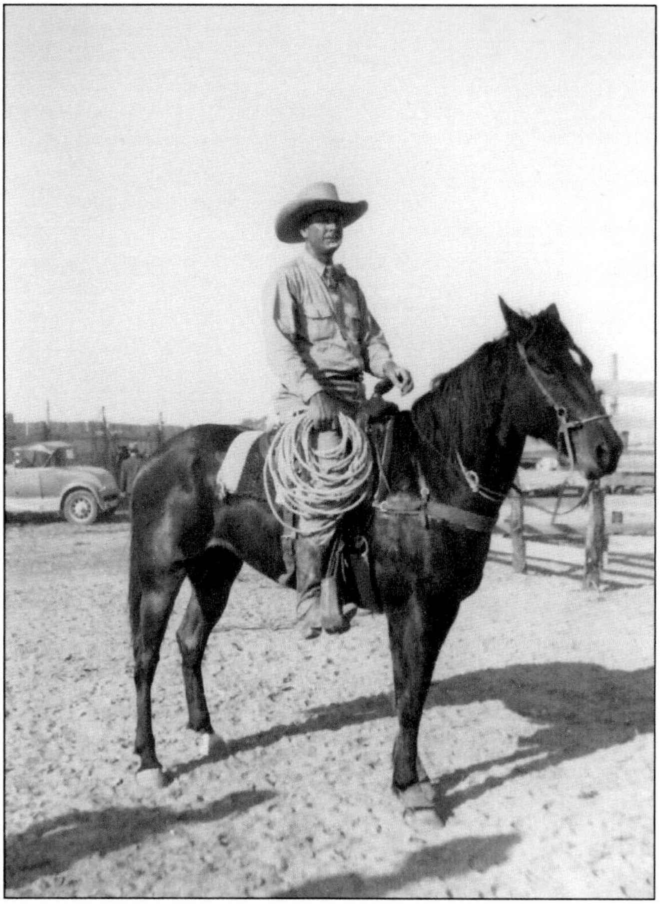

At the annual Frontier Days Celebration and Rodeo in 1931, Juan Salinas, a champion roper, came in second in the calf roping with a time of 32 seconds. In 1934, Salinas won the highest score for all-around cowboy and was awarded the shop-made boots given by Luchesse Boot Shop in San Antonio.

One of the highlights of the Frontier Days Celebration and Rodeo in 1937 was a calf-roping contest between Toots Mansfield of Rio Frio and Juan Salinas of Encinal for a $500 purse. Each contestant roped 10 calves. Salinas had a total two-day score of 248.6 seconds and Mansfield a score of 258.6 seconds.

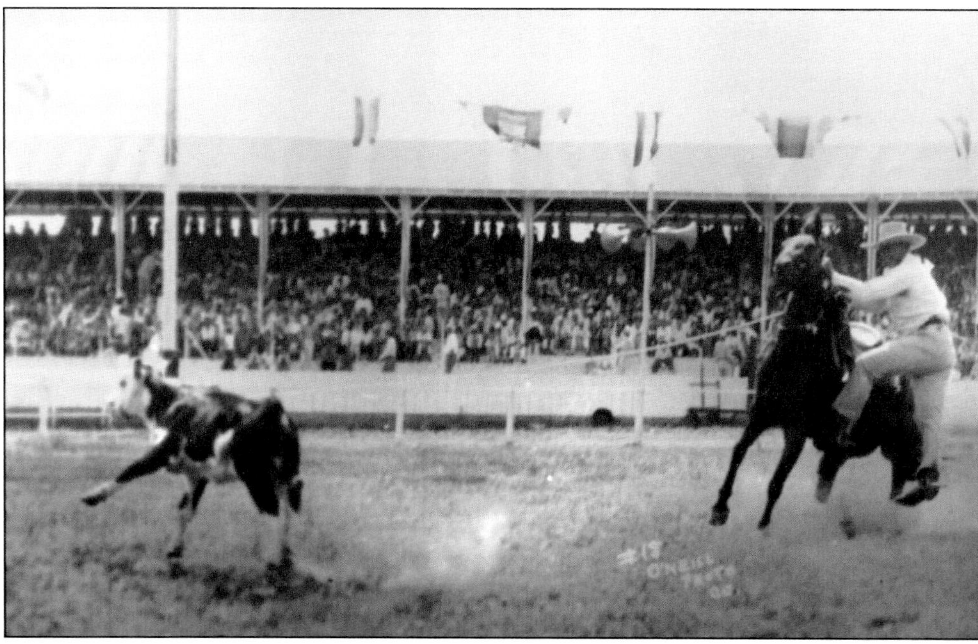

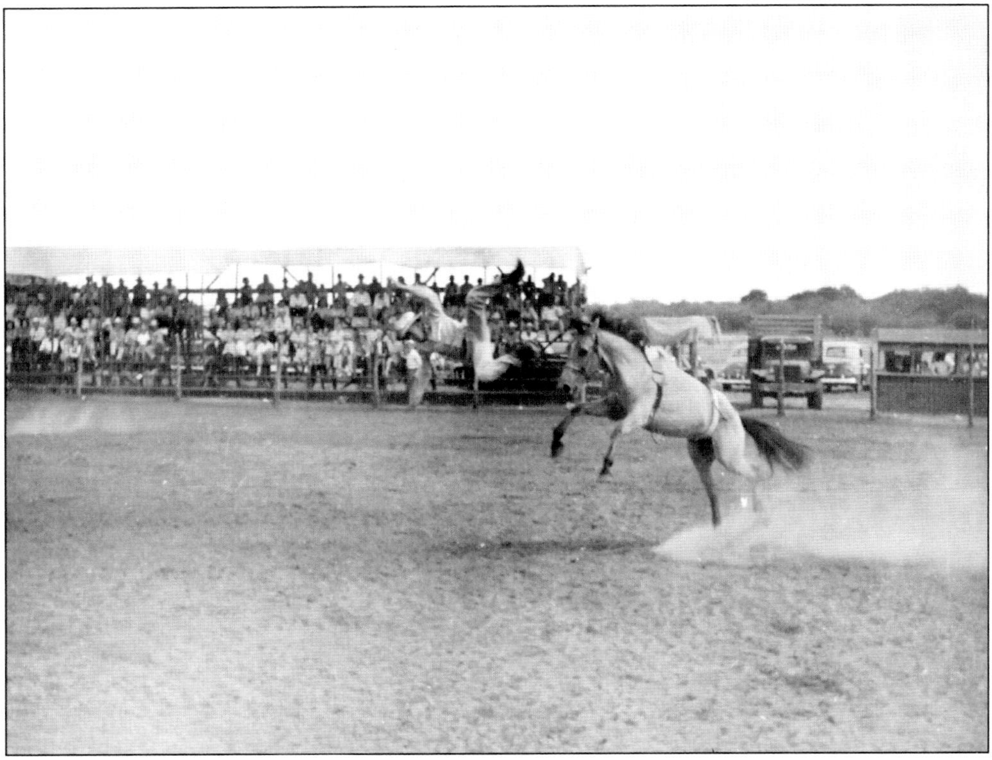

Bronc riding is a popular rodeo event in which the wild horse attempts to unseat its rider. Rattlesnake Brown, a contestant from Carrizo Springs, hangs in mid-air as he loses his battle with the bronc at the 1947 Frontier Days Celebration and Rodeo.

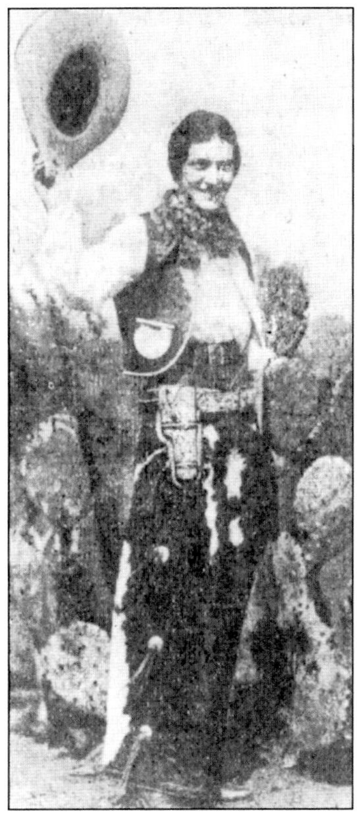

A record crowd attended the annual Frontier Days Celebration and Rodeo in 1933. After the grand entry into the rodeo arena, Helen Storey, daughter of rodeo promoter H. Dudley Storey and wife, Annie Lee Storey, was crowned rodeo queen. This was the first time a queen had been selected for the event.

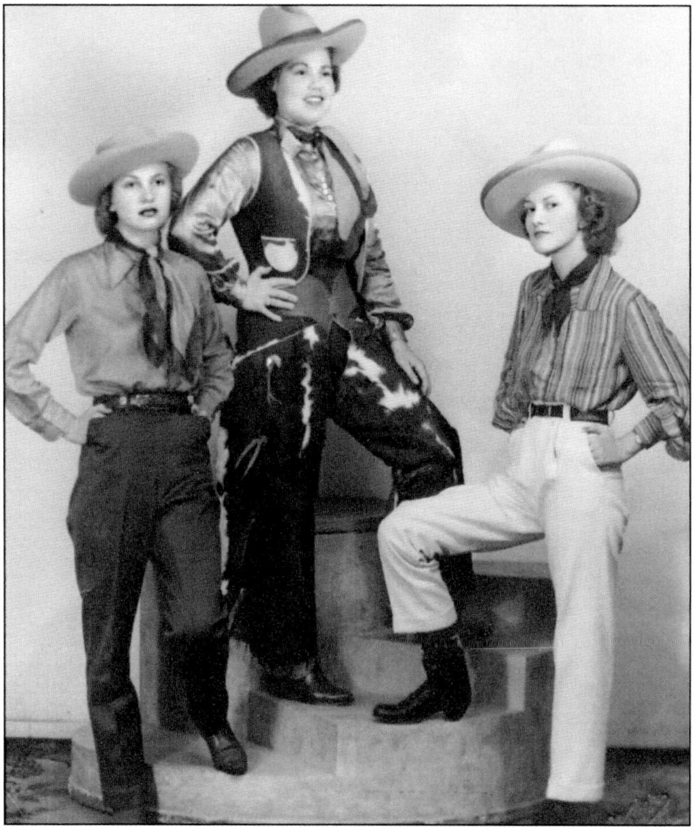

In 1939, Fredna Knaggs (center) was crowned queen of the Frontier Days Celebration and Rodeo in a ceremony held in the high school gym. The gym had been decorated to resemble a typical corral, with cactus, mesquite, and black brush. Bales of hay were used for the queen's throne and other rodeo royalty. Other rodeo royalty were Polly Poole (left) and Snookie Ballard.

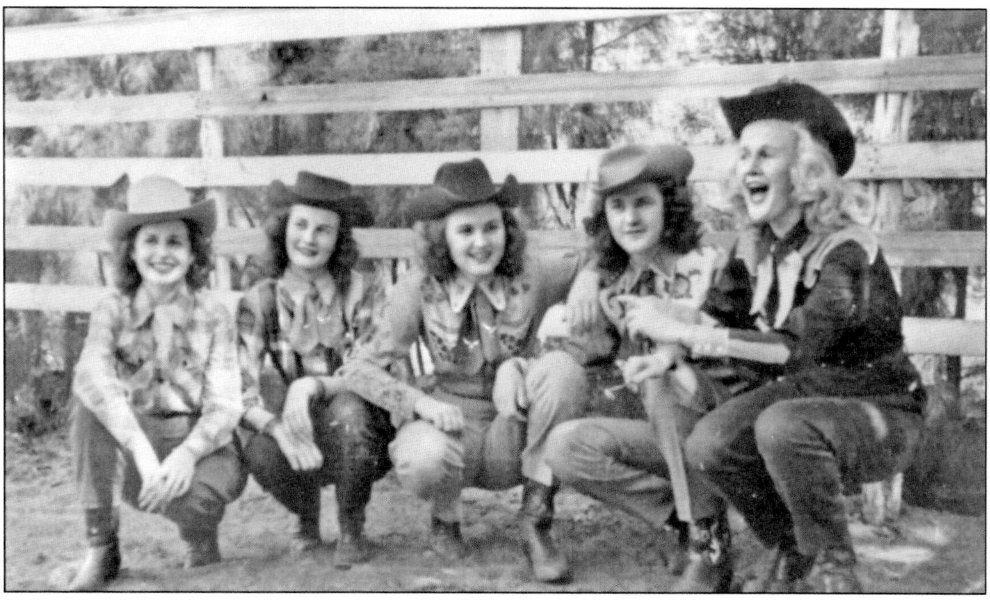

Lottie Lee Franklin was crowned queen of the 1948 Frontier Days Celebration and Rodeo. Pictured from left to right are Dorothy Mangum, Lottie Lee Franklin, Margaret Ann Kimball, Valda Daughtrey, and Jean Pagel, who made up the rodeo royalty. Girls from surrounding towns were invited to be part of the queen's court also.

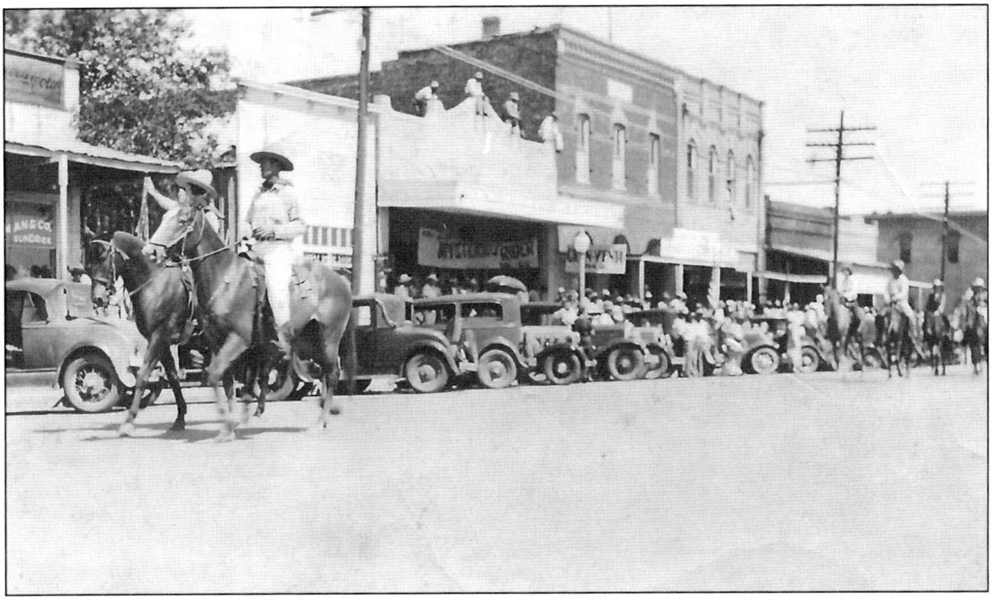

The parade on the Fourth of July was always as popular as the rodeos at the annual Frontier Days Celebration. People would line up along the streets in the early morning in order to get a good spot from which to watch the parade. Front Street was always the best place to be.

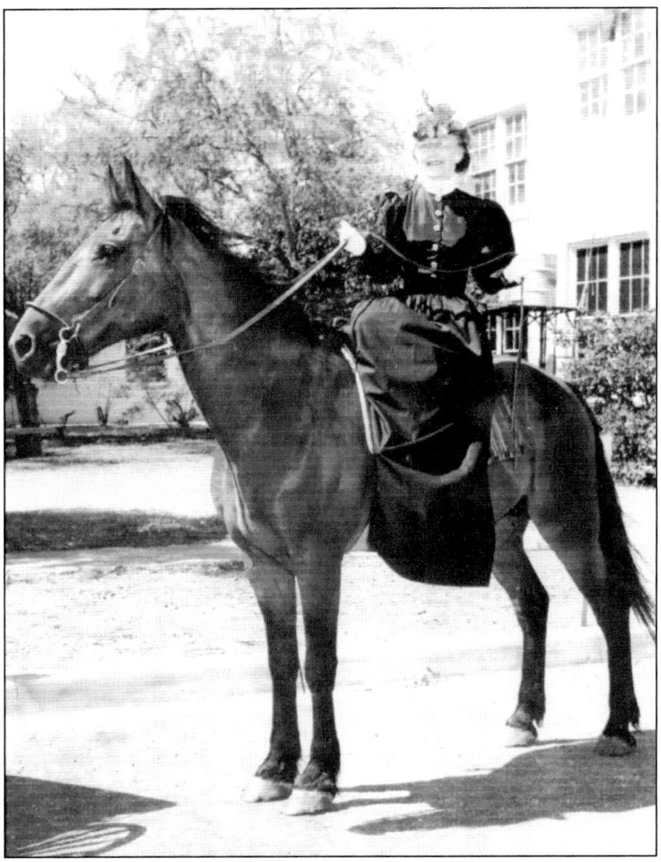

The Frontier Days Celebration parade always started at the school and then made its way down Tilden Street and along Front Street. In 1936, Ethel Dubose rode her horse sidesaddle along the streets of Cotulla waving to the crowd as she passed by.

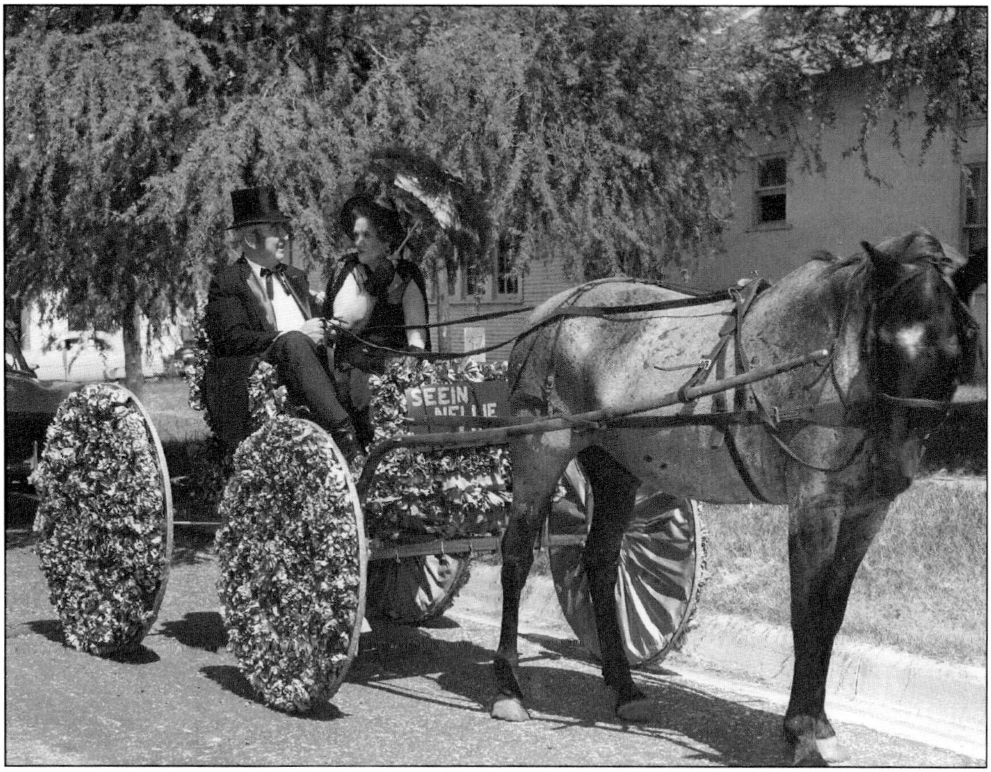

In 1937, a chartered bus brought 25 old trail drivers to participate in the Frontier Days Celebration parade. They were guests of H. Dudley Storey and he furnished horses for them to ride. The parade that year was so long it took more than an hour to pass. A. B. Alexander and Carrie Peters rode along in a decorated buggy.

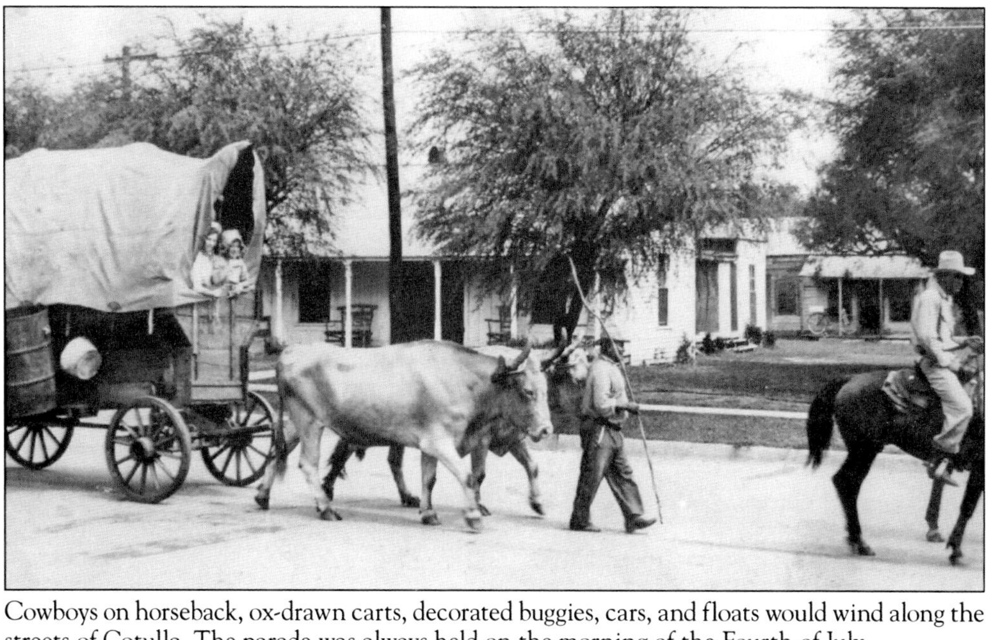

Cowboys on horseback, ox-drawn carts, decorated buggies, cars, and floats would wind along the streets of Cotulla. The parade was always held on the morning of the Fourth of July.

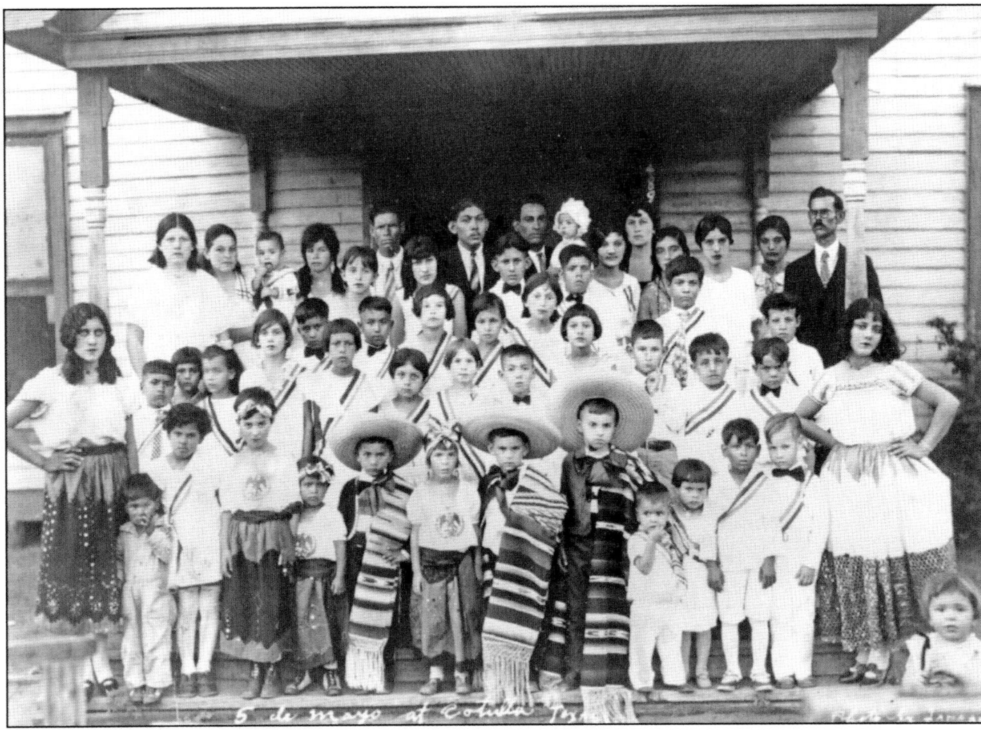

Cinco de Mayo celebrations commemorate the victory of the Mexican army over the French at the Battle of Puebla on May 5, 1862. Cinco de Mayo is observed by many cities and towns along the Texas-Mexican border as a celebration of Mexican heritage and pride. In 1945, Lucia Martinez was crowned May Queen in a Cinco de Mayo celebration.

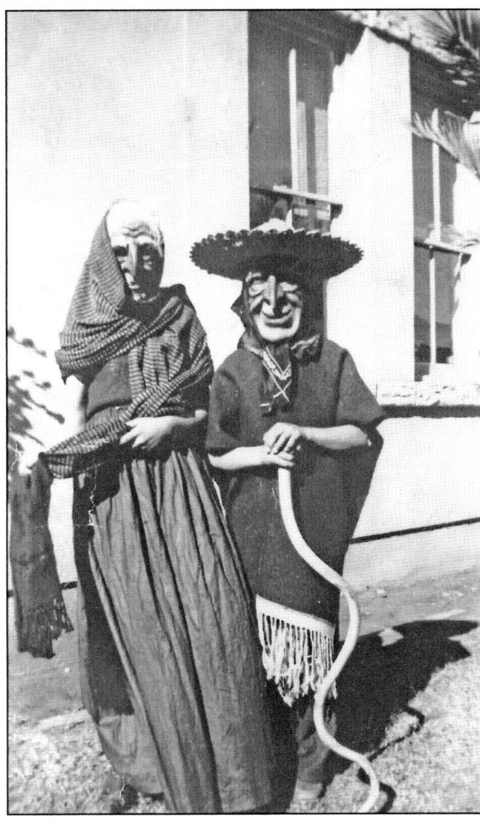

Oralia Gonzalez and Joel Rodriguez are all dressed up in traditional Mexican dance costumes, standing beside the high school auditorium waiting their turn to perform the *baile de los viejitos* or "dance of the little old men" for the crowd assembled inside.

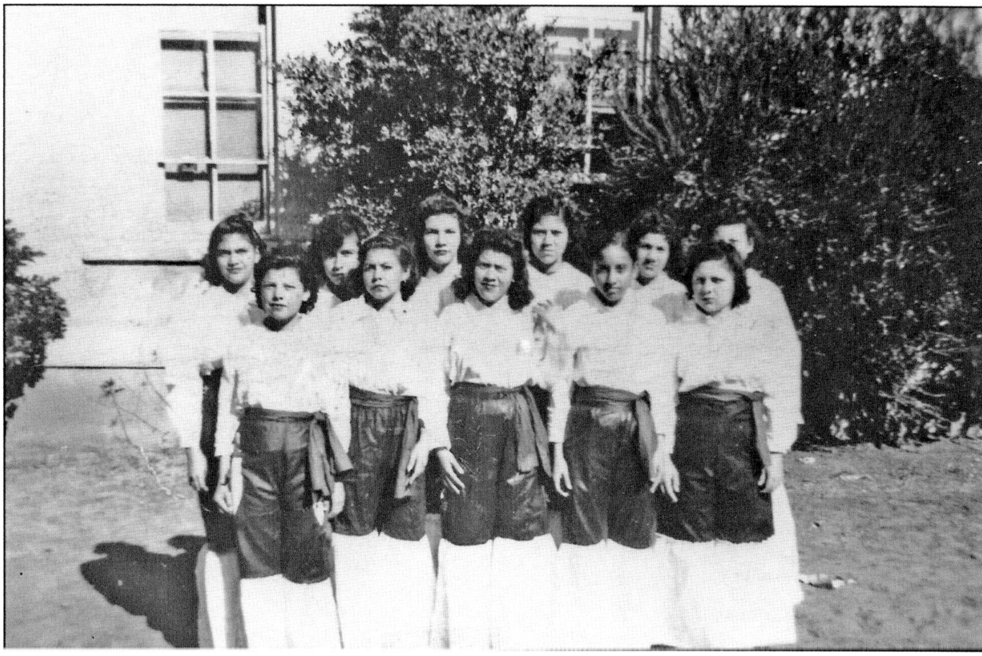

This Cotulla dance group performed at local celebrations including Cinco de Mayo. Pictured from left to right are (first row) Domitila Saldivar, Oralia Gonzalez, unidentified, Margarita Vasquez, and Aurelia Santos; (second row) unidentified, Angelita Alvarado, Beatriz Lopez, Azucena Jaimez, Celia Martinez, and unidentified.

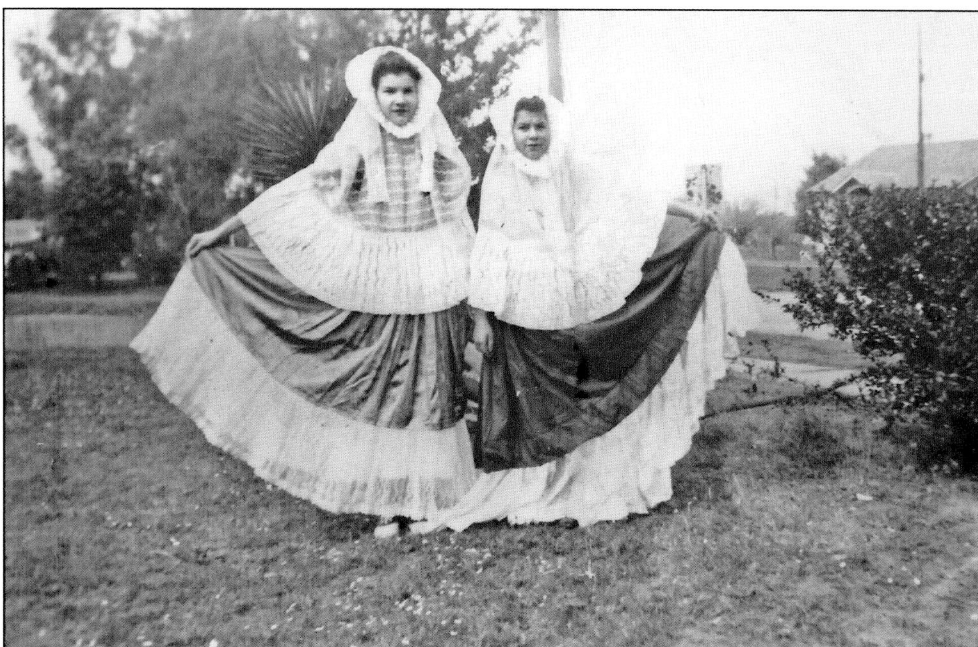

Mexican folk dances often retell the country's colorful history and honor the Mexican culture. The music and colorful costumes add to the beauty of the dances. Beatriz Lopez and Oralia Gonzalez, members of a Cotulla dance group, are dressed in traditional dance costumes.

BIBLIOGRAPHY

Casto, Stanley D. and Eva M. "Businesses at Millett." self-published, 1976.
Casto, Stanley D. A *Chronicle of La Salle County to 1883*. Lubbock, TX: self-published, 1970.
La Salle County Clerk's Office.
Ludeman, Annette M. *La Salle County*. Quanah, TX: Nortex Press, 1975.
Wollff, Henry Jr. Henry's Journal. *Victoria Advocate*. Victoria, TX: 1981.
www.newspaperarchive.com.

Consistent with our mission to preserve history on a local level, this book was printed in South Carolina on American-made paper and manufactured entirely in the United States. Products carrying the accredited Forest Stewardship Council (FSC) label are printed on 100 percent FSC-certified paper.

MADE IN THE USA